Nobody Is a Nobody:

The Story of a Harlem Ministry
Hard at Work to Change America

by

the Reverend Eugene S. Callender

as told to

Lorena K. Rostig and George A. Zdravecky

DEDICATION

This book is dedicated to the glory of God. In Him we all live and move and have our being. Through Him, through Her, all things work together for good.

I thank my divine parent for helping me to know what and who I was created to be, and where I was created to work, as part of the divine creation and order.

Wherever I have traveled and whatever I have done, it has really been consciousness of God that was speaking; it was consciousness of God that spoke at all of the events that are recorded on these pages. So I say, to God be the glory.

This life I have lived was made possible because of all the people that have touched me and my life. Many I don't even know, but their prayers, their associations, their conversations, their cooperation, and even their opposition have made my life what it is. They were the instruments that were used by the creative life force to enable me to dance the dance of life that appears on these pages.

So to all of them I extend a deep, heartfelt thank you. To all the little babies I baptized, to the couples I married, to the thousands of people I counseled, to the young people who helped me dream the dream and have that dream unfold through the Street Academies and Harlem Prep, to the many politicians, preachers, teachers, and friends—to all of these, I give my thanks.

i

George Bernard Shaw said it better than I ever could, and I thank him for these words:

> This is the true joy in life, the being used for a purpose recognized by yourself as a mighty one. For being a force of nature instead of a feverish selfish little clod of ailments and grievances complaining that the world will not devote itself to making you happy. I am of the opinion that my life belongs to the whole community. As long as I live, it is my privilege to do for it whatever I can.
>
> I want to be thoroughly used up when I die, for the harder I work, the more I live. I rejoice in life for its own sake. Life is no brief candle to me. It is a sort of splendid torch which I have got hold of for the moment and I want to make it burn as brightly as possible before handing it on to future generations.

Thank you all.

Eugene S. Callender

To God be the glory.

Eugene S. Callender

Table of Contents:

Cover design by Janeen Koconis: www.kocony.com

PREFACE

I am honored and excited to share my life with you: My experiences, my recollections of important events, and my interactions with people whom I've been blessed to know. The words on these pages tell the story I have wanted to share.

I have tried to recreate events, locales and conversations from my memories of them. While I'm told my memory generally is a good match to history, I may have missed a few beats here and there. Please accept my apologies in advance.

The seeds for *Nobody Is a Nobody* were first planted in 1969 by Alex Haley exhorting me to start writing down my stories. Then, in 1996, when I was visiting a small African village with The Hunger Project, the idea came up again. My thanks to Lynne Twist for coordinating the fundraising and to those who generously chipped in to make it possible for Tracy Howard Apple to sit with me for three months and turn my stories into a 150-page seminal document.

Tracy compiled my stories, connected dots, and framed a life portrait which helped support our work on *Nobody Is a Nobody*. Some of her sentences and paragraphs remain, as they were just too good to change.

Today, with the book now in its final form, my thanks extend to the many, many others, and most notably to Lorena

Rostig and George Zdravecky, who made *Nobody Is a Nobody* possible.

I chose the title of this book from a sermon I first delivered in 1966 at the Cathedral Church of Saint John the Divine in New York City and have re-purposed many times over the years. The message of that sermon appears in full at the end of this book. I hope you will find it relevant to your life, today.

Always remember: God loves you, and I love you, too.

Eugene S. Callender

www.eugenecallender.com

FORWARD

by

The Honorable Charles B. Rangel

The life of Dr. Eugene Callender is a fascinating tale stretching from Barbados to Cambridge and anchored in the great community that is Harlem. I have valued Eugene's friendship for over 50 years and yet there are so many terrific stories in his memoir that give me a more complete picture of such a remarkable man.

Eugene has served the people of Harlem and New Yorkers of all stripes in so many ways. His years of ministry have uplifted the downtrodden, inspired the despondent, and comforted the distressed.

A man of deep thought and continuous action, Rev. Callender developed programs to put people to work, secured adequate housing for families in need, and pursued social justice through countless avenues.

The scourge of drugs was devastating Harlem in the 1980s. My work in the Congress as Chair of the Select Committee on Narcotics would have been in vain if not for the work on the streets that Eugene put his heart, soul and gifted mind into. As I waged war against proposed cuts to the federal antinarcotic budget on Capitol Hill, and advocated for additional funding for homeless shelters, Rev. Callender was my invaluable partner on the ground.

The largest drug rehabilitation center in New York City stands today because of Eugene's early work as its founder. The Addicts Rehabilitation Center has helped our community immensely, and so many families remain appreciative of Rev. Callender's tireless efforts to combat addiction.

At a time when I believe our religious leaders should be more vocal about the plight of the least among us, I hear Rev. Callender's voice and reflect on his deep commitment to helping the common man and woman.

In reading this memoir, you will discover what I have known for quite some time: Eugene Callender is one of New York's treasures in the historical lens of public service and social justice.

As I reflect on our current national crises and observe our young people protesting and demanding that their voices be heard, I think of the work of Rev. Callender. He came of age on the cusp of a young people's movement that changed the world.

Dealing with issues of inequality, colorism, discrimination, racism, segregation and injustice, he adeptly used his resources, connections, and thoughtful nature to address these challenges. It was also his passion that propelled his objectives.

Eugene interacted with the some of the best our country has had to offer. From Ralph Bunche to Jackie Robinson, from Joe Louis to Sugar Ray Robinson. He was even responsible for bringing Martin Luther King, Jr. to Harlem in 1957. The Civil Rights movement inspired him deeply, and the words of Rev. King taught him so much about the power and difficulty in non-violent protest.

Rev. Callender and I also share a love of jazz. His tales involving Duke Ellington, Thelonius Monk, Billie Holiday, and Lena Horne are snapshots of a wonderful musical and artistic world; a world that emanated proudly from the Harlem we both call our home.

Being so involved in our community, made it impossible for Eugene to escape the political tide completely. Our mutual friend Percy Sutton may have beat him to become President of the NAACP, but he would soon become a powerbroker for Presidential candidates and be briefly drawn into local political turf wars. His reflections on dealing with Bobby Kennedy and Eleanor Roosevelt are just a few of his valuable recollections.

Eugene's story is an intriguing portrait in time, from the 1920s through present day. It not only follows his life amidst the vivid backdrop of some of the decades' biggest events, but it also focuses on his familial relationships and boyhood.

Some of the most poignant moments can be found as he processes his upbringing. His relationships with and between his relatives are informative. Rev. Callender reminds us that we all have stories to tell, which others can learn a great deal from. I know I have.

Charles B. Rangel
U.S. House of Representatives
Washington, D.C.
January 2012

INWARD

by

Janeen Koconis

When I think of Eugene Callender, what comes to mind are pressed shirts and ties, the question "How is this relevant?," and his daily copy of the New York Times.

Of course, other things come to mind, too — like his Sunday-morning sermons that turn Matthew and Mark into a self-awareness seminar and Luke and John into a course in civics; or the spelling bee he cooked up one time to raise the literacy level at Harlem PS 134. There was the time he started a political speech with a poem by e.e. cummings; the time he ended a speech with "God loves you. And I love you too"; and there was the time he started the first and largest anti-poverty program in America.

But let's start with his ties.

Some of his ties are business casual. One of them is matte black. He's got a preppy one for the 21 Club and trendy ones for all the other clubs. There are his understated "funeral" ties. His conservative "board meeting" ties. His bright ties for baptisms and inter-racial weddings. And his "black power" ties for keeping it real. There's his Kwanzaa tie. His peace-sign tie.

His pastel, striped tie for Easter. And, of course, his Rudolph, the Red-Nosed Reindeer tie for the Sunday school kids Christmas morning.

If you're meeting Eugene for dinner (P.S., his favorite restaurant in New York is La Mirabelle), he'll either be on time or five minutes early, and most likely he'll be wearing a tie. He holds his fork and knife the classical European way, maneuvers an escargot clamp like a pro, and will wrap up the evening with a tidy "recap" over a double, decaf espresso. There's almost always somebody who will know him from somewhere — the Movement days, the Lindsay Administration, the Ashram, or the church — and they just come over naturally and hug him or thank him or "hi-five" him or shake his hand.

It could be a cafeteria on 125th St. or a concert at Carnegie Hall: Somebody will know him. And be excited to see him. And will wave across the aisle or the room or even three lanes of traffic and shout, "Hey, Rev!," "Hey, Doc!," or "Hey, Gene!"

It's no big surprise, really, that people feel lit up around him or feel like a "somebody" around him or that Governor Mario Cuomo happened to call him a "civic saint." Because the world Eugene stands for is a world called "you and me." A place where nobody is a nobody and everybody is a somebody and where everyone brings something to the world. He was on the Rolodex of five Presidents and the celebrity star of "Positively Black," but the glamour never eclipsed Eugene's mission to serve people. To be the church; not just do the church. Eugene believes in the dignity of people. In the potential of people. Feels "one" with people. Feels the soul of people. And nowhere is this more evident than on the streets of NYC where he has worked tirelessly for the rights of black America since 1950. Or in a jazz club where he might be wearing that matte black tie.

Eugene Callender is a jazz lover. And included in his repertoire of things he knows by heart — along with Biblical passages, religious chants, Articles of the Constitution and the Bill of Rights — are all the old jazz standards: "Lush Life," "Good Morning Heartache," "Up Jumped Spring," "Satin Doll" — as if they were stock material from a Presbyterian hymnal at church. His history with jazz and jazz musicians verges on cinematic and, right here, you may as well just get out a bag of popcorn because it plays back like a movie reel: from Johnny Hartman's ballads to Billie Holiday's funeral; from Ella Fitzgerald at the Apollo to hanging out with Thelonius Monk. Eugene was the one who helped Charlie Mingus and Jackie McLean get it together in the detox clinic above the church; and was the one who helped push a piano down the street and onto the back of a truck so Duke Ellington could play for Martin Luther King's first trip to Harlem.

To most people who know jazz, jazz is jazz. But to Eugene, it's a manifestation, too. It's the soul of the black community. And the pulse of a constituency he, himself, is a part of. Above Eugene's little mahogany desk in his apartment — and amidst all his various political, religious and new-age books and memorabilia, the many plaques and awards and honorary badges, the framed photos of gurus and mayors and family and friends — there is a large, black & white vintage photograph (circa 1955), a poster of all the jazz greats lined up on a stoop in Harlem. Each time I glance at that photograph, there's a split second where I catch myself searching for Eugene in the lineup, too.

So whether it's a jazz joint up in Harlem or the Blue Note downtown, Eugene finds the groove and keeps the beat with the rhythm section as if he were part of it, himself. And, in a way, I suppose, he really kind of is.

I first met ESC in 1994 at an event planning meeting for The Hunger Project. I was one of many Hunger Project volunteers then, and he was the honorary and designated point person for a gala event which would award Nelson Mandela the Africa Prize for Leadership. Eugene's not-so-secret mission was to get President Clinton to introduce the event. It was summer in the City, and Eugene led the meeting wearing wing-tips and a blue and white striped, sear-sucker suit. As hot as I remember it being that August evening, Eugene was also wearing a tie.

While Hunger Project meetings are known for their own brand of charisma, this time it felt like part of the charisma in the air was uniquely Eugene's. The event happened. Bill Clinton was the keynote speaker. Nelson Mandela came on stage to accept the prize. And, from that time on, I lucked out and got Eugene Callender as my very own, charismatic friend. Not much different, I'm sure, than the hundreds and hundreds of other people who have had the same stroke of luck to call Eugene Callender their very own friend, too.

"Nobody Is a Nobody" is a historical memoir tracking one man's tireless work to help build a better America. The setting is Harlem, U.S.A. The time is 1950 to present. The cast is legendary. And the main character — the man with the hard hat, the soft heart (and perhaps a tie) — is The Reverend Dr. Eugene S. Callender. From the rent strikes on 122nd Street to the election of Barack Obama, "Nobody Is a Nobody" is a book of hours and episodes, weeks, months and years illuminating a 60+ year ministry that has made its mark on American Civil Rights history forever.

As we follow Eugene's narrative through this watershed segment of American history, we, at the same time, follow him on his own personal inner journey of Self. Self-worth. Self-respect. Self-understanding. And self-love. To live in the question, "Who am I?" is part of the mystery of the human journey

— the journey we are all on separately as individuals and together as a whole. And while Eugene's answer to this question has reshaped itself over the years of his ministry, the essence of his answer is still the same: "You and I are not nobody. We are manifestations of the eternal spirit of the universe. And each of us—each you and each I—matters."

Love, with a capital L, calls us to do the things of this world. And I don't know of anyone—poet, preacher or king—who rejoices in the privilege of being alive in this world with other human beings more than Eugene Callender.

At age 86, Dr. Eugene S. Callender still wears pressed shirts and ties to La Mirabelle; still discusses the relevance of things with kids in grade schools, high schools and universities worldwide; and still reads the New York Times every single day.

Janeen Koconis
Paris, France
January 2012

PROLOGUE

I know very little about my relatives in Barbados. What I do know, I mostly discovered on my own through handed-down stories, personal journeys to the island to meet relatives, and digging into archives that were made available at the time. I knew of my grandparents and great-grandparents. The name Callender came from a Scottish plantation where Arthur Callender, my great-grandfather, worked.

By 1833, slavery was ended in all British colonies. My parents had no memory of slavery; their parents had never spoken of it. I had several aunts who remained in Barbados, but most of my uncles were in the United States. Through family stories and research, I determined that my family were slaves until 1832, when Britain freed them. Records from their church indicate that the first-known baptisms of my lineage were around the time of liberation, which makes sense because only free people were allowed to be baptized. Life was hard in Barbados for a slave through the 1830s, and for a free person of color into the early 1900s.

I visited Barbados for the first time in 1967 and stayed with my cousin Doreen Mayers. I could tell that my family in Barbados was not nearly as excited to meet me as I was to meet and know them. I could feel a pain that I could not identify. I felt truly unwelcome in both the homeland and homes of my family. This was particularly true of my cousin Doreen. The visit was awkward for most of the time that I was there until I finally asked her if something was wrong. She broke down in tears and told me how much she hated me.

"Hate me? Why, Doreen?"

"Because Grandmother Sophia Callender loved you better than me, and I was here and you were in America."

"But Doreen, I didn't even know her."

"Yes, but she used to send you nice presents. A baby dish, silver spoons, a silver comb, a mirror, and a brush. She made fruitcakes and sent them to you."

"Doreen, I never saw those things. This can't be true."

"She did send those things—and more! Ask your father."

I was flabbergasted. I couldn't get back to America fast enough to get to the bottom of this revelation. I asked my father, "Did your mother send me a silver comb, brush, mirror, baby dish, and spoon when I was born?"

"Yes."

I was suddenly consumed with such a sense of loss, not for the things that were given, but for the comfort of my grandmother who gave them to me in love.

"Well, where are they now?" I asked.

"In my trunk," my father said matter-of-factly. He had never shown them to me. It never occurred to him that these gifts might have been beautiful and important to me. Doreen was angry about something of which I wasn't even aware.

It occurred to me that these gifts from my grandmother were in some way very important to my father. Otherwise, why else would he hold onto them for so long? In ways I'm sure he never even understood, that old trunk contained some of my life's greatest treasures.

The Grahams

My mother, Eva Valeria Graham Callender, was born in 1895 on this Caribbean island. As a teenage girl, she would often work as a babysitter for wealthy American families vacationing there. One wealthy white family liked her so much that they asked my grandmother if they could bring my mother back with them to the United States to work for them as a fulltime nanny. My grandmother said yes because they desperately needed the money that my mother could make and send back. So my mother came to America at the age of sixteen and had to lie about her age to enter the country because of the immigration laws.

My mother was brought to Cambridge, Massachusetts, in 1918 to be the live-in help for this wealthy white family. They sent her to the Miss Farmer's School of Cookery, which served her well through the remainder of her years. She never returned to Barbados.

My maternal grandmother's name was Julia Howard Graham. She was a strikingly beautiful woman. She was black but obviously had white blood. She was a child of slaves, and their master was white. My mother had one sister and two brothers who eventually followed her to America, as would several other family members.

I know that my mother missed her parents very much, especially having left them at such a young age. She and her parents wrote to each other regularly, and she dutifully sent money to her family throughout her life. I do not know why, but my mother would not let us read the letters they sent. I would have loved to have read them as I was growing up. Much later in life, I found some of those letters in my father's drawer after he died. In one letter, my grandmother wrote giving my parents permission to marry. In another, she wrote about my birth saying, "Kiss the baby for me."

I cherish those letters so much because they are the only connection I have with my mother's mother. They were filled with such an expression and abundance of love, and they gave me an even more profound appreciation of, bond with, and love for my mother, my family, and my heritage.

The Callenders

James and Sophia Hart Callender were my paternal grandparents. James Callender came to America from Barbados to make money and support his family. He left his family behind, including his wife, Sophia, and my father. While his leaving caused significant angst in the family, we were told that Grandfather James did quite well in America, although we neither knew what he did to make a living nor received any benefit.

I still have an engraved pocket watch that he sent to my father, Arthur—"Archie"—when he was a boy. The engraved message says, "To Archie, Christmas 1909." This is the only actual timestamp I have of his initial journey to America.

Sometime after 1909, James returned to Barbados to bring his family to America. But his wife, Sophia, was so mad at him for having left them the first time that she refused to join him and would not let him take any of their children with him.

While I certainly was not there to experience it, I can feel the pride and pain. I can only imagine the test of will that my grandparents exhibited in those moments. In their determined efforts to "win," which for only a moment either could claim they did, Sophia and the kids stayed in Barbados, and

James went back to America to start a new life, never returning "home."

My father, Arthur Sinclair Callender, was twenty-seven years old when he immigrated to America from Barbados. He came to America for economic reasons. His family was so poor that he did not have any shoes to wear on the boat. Another man from Barbados on the boat felt so bad for my father that he bought him a pair of shoes for his trip to the new land.

When my father arrived in Cambridge in 1922, he came at the invitation of Stanley Lane, a man from Barbados who had moved to Cambridge some years before. Stanley's sister was quite attractive, and she was active in a Pentecostal church. Naturally, my father started going to church. While nothing ever really clicked for my father and Stanley's sister, my father did become a faithful parishioner of that church.

It was Christian Mission Holiness on Main Street. It was also where he met and married my mother. Growing up, this was our church, and it certainly conformed to—or perhaps, shaped—my parents' very strict approach to parenting. It was most likely a synthesis of both. My parents were very religious and very active in the Pentecostal church. My mother knew the Bible backward and forward.

It was during the early days of my father's immigration to America that he searched for his own father—my grandfather. His search reached closure on 120th Street and Lenox Avenue in Harlem. My grandfather, he discovered, was married to a woman named Mary, which would make him a bigamist.

My father was shocked. He asked my grandfather, "Who is this woman, Mary Callender? Your wife? What about Mama at home?" According to my father, all my grandfather said to him was, "Archie, that's the way we do things in America."

These were the only words my father ever spoke to me about Grandfather James. Years later, when I became interested in my family history, I asked my father questions about Grandfather James. He could not even speak about him, his pain and anger were so deep.

This issue of (un)forgiveness played itself out for the rest of my father's life. Interestingly enough, it also played out for the next sixty years of my own.

Chapter 1:
I Am

I was born at four thirty the morning of January 21, 1926.

When my mother was pregnant with me, she wanted a girl. She was so confident that I was going to be a girl that she picked the name Eugenia, after Princess Eugénie of Greece and Denmark. That's one of the reasons I have never liked the name Eugene. My mother bought all pink blankets and lace dresses for the baby girl she was going to have.

I was just the opposite of what she wanted—a boy—and, worst of all, my skin was the darkest in my family. I was the wrong sex and the wrong color. (Even in a family of color, we were very conscious of the difference between light skin and dark skin. White was right, brown was all right, and black was not right.)

From the time my mother brought me home, I wore those little lace dresses and she wouldn't cut my hair. I had those pink blankets on me, and she used to take Pond's Vanishing Cream and rub me from head to foot, hoping to lighten my skin. She would say to me, "This is what you've got to do every day for the rest of your life." She was trying to get my skin lighter so that I would be more attractive. Eventually my

1

kindergarten teacher begged her to cut my hair so she'd know I was a boy.

Prior to my birth, the doctors discovered that I was upside down in my mother's womb. They suggested that, instead of a natural childbirth, she have a Caesarean section. She refused. She said, "I want to have a baby the way a baby should be born." She later told me that, when she went into labor with me in the breech position, it was very painful. It was then that she remembered the prayer of Hannah, the mother of the Prophet Samuel who became pregnant at a very old age.. Hannah prayed daily and asked God for one thing, to have her own child. Her prayer was, "Lord, just let me have this child. If You give me this child, I will give it back to You. It's Yours." My mother's prayer through the pain of delivery was the same as Hannah's.

Leland

My mother gave birth to two other children: a boy, Leland, and a girl, Thelma. I am twenty months older than my brother. We got along as most brothers that close in age do. But we fought a lot, too, as most brothers do. He had a quick temper, very much like my father; however my father was extremely physical and psychological with his abusive quick temper. Leland and I were drawn together when our dad punished both of us and we had to stay in the house together. We bonded through the pain of the punishment, as well as through the imprisonment we shared for our transgressions. Given the fact that we were the favorite, if not primary, targets of our father's anger, we spent a lot of time together. We learned to become very creative in those times. We invented marble baseball on the floor and all sorts of games that we had to play inside, just the two of us.

Leland was always more popular with girls than I was. He was taller, better-looking, lighter-skinned, and more outgoing. He was a charming fellow. I was always shy, reserved, and afraid to speak to girls. When we were in high school, I was dating a girl named Betty who belonged to our church. I was fourteen or fifteen at the time. That Christmas I had given her a beautiful pair of fur mittens and a box of twenty-four Milky Ways, our favorite treat. We had just performed at a Christmas concert and we were going home on the subway when she told me, "I want to be Leland's girlfriend from now on, not yours." I took those mittens off her hands and told her to bring me the rest of those Milky Ways! I was so angry, so hurt, so embarrassed.

Thelma

My sister's birth was a psychological turning point in my life. At that time, I was ten and in the fifth grade. My teacher was Miss Schoonover. I began to notice women that year, and Miss Schoonover was certainly noticeable. She was quite attractive. Her eyes drew me to her lovely face, and while she was slim, she had noticeable curves on her body that moved wonderfully when she walked. I had my first crush. I tried hard to do well, in fact, to impress her with my work. I remember writing some of my best compositions for her. I remember writing one about how I predicted the Red Sox were going to win the pennant that year and why. She liked baseball and my papers. I had a great fifth-grade year.

My sister was born at the end of my fifth grade school year, in May 1936. Leland and I were sleeping in the dining room at that time, and I heard some unusual noises that woke me up. It was three o'clock in the morning. I saw my mother and father getting dressed. My mother was nine months pregnant, but I can't even remember noticing that she had a big belly. Nobody told me that she was pregnant, and I did not notice

3

that there was something different going on with her. There were no conversations about it or signs of preparation.

My mother and father went out in the middle of the night, and my father came back about three or four hours later by himself. Leland and I got up in the morning, as usual, , to go to school. When we came home, my father announced, "You have a baby sister." You know what I thought? I thought my mother had gone to the hospital, looked over some babies, picked one up, said, "I'll take this one," and brought it home. I had no idea where babies came from, not a clue. That certainly sounds naïve, but in my family there was absolutely no discussion about sex, let alone where babies come from.

When my sister came home from the hospital, my mother finally had the little girl she always wanted. She had blonde hair, very light skin, and blue eyes, just like my grandma. I liked her. I thought my mother had picked out a good baby. She said, "Well, you're going to have to help raise her." That was fine with me. I had to hold the bottle, feed her, and change diapers. (In those days the diapers had pins.) I loved my sister. To this day, Thelma and I are still connected.

Prior to that, I remember seeing one of the ladies in the community with a big belly and saying something to my mother about it. My mother said to me, "She probably got that way lying on the grass." I thought she meant she lay on the grass, caught a cold, and her stomach swelled up. Nobody ever said to me she was having a baby.

52 Pleasant Street

I grew up at 52 Pleasant Street in Cambridge, Massachusetts. My mother's older brother, my Uncle Marcus, owned the house. Uncle Marcus was a janitor. He borrowed money from my mother, father, and Uncle Fred to buy the house we lived in, plus three other houses. He and his family lived downstairs, and we lived upstairs. Both families shared the house's single bathroom. It was on our floor, so we had easier access than they did. We had a kitchen, dining room, and two bedrooms. My parents put twin beds in the dining room after my brother, Leland, was born, so that it became our bedroom and Uncle Fred could have the "extra" room.

Uncle Marcus fixed up some rooms in the attic where Uncle Frank and his wife, Aunt Laurie, lived. When Uncle Frank and Aunt Laurie moved out, my brother and I got to move out of the dining room and into the attic. Believe me, this was a welcome step up with the chance of some privacy and solitude.

Uncle Marcus never repaid my parents or Uncle Fred for the loan they made to him.

Uncle Fred was my mother's youngest brother. He was the babysitter for all of the kids in our house. Uncle Fred cooked and cleaned for us. He also was an alcoholic and was in and out of work a lot. He worked as a waiter in the dining rooms on the boats that sailed from Boston to New York by way of the Cape Cod Canal. He knew a lot about New York. As far as I could tell, he knew the most about life.

All the kids loved Uncle Fred. We used to play with him and tease him. He had been married and divorced once and never had a family of his own, so we became his kids. We'd run him ragged.

Uncle Fred was always drunk, and all the adults in the house always talked bad about him. His own brother, Marcus, didn't even want to give Uncle Fred the room upstairs, but my father convinced him that the family needed to look after their own. Uncle Fred didn't pay rent because he was drunk and broke most of the time.

In spite of his afflictions, Uncle Fred was the only adult in our house I could talk with about current events of the world. Every day he read the *Boston Post* and *Boston Globe*. He would tell me about New York and other places he'd been. This was the root of my fascination with life outside of my Cambridge neighborhood, especially life in New York.

I remember one time Uncle Fred tripped on the stairs. I went up to him and said, "Uncle Fred, can I help you?" He was so drunk I don't think he even recognized me. I remember taking him by the hand. I was maybe nine or ten years old. He put his arm around my shoulder, and I walked Uncle Fred up the stairs.

When we finally reached his room, there was no heat and it was the middle of winter. I could not understand my family's awful behavior. Uncle Marcus would not put a heater in the room because he did not want Uncle Fred there. My father wouldn't because Uncle Fred was a drunk and a sinner, so he was "punishing" him. I didn't see him as a drunk; I saw him as a sweet, loving man. He fell on the bed and I put blankets over him.

I asked him, "Uncle Fred, why do you get drunk?"

"My wife, Corinne. I'm trying to forget my wife, Corinne."

"Uncle Fred," I said, "Don't you realize that every time you drink to forget Corinne, you are always remembering?"

I sat on the floor until he fell asleep.

Neighborhood

My parents chose to live in Cambridge because many clans from Barbados had settled there and told them there was work to be had. Harvard University and MIT made Cambridge a university town, and there were plenty of jobs open to immigrants who serviced the wealthy or who could rent out shops and provide goods and services to the university staff and students.

All of the kids in my neighborhood were first-generation Americans. Florence Manassian's parents came from Armenia, Peter Ballas's parents were from Greece, and Johnny Walsh's parents came from Ireland.

I had the advantage in our neighborhood because my parents—being from Barbados, an British colony—spoke good English. Barbados may have been the most literate country in the world: The Anglican Church made sure that everyone there was baptized Anglican, and it was the duty of the nuns and nurses to teach English. Although my mother and grandmother never went to school, they learned to read and write perfect English in church by reading the prayer book and the Bible.

The parents in our neighborhood had one clear goal for their children: to get an education. Many of my friends, like Florence, would attend their own parent-teacher conferences with their parents so they could translate what the teachers said. My mother and father would take me to parent-teacher conferences so that I would hear firsthand what the teachers had to say about me.

My parents insisted that I do well in school. If anything my parents did not approve of was brought up during those teacher conferences, I would get a terrible beating.

My mother never beat me, but my father beat me with a strap or a rope. Sometimes he hit me on the butt, but mostly he'd just swing, landing most of the blows on my head. We were graded on our academic performance and our conduct: "E" for Excellent, "VG" for Very Good, "G" for Good, "F" for Fair, and "P" for Poor. I usually got all Es for academics, but I was often marked Fair or Poor for conduct—usually for laughing, whispering, or throwing things in class. I received a lot of beatings because my conduct was unacceptable to both of my parents.

Over the years, there were many times that families in our neighborhood would help each other with key skills necessary to survive in America, their new home. They supported each other as they discovered their way to hope, change, and opportunity. For example, my father helped Florence's father, Mr. Manassian, learn English so he could take his citizenship test.

Race was never an issue. We were all one and we learned from one another. Women took care of each other when they were sick. Our mothers never minded if we played at each other's homes so long as we behaved ourselves. I would ask my mother permission to play at Peter's house and she would say, "Yes, but behave!"

I learned to eat raw spinach and olive oil from Peter's family, which began a long-time love of Greek food. The cultural fabric of the neighborhood served all families well for support, living, and learning.

Being a Boy of Color

Most people who came to America were fleeing from some legacy of poverty, despair, and oppression. They would discard the customs and beliefs that held them back and seek the opportunities offered in their new lives and land. At least, that was my reality growing up as a young boy of color and a first-generation son of immigrants. I would learn that my reality was not the same as that of other young boys and girls of color in my generation in America. For the most part, their family stories were vastly different. They did not come to America by choice. Their forbears were slaves.

While most of the struggles that shaped my youth involved my family, I also experienced what it was like to be black in America—a feeling of being different, unequal, and unwelcome. My first-generation immigrant neighborhood was generally without barriers, probably because we were all in the same boat—coming to America for work—so we stuck together. But when I stepped outside of the neighborhood, a different, starker reality confronted me.

Once, when I was about nine years old, in the spring of 1935, I got on a streetcar in Central Square. There was plenty of room to sit down, but I had a strong feeling that nobody wanted to be near me. I was the only person of color on the car. That's the earliest experience of discrimination I can remember. No one did anything to me, but no one would talk to me. It was like I did not exist, or worse yet, the people on the car wished I did not exist. In my neighborhood, I never felt like a nonperson. That empty feeling on the streetcar certainly left a lasting impression on me.

Later, when I was about fourteen years old, my father sent me to the store to buy a can of tuna fish. I ran to the Stop & Shop, but couldn't find the particular kind of tuna he wanted. I was searching through all the choices on the shelves when this guy came up behind me, grabbed me, took me to a back room, and started to search me.

"We saw you stealing."

"I didn't steal nothing," I said angrily. He searched me and couldn't find anything, so he let me go.

I was so humiliated.

When I returned home my father asked where I had put the tuna fish. I told him what happened. He grabbed my hand and said, "Come with me!" He walked to the Stop & Shop with a determination, purpose, and stride that I clearly could not keep up with. Upon our arrival, I pointed to the man who grabbed me and said, "There he is!"

He was much taller than my father, but thinner. He ran into his office and locked the door. We reached the office door and my father bellowed, "If you don't open this door, I'll kick it down!" My father was *big*. My father made his way into that office, grabbed the man by his tie, and said, "Look, this is my son. I am not a thief and he is not a thief! You don't do that to my son. I want you to apologize to him or I'm going to knock you out!"

The man was obviously terrified. I was terrified too, but at the same time, this was one of the most connected and loving moments I had with my father growing up. The man said he was sorry, but that someone had come up to him and told him I had been stealing tuna fish. At that, my father just snapped, *"You didn't hear me! My son is no thief!* I am not a thief, he is not a thief! Maybe I'd better write your boss!"

The man offered my father anything he wanted in the store that day. My father, still furious, replied, "I don't want nothing from your store. I want you to apologize to my son." He did. Within a week or so, we got a check for twenty-five dollars from the Stop & Shop for a generous amount of groceries.

Chapter 2:
Family

My parents weren't affectionate with each other, and they certainly weren't affectionate with my siblings and me. We never hugged or kissed our mother or father, and I never saw them hug or kiss each other. My mother always walked behind my father. They sat separately in church.

Church was the only place they ever went together. They didn't go to movies or plays. They didn't shop together or sleep together. When my brother and I were older and finally learned how babies were conceived, we used to kid each other that we must have been virgin births.

My parents kept their money absolutely separate, and you didn't dare ask one what the other made. When they married, my father gave my mother $10 a week to run the house. When I was born, he gave her one more dollar. She received another dollar when my brother was born a year later, and one more dollar with the birth of my sister ten years after that. With three children, she received a total of $13 a week.

The only notion my parents had of sharing money was this thing called the "meeting." It was a West Indian kind of tradition for family money management. My parents each put $5 a week into a "pot," and at the end of twenty weeks, they would alternately get the whole kitty. When my father got his "meeting," he put it in the bank. When it was my mother's turn, she spent it—mostly on my brother, my sister, and me. This was usually when we got new shoes.

My mother's spending habits would shape who I thought I wanted to be. She worked hard at home and on the job. When it came to money, she would spend it as soon as she got it. She was always buying gifts for the neighbors' kids and our relatives. A woman of enormous generosity, my mother taught me to help others less fortunate than myself. As little as she had, she always looked out for others.

Father

Back in Barbados, my father had worked as a chauffeur. He drove a lot of dignitaries and rich white people around— especially those who regularly vacationed in Barbados.

My father rarely talked about his childhood in Barbados, and when he did, all he would really say is that they were poor and that he'd lived a hard life. He only had sad memories of Barbados, most of which stemmed from the sense of abandonment he felt when his father left his family and came to America. I believe that is why being a chauffeur was so meaningful to him. He actually had a job when jobs were hard to find for freed slaves in Barbados, and he was fulfilling the role of his absentee father by providing for his family.

One of his proudest moments occurred when he became a U.S. citizen. While it could not remove the scars from the hardship of his early years, it did give him the hope of better opportunities that come with new beginnings. He became an active citizen in the church, and in the community. My father worked extremely hard to overcome so much, for which I now have a much greater appreciation. I now can go so far as to claim benefit from not only what he did, but also how he did it.

I certainly did not see things that way throughout my childhood. My father was raised in a very religious family. They lived
by the Ten Commandments and took the Bible literally. My father ruled by "He who spares the rod, hates his son, but he who
loves him is careful to discipline him" (Proverbs 13:24).

My father was a tall, handsome man, a very hard worker, and a great steward of the few things he had. He saved his
money in miraculous ways. Work and church were his life. He
had no real social life, and I have no memory of what he did for
fun, and little memory of having fun with him. Once a year he
took my brother and me to the beach and gave us each a nickel.
I took my nickel and played a carnival game and won a big
prize. It was a stuffed Collie dog. I was so happy. When I
showed him my prize, he called me a jackass. "You didn't put
that nickel in your stomach. You got this stupid dog." I was so
ashamed. I took the dog home and my father used it as a door-
stop. He could tell a funny story every now and then, but for
the most part, my memory of my father growing up had little to
do with loving and fun.

My father took great pride and identity in the service he
provided as a chauffeur in Barbados. He thought there would
be an even greater demand for his services in America and that
he would be able to utilize his skills as a driver as well as lever-
age his knowledge about how to service a vehicle. So you can
imagine his delight when he saw a sign in the window at a garage on Windsor Street in Cambridge that read, "MECHANIC
WANTED." My father applied for the job, but the garage owner looked at him and said, "We don't hire your kind here."

I can remember the excruciating sadness in his voice
when told me this story for the first time. It seemed as if that
bitter moment had been transported to the front steps of Stanley's house, where he first lived when he came to America. The
poison from the sting of the garage owner's words wrested all

control of his ability to feel and consciously process thoughts. He was finally rescued from his hypnotic state when Stanley came home from work. It took all the energy my father had to ask him, "Stanley, I saw a sign saying they wanted a mechanic. I went and applied for the job and the man said he didn't hire *our* kind. Why doesn't that man like West Indians?"

Stanley took him into the house and said, "Archie, let me tell you something. It wasn't that the man didn't like West Indians."

Archie interrupted, "But he said he didn't hire *my* kind!"

With a calm resignation, Stanley said, "Archie, he didn't hire you because you are colored."

My father was astonished. "What do you mean *because I'm colored?*"

"That is the way things are in America. There are some places where they won't hire you if you're colored."

That was my father's first experience with discrimination in America. It was unfathomable to him.

The first time I saw my father cry occurred when he started working for the John P. Squires Company. He made $8 a week. Through time he moved up the ladder of responsibility and seniority. He had been with the company for many years when, one day while I was doing my homework, my father came home and he was crying.

I asked my mother, "Why is Daddy crying?" She told me that he thought he was going to become the foreman of his section, but Eddie Coogan got the job instead.

Every day, Eddie Coogan and my father would go to work together. They would go to the drugstore and have a cup of coffee, and then go off to their jobs. My father showed Eddie the ropes and welcomed him from the day he joined the team. Eddie had emigrated from Ireland and had only been in America for five years at the time my father was passed over for the foreman position. My father had been working at John P. Squires twice as long as Eddie had been in America! At first, my father could not understand what had just happened to him. He had always worked so hard, he was so well liked, and Eddie was *his* friend. Surely this was not happening to him. But it did, and it ripped his heart out.

What hurt him most was that this dear friend, Eddie Coogan, the one my father took under his wing, never told him that he was going to get the job instead of him. This took a toll on my father, but to his credit, he found the strength and determination to press on. It was this event that inspired my father to become active in the union. He eventually became the shop steward, and Eddie had to deal with *him*. My father made him pay for not having enough faith in the bonds of friendship.

Even though my father's job at John P. Squires was to stand on an assembly line and slaughter pigs, he still always thought of himself as a chauffeur. He never owned a car, but he got his driver's license renewed every year to the day he died at the age of ninety-eight because he was a chauffeur.

I remember one day as a child, my third-grade teacher asked each of the students in the class to describe what their fathers did for a living. I remember saying, "He kills pigs." That night at the dinner table when my parents asked about my day at school, I excitedly said, "They wanted to know what you do for work, Daddy!"

"What did you tell them?"

"I said you killed pigs."

He was furious. I thought he was going to kill me!

"I'm a chauffeur! You go back and tell them that your daddy is a chauffeur!"

I could not understand his outburst, but the next day at school I did what he asked me to do. When he died, he still had his chauffeur's cap from Barbados sitting on his dresser.

He loathed the thought of my ascribing "pig killer" as the description of his life's work, but for forty-seven years he was a dedicated worker in a job he hated. I now understand how amazing that level of commitment was, and in some way, large or small, was motivated by that hope and opportunity to make things better for his family—something his father never did. His commitment was eventually recognized during his tenure at John P. Squire, when he became a shop steward. It was neither an easy nor a painless path. My father was a notorious collector and saver of things; nearly all of his treasures were stored in his dresser drawers. He was particularly attached to the watch his dad had sent to him from New York when he was a boy in Barbados. Once a year he'd take it out, polish it, and clean it.

I loved that watch. He never used it. He held onto valuable and precious things. He'd take this watch out and I'd admire it. He said to me, "When I die, this is going to be your watch, because your grandfather gave it to me and I'm going to give it to you and then you can give it to your son."

One day when I was about nine, I went into the dresser drawer when he was at work and took out the watch just to look at it, feel it, and hold it. As I lifted the face off the watch, I broke the crystal. I panicked, as most children do when they do stupid things. If I had put that watch back in the box, back in the dresser, it may have been several months—maybe a year— before he knew that it was broken. Instead, I stuck it under a pillow on my bed.

At that time, my bed was at the foot of my parents' bed. When my father came home from work that night, he pulled the covers over me and he saw the watch chain hanging from under the pillow. He pulled it out and saw the crystal was broken.

I had a little baseball bat in the corner of the room and he gripped that baseball bat as if he were Josh Gibson, the "Black Babe Ruth" of the Negro League. Instead of a baseball, my head was the target of his anger. I was still asleep, but in my dream I heard this strangely familiar voice call out, *"Archie, don't hit him!"* It was the voice of a woman, one that I'd never heard before, but I felt as if she knew me. It woke me up. There was my father with the bat raised over his head with a fire of fury in his eyes. He must have heard that voice, too; when our eyes connected he seemed paralyzed. It was not my mother's voice; she was still fast asleep. He said to me as he put the bat down and walked away, "Your grandmother just saved your life. My mother in Barbados told me not to hit you."

In that moment, I had been saved by an angel from God.

Four weeks later, we got a letter from Barbados. In those days when someone died in your family, you received a letter with black trim around the edges. So we knew it was a death letter. My grandmother had died the night that I heard the voice.

Many years later when my only grandson, Roshon, was nine years old, he would come to my house in the morning and I would take him to school. I used to keep the watch my grandfather gave to my father on the table. One time, while Roshon was waiting for me to take him to school, I came out of the shower and noticed the watch was missing.

I asked him, "Roshon, have you seen the watch that was here on the table?"

"No, no, I didn't see it, Poppy."

"But I know that watch was here, Roshon."

"I didn't see any watch here."

So I started moving my books around and there was the watch. I noticed the crystal was broken. I looked at him and he started to cry. I said, "Did you break this crystal?"

"Yes. I was playing with it and it broke."

"Let me tell you a story, Roshon…"

I told him I wasn't going to spank him because a voice of love once showered me with a moment of mercy.

My father had two personalities: a public persona and a family persona. His public personality was ebullient, outgoing, friendly, and funny; people really liked him. I used to sit back and think to myself, "If everybody knew him like I know him, they wouldn't like him at all." At home he was rigid, brutal. Growing up, I could not understand how this man who was so loyal to his church could be so extremely brutal to his children, particularly to me.

I was too young to understand the difference between being part of a religion and being a follower of Christ. I thought church people were supposed to be kind and loving, not brutal and suffocating. My father beat me unmercifully.

One spring when my cousin, my brother, and some neighborhood friends were playing ball in the backyard, the bat slipped out of my neighbor's hand and went through my uncle's window. I wasn't even in the game; I was just sitting and watching. When my father came home from work that night, Uncle Marcus said to him, "Your children were out there playing ball and broke my window." My father asked no questions. He gave Leland and me one of the worst beatings in our lives and then forbade us from going outside for the rest of the summer!

My mother's reaction was always, "He's your father." Sometimes she would help Leland and I sneak out when he was working in the daytime. She would help us polish our shoes if we scuffed them when we were out playing. He always inspected the condition of our shoes when we were grounded and being punished. My mother allowed us to sneak out and play a couple of times, but for most of that summer, we had to stay in that house. The neighborhood kids would laugh at us when we looked longingly out the window.

All the nine- to twelve-year-old boys in our interracial Cambridge community wanted to play baseball, and every one of us aspired to be on Patsy's Midgets. The team was made up of the best players in the neighborhood, and the competition for the limited slots on the team was fierce. That was *the* team to be on. We played our games at Russell Field in Cambridge. The only other important team was the Boston Red Sox. We all dreamed of being on both.

When I was twelve years old, my brother and I made Patsy's Midgets. I can still recall the joy, the pride, and the consuming excitement of a dream becoming reality. The coached picked my brother to be the catcher and me to be the first baseman. These were the positions of honor because we were the only players *given* mitts. I guess we were pretty good—at least we thought so. You became a big shot in the community when you were a member of Patsy's Midgets. Each member would be given a coveted sweater with the team name and your number on the back, and was entitled to walk around town as a boy to be honored, a real prince of the community. You were really *something* when you made Patsy's Midgets.

Our first game was on a Thursday. I can still feel the excitement and anticipation, like we were about to play in the World Series. The night before the game, my brother and I were so excited that we talked all night. "Oh boy, tomorrow we are going to play on Patsy's Midgets!" The second the sun arose, so did we, because we were not allowed to get up one minute before unless our dad woke us up to do a random midnight chore. We got up and ran down to the field as fast as we could. We were a couple of hours early!

The game finally started, and Junior Bradford was pitching. It was midway through the first inning, with a boy on first base. I was beside myself with the excitement and the joy of playing. I hovered close to first base, in position, ready in case Junior wanted to pick off the runner. In order to throw the ball to first base, Junior had to look in my direction, which he did. The expression on his face was a mixture of disbelief and fear. I noticed his glance went beyond me and into right field. An eerie feeling began to consume me. Something was not right. Junior confirmed my feeling of growing terror when he said, "Hey Gene, here comes your father!"

The kids in the neighborhood knew that my father could be consumed by abusive rage, so my friends were afraid not only for us, but also for themselves. Junior could tell that my father was not coming to see his boys play ball. I turned and saw my father slowly walking through right field toward first base, with a rope in his hand. In that moment, it occurred to me that this was also the day of my piano lesson. I'd been so excited about my first game on Patsy's Midgets that I had forgotten all about the lesson. I knew that I was in for it.

I dropped my mitt on the spot and ran home. I got downstairs and leapt on the bench to start my piano lesson. My father came home a few minutes later and walked downstairs, pulled me off the piano stool, carried me to the cellar, tied me up with the rope to one of the columns holding up the house, and beat me.

He beat me so badly about my head that my glasses flew across the room and shattered against a wall. He wouldn't let me cry or scream because he didn't want the people upstairs to hear what he was doing. If I cried, he beat me harder. When he eventually untied me, I fell to the ground, nearly comatose. He picked me up and carried me back up stairs and put me on the piano stool and forced me to finish my lesson.

The teacher said, "Oh, Mr. Callender, he's not in any condition to take any lesson today…"

"He's going to take the lesson. I'm not paying fifty cents for nothing. He had no business going down to that ball field."

She was kind and nice and went easy on me. He stood right there the whole time. I was barely lucid. I was in so much pain, both physically and emotionally.

When my teacher left, I crawled up the stairs, went to my mother and told her, "I don't ever want to be in his presence again. Mama, I'm sorry. I hate him. He tried to kill me."

I then went to the attic, lay on my bed, and cried and cried. I stopped speaking to him and did everything I could to avoid him from the time I was twelve years old. I would answer him if he spoke to me but, for the most part, I stopped reaching out to him and seeking advice that sons normally seek from their fathers.

Whenever my father and I were in the house at the same time, I would hide in the attic. On the occasions he worked nights, I came downstairs to visit and listen to Tom Mix and "Little Orphan Annie" on the radio with my brother and younger sister, Thelma. I didn't care what he said to me, I didn't say anything. I became a recluse in the attic.

I was too embarrassed to go back to Patsy's Midgets. I heard someone else had already taken my position. My father made Leland leave the team as well, and Leland hated me for it.

One day when I was in high school and my sister was just about seven years old, my father was giving her a beating. I was upstairs in the attic, my refuge anytime he and I were in the house at the same time. I heard her screaming. I went *flying* downstairs where I saw him with his great big razor strap in his hand. I grabbed the hand with the strap and said, "You hit her one more time and I'll kill you!" I let go of him and began daring him, "Hit her!" He knew that my bottled-up rage had exploded into a scary place, somewhere in the deep recesses of my mind. I wanted to kill him, and wanted a reason for what he was doing. I don't know how I would have done it but I would have killed my father if I could. He turned and walked away.

I don't know why he was beating her. In our home, children were seen but not heard; we were never allowed to ask questions. Our parents commanded and we complied. If we didn't, we'd be beaten. No matter how stupid or illogical the request, we could not question it. My father would come into our bedroom at two in the morning and say to my brother and me, "Gene and Leland, get up and wash the back stairs." We got up and washed the back stairs.

Mother

My earliest memories, and, for that matter, my childhood memories, created the fabric of what I became. I reflect on them now and understand that there is a purpose for all things, no matter how inexplicable they seem at the time.

In my first conscious memory, I was lying in a crib in my parents' bedroom. I think I was less than two years old. I remember waking up and nobody was in the room. I was reaching up on the bars of the crib and nobody was there and I began screaming uncontrollably from fear of being alone. I can hear myself screaming now. My mother came running up. She was downstairs visiting with my Aunt Sylvia. She yelled, "What are you screaming about?"

I remember her picking me up, and for a moment, I felt immediate comfort. However, instead of hugging and nurturing me, she hit me. In a vain attempt to make me stop screaming, she hit me over and over to scold me. That moment, and that memory, has had a tremendous impact on me. I remember this scene so vividly. I can see that little baby, and then all those whacks.

But even though she was not very affectionate, I knew my mother loved me. I would do anything for her. By contrast, I would do what my father wanted me to do, but only with hostility. I obeyed him out of fear because he would beat me if I did not carry out his wishes and demands.

When I was growing up, my mother would tell me all about the family she worked for, and their son, whom she helped raise. His name was Eric Williams. From the moment he was born, he was destined to attend Harvard. This is how my mother learned about college. Based on the experience she gleaned from serving the privileged, my mother concluded that I, too, would attend college. And because Eric Williams was going to go to Harvard, she was convinced that I should attend Harvard, too. She also picked my major when I was still a child. She wanted me to be a doctor, because she spent so much money on doctors that she wanted me to earn back the money she had spent.

A hypochondriac, she constantly suffered and she would tell me, "Go get the smelling salts and hold it to my nose." Other times I would rub her down with Ben-Gay to ease her aches and pains. She would say, "You put it there, you gotta take it away." So I'd dutifully go get what she thought she needed or I'd apply what she thought she needed to remove the pain…which I had apparently put there.

* * *

Years later, in 1957, I got a call that my mother was in the hospital. The last time that I had seen her, she had come to help me clean one of my churches in Harlem.

That multilevel structure was a collection of stores, and the main store on the ground floor was a butcher shop. The previous tenant had been there for twenty-one years and had never washed the floors; he simply kept putting fresh sawdust on it, so we had twenty-one years of crushed sawdust to remove. We dug through the layers of crud with pickaxes and shovels until we finally got down to the real floor, which was cement.

My mother bought lye, brushes, and a whole bunch of other stuff, and she got on her hands and knees and scrubbed the floor of that storefront where her son was going to minister a church. She did see the cleaned-out shell of our storefront church, but she never got to see our mission and parish in action, nor did she get to witness her son's professional success.

But I knew she was proud of me.

I was the first one from my family to get to the hospital. When I arrived, my mother was asleep in the recovery room, following surgery. The doctor told me she was very sick, that she had cancer of the pancreas and liver. When they opened her up, they saw that the cancer had metastasized so much they just sewed her back up.

He gave her between six months and a year to live.

I remember sobbing uncontrollably.

Although I was married to my first wife at the time, the person I had rushed to Boston with to see my mother was not my wife, it was a woman named Wendy. There's no sugar-coated way to say that except to say that, at the time, Wendy and I were having an affair.

When Wendy came over to comfort me and I told her the news, she started to cry, too. Once we calmed down and the nurse took my mother to her room, Wendy and I went upstairs to see her.

My mother looked at me, and then she looked at Wendy. There was a pause; it seemed like an eternity, but in this moment I knew that my mother did love me unconditionally. I was married and had a daughter, *her* granddaughter—but as she looked at Wendy she said to me, "Do you all know what you're doing?"

"Yes, Mother."

And that was it. No rebuke, no Pentecostal condemnation, simply accepting me, loving me through all of my success but, more importantly, through my failures. Then she reached under her pillow and took out a twenty-dollar bill, and, sick as she was, she put it in my hand and said, "Here. Go buy the young lady something to eat before you go back."

Of all the things my mother ever did for me in my lifetime, that little act said more to me and taught more to me about love than anything she'd done before.

When Wendy and I returned from Boston, it was the beginning of the end of our affair—and not because of *my* moral compass, but because of Wendy's. Wendy read me the riot act and pleaded with me to see a therapist, to work through my issues with being a family man. Her ending the relationship was an act of wisdom and, in hindsight, of love. My deep disappointment forced me to step back and observe my own personal behavior from the outside. For the first time. It also got me to my first of many sessions in therapy.

* * *

My childhood was sad, lonely, and oppressive. My parents' religion, or their implementation of it, was steeped with
rules and consequences—something with which I became all
too familiar. But the experience of my youth was not biblically
based. It was not the Word of God, The God of Love, but the
religious ceremony and interpretation and application of rules
to fit the needs of the congregation. Consequently, I had the
fear of God. I was afraid God was going to punish me just like
my father did.

Chapter 3:
Education

The prospect of college was the source of one of the biggest arguments my mother and father ever had. My father insisted that, after I finished high school, I should work and contribute to the family expenses

"No," my mother insisted.

I can still remember my mother's voice: "Even if I have to scrub toilets for the rest of my life, he's going to college."

To fulfill her dream, my mother found a job for me when I was eleven years old. I worked in an automobile sales factory cleaning floors. Later, when I was thirteen, my mother got me a job filling bottles with rubbing alcohol. I always brought my wages home to my mother, and she would count it out: Two dollars for me, and the rest for my education.

When I graduated from Cambridge Latin High School in 1943, I took exams for college and passed easily. These exams were a blend of aptitude and intelligence. All the schools that interviewed me said that the exams showed that I should study social science. I said, "No, I'm going to be a doctor."

The school admissions officers would say, "You could do the physical sciences, but you would be superb in the social sciences."

I insisted on staying with the physical sciences. They couldn't understand my resistance. "I'm going to be a doctor."

I was finally asked, "Why?"

The only answer I could give was, "Because my mother wants me to be a doctor." Whether or not my mother willed it for me, her dream became my dream. I really wanted to go to Harvard to become a doctor.

Every year Harvard awarded a four-year scholarship to the top three graduates from Cambridge Latin High School. I was the salutatorian in my class, but, when I went for my entrance interview, I was told that Harvard had an admissions quota: Two colored, two Jews, and two Catholics. The interviewer added that Harvard had already admitted two blacks for that year but they'd be able to accept me if I came back next year. I said, "No way," and went to Boston University instead.

Boston University was glad to admit me as a student based solely on my qualifications. Interestingly, there were three other students of color in my freshman class. Our freshman class had double the number of black students admitted to Harvard in 1943! I registered for pre-med, but they, too, told me I might want to consider specializing in the social sciences, based on my exams.

Early on at Boston University, I had a friend named Newell Booth, Jr. Newell's father was a Methodist bishop in the Belgian Congo, and Newell's passion was very similar to his father's. Newell knew exactly what he wanted to do with his life, which I admired and envied. He knew that he was going to finish Boston University, go to seminary, be ordained as a Methodist minister, and someday be a bishop like his father.

One day he asked me, "Gene, what do you want to do with your life?"

"Well, my mother wants me to be a doctor."

"No," he said, "What do *you* want to be?"

"I'm going to be a doctor," I repeated.

"No, that's what your mother wants you to be. What do *you* want to be?" he asked again.

I respond

ed incredulously, "I'm going to be what my mother wants me to be!"

Newell said, "Gene, I'm not saying not to become a doctor, but do not do what your mother wants just because she says so."

He looked up at me and asked, "If you had a chance to do what you wanted to do, what would you do?"

I said, "Well, to tell you the truth, what I would really like to do is get involved in the struggle for equality and opportunity for colored people." (Even I called us "colored" back then.) I was stunned and wondering if I really just said that out loud.

"If that's really what you want to do, you ought to be a minister."

My *white* friend Newell assured me and went on to say, "Don't you know that most of the presidents of the NAACP chapters in America are ministers? Don't you know that the only colored congressman we have in Washington D.C. is a minister? If you really want to lead your people, you should be a minister."

I was dumbfounded. True to form, I said, "No way! My mother would never allow me to be a minister."

Basketball

My mother always instilled in me the mantra, "Never settle for being just good when you know you can be better." So when I got to Boston University, I decided to try out for the basketball team my freshman year. While I lacked formal experience, I really enjoyed the times we played pick-up basketball at the playgrounds growing up. I made the team. I was really excited. I was so happy to take this big step.

Being at college, I felt an emerging strength, if not a liberation toward manhood. Things were going quite well, and I was actually making a difference for the team. One day an article appeared in the back of the *Boston Sunday Herald*: "Callender Leads Terriers to Victory." I was overwhelmed with excitement. The closest I ever came to this feeling occurred during my first and only inning with Patsy's Midgets.

My mother knew I went to practice every day. She even washed my uniforms two or three times a week. She knew I went on Friday nights and Saturdays to play games. I assumed I had her blessing and approval, and that she shared my joy.

I was wrong. She saw the article, and it brought about feelings of complete and utter embarrassment from the scorn and possible retribution she anticipated she might receive for my "careless" decisions, which, she felt, compromised her commitment to modesty.

Modesty?

She told me I had to quit the basketball team. I asked why. She said, "Now the Pentecostal saints know that I allow my son to walk around in public in shorts, and that simply is unacceptable. That sin will not be tolerated in our family." I was so shocked and dismayed. My newly found wings were clipped in an instant.

And so I went back to the coach on Monday and told him I was leaving the basketball team.

"Why?" he asked.

"Because my mother wants me to."

This was my freshman year in college. He couldn't believe it. "What do you mean, your mother doesn't want you to play?"

"She's upset because my picture was in the paper and the people in her church are going to see and be mad at her for letting me run around in public in shorts."

"Does your mother know you are in college?"

"Yes, she knows."

"Does she know that in college you make decisions for yourself?"

"I don't know if she knows all that, but if she wants me off the team, I'm getting off the team."

I told my mother that my coach wanted to talk to her.

"About what?" she asked.

"About my getting off the team."

She said I should invite him over for dinner.

He was a southern guy from Texas, and she made him a nice southern-fried chicken with collard greens and all the foods he used to eat at home. After dinner, he tried to tell her that, when you get to college, you begin to get some independence and begin to make decisions for yourself. He said that I was a good basketball player and that it would help me in my future. She just listened.

"Do you understand?" he asked.

"I understand everything you're saying."

"Well, are you going to let Eugene stay on the team?"

"No. I'm not going to let God punish me because of basketball."

The coach couldn't believe it. I quit the team, just like that.

Eventually, my mother let me play recreational basketball as long as I wore slacks and a T-shirt. I started a little informal team on my own, and we would play pick-up games around the city. I would bring the team home, they would have fellowship in the house, and my mother would feed us. This was my "March Madness."

Paying for College

I needed to earn money to help pay for college and to contribute to the family, so I became a custodian at a printing company. It was the only job available that allowed me to maintain my classroom commitments. Once basketball was formally out of the picture, I started to look for other additional opportunities.

One night, while I was cleaning the floors from four o'clock until midnight, an opportunity fell into my lap. I noticed the foreman of the printing company doing his calculations longhand with a pencil. I said, "Joe, I can help you do that much easier. I'll teach you how to use a slide rule."

I told him I'd teach him more on one condition: I wanted to learn how to run the printing press. I knew I wasn't going to be a printer, but I didn't want to be a custodian anymore. I was *seizing* an opportunity to not *settle* for less. Surely my mother would be proud. Joe taught me the essentials of the printing trade, and I taught him how to be more efficient by using the slide rule to help him do his job. It worked out well for both of us.

Even though this was a union shop, every now and then there'd be a last-minute priority order and he'd say to the guys, "Gene knows how to run the press. Mind if he helps?" And they'd say, "Fine, fine." I had him teach me how to run every press in that place. I wasn't getting paid as a printer but I didn't care. They eventually found enough work for me that I didn't have to do the janitorial work anymore.

One day, the big boss, Mr. Seigel, came in, and he saw me running the press. He asked me what I was doing there, and I explained that I had taught Joe how to use a slide rule and mathematics that helped him do his work faster.

Mr. Siegel said his son was having difficulty with math and asked if I would mind helping him. I told him I couldn't do both jobs; he said to forget the press, just come to his office. So I became tutor to the boss's son.

I got a big raise. It was liberating to observe a need and provide a solution that would lead to something better. This experience helped me become confident in myself. Little did I know that that event planted the seeds that would inspire me to turn to the ministry and participate in social reform and public service.

With the goodwill I earned from the foreman and Mr. Seigel, I was able to find jobs for my girlfriends, other friends at school, and people from church. They were quality people and the printing company prospered from all of their efforts. This was a good time in my life.

Becoming a Doctor

During my sophomore year at Boston University, I was exposed to and learned a lot about what was going on in the world, especially the cultural and social disparity for a person of color. I had been so sheltered and unaware of so much up to this point in my life.

The same was true of my parents. They knew nothing about the NAACP; church was their life. It would seem that there would be a connection, and I had hoped my parents would look favorably on my desire for ministry. My hope was misplaced.

In their view, social change and reform were completely foreign, if not forbidden—a complete waste of time and money for a college education. I was there to become a doctor, not a minister!

But, oddly enough, my Uncle Fred knew about the NAACP. He also knew about the social disparity in America, and the role of ministers in the struggle for social reform. He seemed to know everything about the world outside of my sheltered, immigrant neighborhood. While unfortunately disconnected from my family, Uncle Fred seemed completely connected to the world of, and the reality of, being black in America. I sought him out soon after my conversation with Newell Booth, Jr.

Uncle Fred confirmed that it was true, that the heads of the NAACP he knew were ministers. I asked him, "Do you have any evidence for that?"

He said, with a smile and compassion for my distrust, "Yes."

Thanksgiving in Harlem

I was ten years old when I first read the book *New World A-Coming: Inside Black America* by Roi Ottley. It was a gift from my Uncle Fred. Each time I read that book, I learned something about my culture and history as a colored person; it helped me better understand who I was. I read about the struggle of people of color in their countries and in early America. It was as if the words and message of the book were written for me, encouraging me to find a role in the struggle for social justice, especially for people of color.

I longed to experience the reality of the vision I'd read in *New World A-Coming*; I wanted to see first-hand this mecca of culture, religion and churches, and the people called Harlem.

Ottley's book taught me about black leaders like Adam Clayton Powell, Sr. and Marcus Garvey. Then Uncle Fred started bringing me editions of *The Afro-American Newspaper* and *The Pittsburgh Courier*. I found out *we* had a Negro baseball league, and black opera singers, and entertainers. A whole new world opened up to me.

I had been on the sidelines of life up to this point, but my eyes had been opened. I became aware of God working *with* me so that He could begin His work *through* me. *This* is what I wanted to do with my life; I wanted to be like the leaders Roi Ottley introduced to me.

After I read *New World A-Coming*, I told my mother that I wanted to go to New York. She didn't want me to go, but Uncle Fred said, "Oh, let the boy go." This might have been the only time my mother paid much attention to Fred, but, reluctantly, miraculously, she arranged for me to visit her cousin Elma Corion-El in New York City during Thanksgiving break. My mother and Elma grew up together in Barbados, but had not seen each other in a very long time.

I was eighteen years old when I took my first trip to New York City, in 1944. My mother woke me up early on the morning of my first day of Thanksgiving break so that she could get me to the seven o'clock train from Boston to New York.

We took the subway to South Station. She put me on the train, kissed me and said, "Good-bye, son. Behave yourself." I was a sophomore at Boston University, but my mother was still concerned about my conduct.

I sat by a window so I could see everything. The train was crowded and noisy due to the Thanksgiving holiday. College students were going home; adults were visiting their relatives. The train went from Boston to Providence and then to New York.

My mother had arranged for my cousin Elma to meet me at the information desk in Penn Station. The station was so crowded; people were pushy. I clutched my suitcase and searched for anything or anyone familiar.

I walked around and finally asked a man in a uniform, "Where is the information desk?"

"Right behind you."

I was nervous. For a moment, I wondered if I had done the right thing. A sweet voice asked, "Are you Eugene, Eva's child?"

I said, "Yes."

We hugged and kissed and I met, for the first time, one of my relatives outside of Cambridge, Massachusetts—someone actually related to me who did not live at 52 Pleasant Street. Elma took my bag and my hand and we walked to the subway.

Suddenly, a train pulled into the station. There was a great big letter *A* on it. I could feel my excitement from something that seemed strangely familiar. I asked, "Cousin Elma, is that the 'A' Train Duke Ellington wrote the song about?"

"Yes," she replied.

I had that record at home; I played it many times. I could hum it; I could sing it; I could dance to it. But I never knew there was a *real* A train.

I was so excited and so happy. It was as if the Lord had brought me home. It had never occurred to me the song could be about something real, but here it was, my life rushing forward. My first steps into my life as a man.

The train sped through the dark tunnels of New York. When it stopped at Fifty-Ninth Street, most of the white people got off. I thought that was strange, so I asked Elma, "Don't any white people live where we're going?"

She said, "Most of those folks live in the Bronx."

The train went on to 125th Street, which was the dividing line for the ghetto, where a large number of colored people got off along with the few remaining whites. There were only a few of us left. I asked, "Are we going to be left on this train by ourselves?"

My cousin Elma said, "No, we'll get off at the next stop."

We went one more stop to 145th Street and Saint Nicholas Avenue, where we left the A train.

In Cambridge, I lived in an immigrant neighborhood full of mixed nationalities. The greatest concentration of blacks in one place was church. Ours was the only colored family in the neighborhood. Never before had I seen so many colored people in one place as I did in Harlem.

A bus came, and the driver was colored. I'd never seen a colored bus driver before. I saw colored policemen. There were colored bars and restaurants. I was so moved with all that I was seeing.

"Elma," I asked, "is this *our* land? Do *we* own this?"

"No, Gene, we don't own it. We live here, *we enjoy it*, but we don't own it."

We crossed over Saint Nicholas Avenue and walked from 145th Street to 141st Street. Cousin Elma seemed to know everyone. She introduced me as her little cousin from Boston. All the people welcomed me. I felt I'd found something special. I felt connected to something, but I wasn't sure what it was.

We reached the front stairs to her apartment when I noticed the building next door was called the Woodside Hotel. I asked Cousin Elma, "Is this the same 'Jumpin' at the Woodside' as the song by Count Basie?"

She said, "Yes." Then she told me that when Count Basie came to Harlem, he would stay at the Woodside Hotel, right next door to where she lived. That night I went to bed and thought, "Wow! I'm finally going to see all of those places I had only read about in the books, magazines, and newspapers that Uncle Fred gave to me."

The next day, Cousin Elma took me on a walking tour of Harlem. I saw the Savoy Ballroom and the Golden Gate Ballroom where years later I would hear Indira Gandhi, the prime minister of India, speak. We visited the Abyssinian Church, the Apollo Theater, and the Lafayette Theater. She taught me the history of all those places.

Elma tried to interest me in The Ethiopian World Federation Movement, in which she and her husband, Herbert, were involved. The Federation was made up of people who were planning and saving to go back to Ethiopia because they felt that America was not a safe or comfortable place for black people to live and strive and raise families.

Elma and Herbert passed out literature about the movement throughout the community and attended meetings. They became followers of Marcus Garvey, the Jamaican orator who began the movement called the Universal Negro Improvement Association (UNIA). This movement aimed to motivate U.S. blacks to go back to Africa. She told me about Elijah Muhammad and the Nation of Islam. She told me about Lewis Michaux's bookstore, located at 125th Street and Lenox Avenue; it had the most extensive collection of black nationalist literature and a broad collection of black newspapers from across the country.

And she told me how she marched with A. Philip Randolph, Shelby Bishop, Adam Clayton Powell, and Reverend William Lloyd Imes to integrate the stores on 125th Street.

A. Philip Randolph founded the first all-black union, The Brotherhood of Sleeping Car Porters. Reverend Bishop was the minister of Saint Philips, the famous and largest Episcopal Church in New York. Adam Clayton Powell was the young pastor of the Abyssinian Baptist Church, and Reverend Imes was the pastor of Saint James Presbyterian Church. These four men led the picketing and marching on 125th Street to force the businessmen to hire black workers.

The vision of Sunday morning after Thanksgiving remained so vivid and so alive that I can picture it today. Memories drift back of men walking around in tuxedos and spats going to church. The community was a collection of connected and caring families. There was so much love and trust. People didn't even lock their doors at night! It was a beautiful, beautiful place that was made so by its people. I had never seen anything like it in my life.

I was determined that, someday, I would come back to Harlem and it would be a part of my journey and struggle. I didn't tell anybody about this consuming fire when I returned to Boston because, in my family, no one ever talked about their dreams for the future. The Harlem essence and spirit was beginning to take hold of my life. For me, it is always Thanksgiving in Harlem.

Changing Majors

I was so moved by all that I saw, experienced, and learned from my first visit that, on the Monday morning after my Thanksgiving in Harlem, I rushed to the registrar's office to switch my major.

I switched to a major in philosophy with a minor in psychology. The registrar said he was so glad I had made this decision, and he reiterated that that I was going to do great in social sciences.

While I was emboldened to make a decision to change my major, it had been one thing to tell the registrar and something completely different to tell my mother. My solution? I didn't tell her.

I kept in touch with Cousin Elma during this transition in my life at Boston University. She was connected to the inspirational changes occurring in me. While we did not always agree on things, we were able to share our perspectives, our differences, and our passions in a way that was mutually enriching.

She continued to tell me all about Marcus Garvey, and I started reading about the black nationalist movement. I learned how Marcus Garvey owned a ship, got arrested for fraud, and got deported. Marcus Garvey was the forerunner of Elijah Muhammad, who founded the Nation of Islam. This was a great period of enlightenment for me, but it also started to challenge many of the beliefs I had. At times the enlightenment led to struggles.

At that point in my life I was confused about God. The God of my childhood was angry, severe. He wasn't the God of love I sang about. I was afraid of this God, but not so fearful that I wouldn't do wrong things. Yet I suffered when I did, internally and mentally.

Sometimes I deliberately and devilishly did wrong things with my peers or by myself, or sometimes I just did wrong things that I didn't know were wrong.

After my mystical experience with the Holy Spirit in the Pentecostal Church, I started to carry a King James Bible on top of my textbooks. In fact, my colleagues at school started calling me King James.

One guy named Nick said, "You walk around with that King James Bible. What do you think? Think you're better than any of us?"

"No," I said. "I don't think I'm any better than any of you guys. But I've been converted, and I've been saved. I love the Lord, and I'm proud of it. I'm not ashamed of the Gospel."

I didn't say a lot, but I thought I could at least carry my Bible and let people see the Bible-totin' Christian. This was in college, where I had the intellectual ability to do the work well. At the same time, I had this naïve, simple kind of religious practice and awareness. All the religion I knew was the Pentecostal church.

Changes in my social and spiritual life began to really take shape during my time at Boston University. I joined a fundamentalist Christian group on campus known as the Intervarsity Christian Fellowship. This was a Bible-believing group, and

I eventually became the president of the BU chapter. All the other members were white.

My shift to philosophy at BU exposed me to interesting, challenging, and at times conflicting theories. Commentaries on Hume, Berkeley, Locke, Kant, Nietzsche, and Schopenhauer were some of the more memorable academic exercises I recall from my undergraduate experience.

Internally, I struggled with many of the philosophies, especially those that focused on the beginning of the universe and whether God actually exists. I had a kind of detachment that was rooted in my Pentecostal upbringing: I had to do the work, ascribe to their positions, and appeal to their proclivities to get good grades. While their beliefs might not have been my beliefs, I wasn't going to let those professors interfere with my belief in God. I also was not going to let them give me bad grades when I knew how to earn good ones.

I had three favorite professors at Boston University: Dr. Wayland Vaughan, my professor of psychology; Professor Edgar Sheffield Brightman, who taught philosophy; and Professor Bouman, who taught a course on the Bible.

Professor Bouman made a tremendous impression upon me; I will never forget him. He was a retired professor emeritus, with white, silky hair and glasses, kind of bent over. Bouman had a more profound effect on my life than the rest of my college experience.

Vaughan made psychology personal and interesting. He had a great sense of humor. I was really involved in what he had to say, and I loved his work. Vaughan made accessible aspects of human behavior that had been shut out of my life by the Pentecostal church. He made me see why religious bigotry and so-called piety should be shunned—particularly in matters involving sex, women, movies, dancing, playing cards, or even telling the truth.

Brightman was one of the founders of a philosophical school of thought in America known as Personalism. Parker Bowne was the original inspiration, and Brightman was his pupil and successor. Brightman was instrumental in evangelizing Personalism throughout academic philosophy communities.

Personalism had as its roots a belief in God. At its core, Personalism expressed that personality is the essence of the universe, that God is a personality, and that we are individual personalities emanating from this universal personality.

Brightman was engaging, a loving and consistent pacifist. I liked what Brightman was saying, and he practiced what he preached. Brightman brought philosophy to the level of daily experience.

I found it fascinating and began gravitating toward his beliefs, but as I did I began to struggle with my own foundational beliefs—which conflicted with the private intoxication of brilliantly presented philosophies that were counter to mine. Especially challenging to me was Brightman's idea that God was finite. If true, then everything else that I believed—everything that was real to me—had to be false.

The Personalists looked at Jesus as a mere personality who evolved into awareness of God and recognized the divinity in Himself and in all people. They believed that, like Jesus, we all could achieve the same awareness and divinity. That was heresy to me; yet, as I was experiencing it, there was something about this belief system that attracted me.

At this point in my life, the lines of religion and philosophy were dissolving into one another. I had an all-consuming desire to learn and feel more. I loved and still love the academic environment, but I found that, paradoxically, the more I pursued knowledge, the less I knew and, most of all, I was less connected to a "personality" and even less qualified to share my incomplete knowledge for anything purposeful. For me, religion and philosophy had become the same self-indulgent, exclusive, intellectual endeavor—not at all what I'd learned in my Christian experience about God being a God of love.

Professor Bouman displayed a keen ability to understand and relate to people. He was a retired professor who came back to teach a course, without pay, called "'Appreciation of the Bible." Bouman took a liking to me, I think because he saw my struggle to reconcile what I was learning in his class with what I had learned growing up in the Pentecostal church.

For example, he taught us that sex was a natural, healthy human experience, whereas I had been raised to believe that it was dirty, nasty, and sinful. He delighted in challenging young minds to think critically, and this was happening to me in his class.

I had a preconceived expectation of what the class would be about. Since I was already known as King James, I assumed I would be helping him teach the class. Yes, I was full of myself, and I learned one of many lessons in my life when, by the grace of God, He gave me an opportunity to be humbled.

After I registered, I found the class was not a discourse on the true Word of God, or a history lesson on the Bible. Instead, the course consisted of an analytical interpretation of how the scriptures came into being. Most challenging of all, it posited that the Bible was not inspired by God. This point of view contradicted everything I believed and had ever been taught. It really shook me up. But I found it enriching because it opened new intellectual windows and introduced me to new experiences.

Professor Bouman was keen on encouraging people to experience new things; he exposed me to a whole new kind of life. For the first time in my life, I went to a performance by the Boston Symphony Orchestra at Boston's historic Symphony Hall. I loved it! The music was delightful, but the fellowship and mentorship were even more compelling to me.

It was during this time that the United States dropped atomic bombs on Hiroshima and Nagasaki. Bouman came to the class the morning of the raid on Hiroshima. He was shaking. We were stunned as we watched this little old man with a hunched back and white hair with tears pouring out of his eyes. We just sat silently in the class and looked at him.

He finally said, "I wonder if the mercy of God is big enough to forgive America for what they did today." For the first time, at the age of nearly twenty, I began to understand that it is not so much what you believe, but who you are that matters. Bouman and I were often miles apart in our beliefs, but there was something in his persona that touched me.

It was through Bouman's direct and indirect mentorship that I began to pray about my questions about God. I was lost in my intellectual pursuit of God and life, but those prayers were the first steps from simple knowledge of God toward a relationship with God. In a lonely pursuit, I had tried to find God on my own until Bouman led me to the meaning of a healthy and wholesome relationship with people with different religious experiences.

Through my meaningful relationships and experiences during my undergraduate years, I felt a calling to serve people. My prayers and baby steps toward a relationship with God inspired me the same way as my experiences with Cousin Elma in Harlem. I now realized I was going to be a minister of some kind, but I also knew I didn't want to be stay with the Pentecostal church.

Chapter 4:
Ministry

When I was eighteen, I had had a mystical experience. In the Pentecostal church, you believe in the baptism, the Holy Spirit, and evidence that you received the Holy Spirit such as speaking in tongues.

At a revival in Cambridge, my brother had had this experience and he started speaking in tongues. Of course everyone clapped and acknowledged "Brother Leland." I said to myself, "Oh my God. They're going to like Leland more than they like me now." He was in, and I was not!

The first Monday after the revival, I faked speaking in tongues in the Gospel Hall. I got away with it! Many of the people in the church didn't seem to know the difference between the real thing and someone acting. But oh, did I feel guilty.

I just knew that God was going to punish me for sure. I prayed like I'd never prayed in my life, "Lord, please forgive me. I didn't mean to do that. I only did it because I didn't want people to like Leland more than they like me."

I prayed and prayed. My guilt was all-consuming. I couldn't study, I couldn't eat, and I just felt a horrible shame. I couldn't do anything. I thought I was the most miserable sinner in the world.

Two weeks later, I went to a young people's service at a church on Columbia Street. I was sitting in the front seat because I was the piano player and head of the youth group. I wore a hand-me-down suit. Then the congregation started singing the song "Jesus, I Come." As they were singing that song, I started to stand up. I could feel myself rising into the air.

For the next forty-five minutes, I was not conscious or aware of my surroundings. People told me that they saw me rise up into the air, come back down, then march around the church touching people who began to speak in tongues. I then found myself up at the pulpit speaking a strange language I did not understand. The church was packed and the members of the congregation all celebrated in the Holy Spirit and told me, "You're going to be a preacher." The people in the pews said, "Oh, the Lord's calling you to preach. Look at what he did to you." That experience was as real as my being here right now. It changed my life.

* * *

The minister and several members of our Pentecostal church in Cambridge were convinced of my calling based on my experiences with the Holy Spirit years earlier. They ascribed those experiences in the church as evidence of my calling. My path to the ministry became the subject of many sermons.

The ministers would declare, "How can he go to college to be a minister? You don't need college. You get a call from the Lord." The bishop came to me one day and said he was so glad I was with them and that if I remained in the ministry, one day I'd become a bishop. In those days, I'm not sure there was any place in the Pentecostal church for someone who was seriously interested in university education.

After I got my degree from Boston University, I wrote to numerous seminaries to inquire about enrolling. I didn't tell my mother of my career change. I still hadn't told her about changing my major three years earlier. I was accepted at several seminaries, but I chose Westminster Theological Seminary in Philadelphia. My mother thought I was going to medical school. She was very excited. She even packed my trunk for me!

When I finally got settled, I found twenty-one bottles of Pond's Vanishing Cream in the top compartment of my trunk. She hadn't given up yet.

Westminster Seminary

In the fall of 1947, I arrived at Westminster Seminary, a fundamentalist seminary that I discovered was very Calvinistic and very conservative. The seminary opened its doors in 1929 when it broke off from Princeton Theological Seminary, which was generally considered conservative; the founders of Westminster, however, viewed Princeton as too liberal. At Westminster, they believed in the infallibility of the Bible and that Jesus's was a virgin birth. At the same time they believed in a vigorous, scholarly education. I liked that.

I arrived just before classes were to begin. I remember walking into this beautiful building in the Chestnut Hill area of Philadelphia. It had once been an old gothic mansion and private home. There were acres and acres of land with a gatehouse on both sides of the property. The first person I saw was a black man vacuuming the rugs in the lobby.

"Pardon me, sir, can you help me?"

"Who are you?" The custodian asked.

"My name is Eugene Callender. I'm a student here." The man dropped the vacuum and ran fast into an office beyond the lobby. He looked terrified.

Out came a white lady who said, "My name is Margaret Robertson. I am the secretary to the registrar. I understand you are Eugene Callender?"

"Yes I am."

She turned around and left for what seemed like hours. Then a man entered the lobby to greet me. He said, "My name is Paul Wooley. I am the professor of church history here, and I am also the registrar. I understand that you are Mr. Callender. Please come to my office and have a seat."

"Mr. Wooley, may I ask you a question?" I told him what happened when I arrived and encountered the custodian and Ms. Robertson. "What's going on?"

He got a sheepish look on his face. "Well, I guess we were kind of taken aback because you're colored and we have never had a colored student here."

"Mr. Wooley, do you know why I picked this seminary? I could have been in a dozen seminaries. But I picked Westminster because yours was the only application that didn't ask me what race I was."

"Well, I guess that's because we never had the experience of having anyone but white students here."

Mr. Wooley honored Westminster's commitment and processed my registration. In the end, we were both glad we chose each other. The seminary never conceived that it would have a non-Caucasian applicant. I learned so much from the experience. I learned fundamentals like Greek and Hebrew and how to read the Bible in its original language. It was a very good, disciplined education for me, particularly coming out of the Pentecostal church.

Fortunately, I received a scholarship. However, I still had to work to make ends meet, so I became the weekend cook at the seminary. My sole qualification came from my mother, who taught me how to cook from the time I was nine years old.

When I had been at Westminster for no more than one week, I decided to eat at a restaurant downtown in the City of Brotherly Love. I sat at a table for over an hour. The waitresses walked all around me. People came and left; nobody said anything to me. It finally dawned on me: They weren't going to serve me.

I walked out of that restaurant, sheepishly, totally humiliated. This experience reawakened my feelings of being different that I'd had on that trolley car in Boston. I know it seems naïve for a young black man in the late 1940s to have no concept of the real world. I was embarrassed, and crushed.

When I returned to my room, I despairingly told my best friend, Lewis B. Smeeds, that I was going to leave. He said "Oh, no! You are *not* leaving. Let's go tell Mr. Wooley what happened."

Professor Wooley spoke to the faculty and called a meeting of the student body. He asked, "How many of you would like to go down to that restaurant with Eugene tomorrow?" When faculty members and students—all of them white—took me to that restaurant and sat down with me, and I was served. I was overwhelmed.

Professor Kuiper, the chairman of the faculty, told the restaurant's staff, "We understand that our student came here the other day and you didn't serve him." The restaurant denied it. But the faculty and students who had been there knew better. I will always remember the unity and fellowship of that time. A group of people who owed me nothing served me, aided me, and lovingly sent a strong message of equality for all of God's children.

I do not know if those working in the restaurant knew what was happening, or if they began treating all people of color equally. But I do know that I was always served there for the rest of my time at Westminster. I learned that a peaceful but poignant message of love for all through serving one's fellow man is a recipe for good.

Once I was settled in at the seminary, I wrote my mother a letter telling her the truth. The day after she received the letter she got on a train. I'm sure she came with a mission to get me out of there, but her attitude changed within the first few hours of her visit.

As we walked around the campus, she noticed that none of the students were black. She also noticed that none of the professors to whom I introduced her were black. She finally asked me, "Eugene, are there any colored folks here?"

When I told her that I was the first colored student ever admitted to Westminster, I saw her smile in a way she had never smiled before. I hadn't known how much my being their first black student would mean to her. It made her feel so proud—and that was one of the most important gifts she gave me. In that moment, I had a glimpse of the acceptance I'd yearned for throughout my childhood. I also had a glimpse of the first steps toward confident self-sufficiency. In that moment, I was so proud to be her son.

My mother had what I call an unconscious acceptance of white supremacy. If white folks did it, it was right. And here I was in this totally white environment, so I had to be somebody special. She would return home proud—so long, she said, "As long as you don't lose your faith in God."

"Mama, how am I going to lose my faith in God in a seminary?"

But what she really meant was, as long as I didn't lose my Pentecostal faith. Her acceptance of my pursuits at Westminster was a big step, and I was happy to have taken it with my mother. Needless to say, a very large, seemingly impossible weight was lifted from my life. It is so oppressive to live a life in secret.

Professor Cornelius Van Til was one of my most memorable teachers at Westminster. He was a professor of apologetics, and he used to talk about God by putting a big circle on the chalkboard and saying, "This is God." Then he'd draw a line and say, "This is creation," and never the two should meet. He said we relate to God because we are in the image and likeness of God, and we think God's thoughts after him. I learned the philosophy of Til's teachings very well, but I never fully understood it. In fact, I struggled to apply it to my life. I had the "book smarts" on the topic, but found myself conflicted in trying to live a compartmentalized spiritual life. Something was missing.

One of my most helpful growth experiences during my time at Westminster occurred while I attended North Penn Baptist Church, whose minister was the Reverend Dr. Charles Churn. It was my experience in that church that made me feel an energy that I never had felt in any Pentecostal church.

Like all the black Baptist churches in Philadelphia, people came to church in large numbers on Sunday morning. They sang moving hymns of Zion like "Precious Lord, Take My Hand," "In the Garden," and "King of My Life." They gave beautiful testimonies to the goodness of God. People were happy and jumped for joy, clapped their hands, and praised the Lord. It was in the Baptist church where I began to read and study all I could about the beginning and development of what we call the "Black Religious Experience."

I gave myself over to the feelings that welled deep within me. Dr. Churn was an inspiring leader. He asked me to become his assistant while I was still studying at the seminary, and several families of the church took care of me when I came to the city on weekends.

Dr. Churn preached with great feeling. He started off in an easy or smooth way, taking his text from some passage from the Bible and likening it to life as people in the congregation knew it. He often spoke of our old folks' hard times, and how they came through slavery.

He spoke of what he called the bad time, the Reconstruction Era after the Civil War, when the white folks set up "Black Codes." The whites did away with all of the good changes sought by the black men who were elected to the U.S. Congress and Senate during the Reconstruction Era after the Civil War. He spoke often of the evil doings of the Ku Klux Klan.

These things really stirred up the congregation; some of the people used to say that Rev. Churn was "moved by the spirit." One of members of the church gave me a copy of her shorthand notes on one of Dr. Churn's prayers. During these prayers, he would chant, moan, and plead for God's mercy on his children. I'd like to include one of those prayers at this time:

> Lord! Oh my good Lord, hear my prayer. Look down on these, thy children in this place. We hunger, oh mighty God, we hunger and thirst for thy love. We hear thy word and follow thy commandments. Blacks we are, Lord, and you made us. Sinners we are, as man born of woman is made to be. We kneel at the feet of thy son, Jesus Christ, who died on the cross for our sins.

Lord! We come before you praying your blessings on black people here and away. Oh merciful God, have mercy upon our people through thy son, Jesus, social justice to come to pass in this harsh land where we have known such sorrow and where we have known no peace. Hear our prayers, blessed God! Send down thine angels to watch over us as they watched over the babe in Bethlehem. Open a sure way for us as you parted the Red Sea for the children of Israel. Save us from those would destroy us, as you preserved Daniel in the Lion's Den. Have mercy on us,

Oh Lord, for we too are surrounded by those who would keep us in bondage forever. It's a long time, Lord…since I heard my mother pray, a long time. She's gone now, in the sweet by and by, up in heaven, sitting at the right hand of Jesus. But I remember my mother used to say—don't you worry, children; my God will make it right. One day King Jesus will come back again to see about this old world. And when that day comes, He's going to separate the wheat from the tears, then He'll wrap us up in the royal cloak of His love and everything will be all right, great God.

So brothers and sisters, don't you worry, the God of our fathers has not forgotten us. The God of our slave fathers and our slave forefathers and our kinfolk back in long lost Africa. The Great God will see us through.

By the time Dr. Churn had come to his high point that church would be on fire! Cries of "Amen!" and "Hallelujah!" would pour forth from every brother and sister. The whole building would rock with the spirit and the faith we all had to hold on to—a faith that God would see us through. Then Dr. Churn would announce a hymn, and we'd sing. Lord, how we'd sing.

The unsaved would fill up the mourner's bench. A member of the Deacon Board would go over and put Dr. Churn's prayer shawl over his shoulders so he wouldn't catch cold from all of that sweating he had done. North Penn Church didn't want anything to happen to their pastor, and neither did I. I loved that man.

Dr. Churn left the church while I was still in seminary. Then the church's board of trustees, led by Dr. Broomer, invited me to succeed Dr. Churn as pastor. I was a senior in the seminary at the time, but I thought I was too immature. I was also too frightened by Dr. Churn's excellence as a preacher to say yes. But I did preach each Sunday for two months after Dr. Churn left.

By the time I finished seminary I was in a complete state of confusion. I was lost in a conflicting sea of knowledge and experience. I would learn about God at Westminster, but I would experience God only when I participated in the black Baptist church on Sunday.

For those folks, God was like their granddaddy—he was with them all the time. They talked about God like he was a member of their household. For many years of my life, I struggled to reconcile the chasm between knowledge and experience of God.

In spite of my heightened internal wrestling match between philosophy and religion, I loved my time at Westminster Seminary. It challenged me in many positive ways, and it was a great time and environment in which I grew both spiritually and as a man. I was blessed with great faculty, classmates, and friends that I value to this day. I was president of my first-year class, second-year class, and graduating class. When I graduated *cum laude* from Westminster, I had a real sense of accomplishment. My mother was so proud of me.

There was one downside to this successful chapter of my academic journey. Since I was its first black graduate, Westminster was ill equipped to help me find an opportunity to go into the world as a minister. It had no place for me to work and no church to send me to. This was a real dilemma for which we could not figure out a solution. But God did.

Graduation

The speaker at my graduation was a man named Peter Eldersveld. He was the radio minister of the Christian Reformed Church, an all-white, all-Dutch church that I had never heard of. There were no non-Dutch members, no non-Dutch ministers. The church was isolated, insular, and very conservative. Its members did not shop on Sundays; they cooked their Sunday meal on Saturday nights. The kids did not go to public schools. They created their own "Christian schools" and a college, Calvin College. Those young people received a brilliant education. They really knew the classics.

Like many other denominations, the Christian Reformed Church broadcast nationally over the radio with a show called *The Back to God Hour*. Many ministers from this church gave me the impression that they considered other churches to be too liberal, not really holy, and lacking in biblical faith. The people of such churches, they believed, had backslid. They needed to be reached.

Peter Eldersveld had an assistant radio minister, Harold Dekker. Both were considered rebels. They were Dutch, but they felt that the church could not remain what they considered to be a narrow, insular Dutch institution in America. They sought to incorporate a broader perspective with their Christian Reformed experience.

So Eldersveld spoke at my graduation, and I also spoke as president of the graduating class. He came to me afterward and asked what I intended to do now that I had finished school. I told him I thought I'd go home because I didn't have an assignment.

He informed me that *The Back to God Hour* received a lot of mail from Harlem and they'd always wondered why. "How about working for us this summer in New York City and seeing why we are getting a significant of response from that community?"

"Fine," I said.

The one thing I knew was that I didn't want to go back to Boston, so this invitation was an answer to my prayer.

Within days of graduation, Adrian De Young, a minister from the Dutch Reformed Church of America, contacted me to ask what I was doing after graduation. I told him about the *Back to God* Hour and the opportunity to work with the Christian Reformed Church. While both are culturally Dutch-based, they are different denominations.

De Young said his church had an opening in Patterson, New Jersey, in the heart of an all-black community. Every Sunday, the white population came to the church from the outlying sections of Patterson, but they had no relationship with the black community. He explained that his church had a forward-looking minister, Mr. Vanderwegh, and asked if I'd like to work there for the summer as an intern minister.

With two choices before me upon graduating from Westminster Seminary, I spent a short time in New York to weigh my opportunities. I reconnected with a young woman from a Pentecostal church I had visited.

Her name was Gladys McClendon and she was the prettiest and the brightest girl in that church. We didn't have any real courtship, but I believed that she was the girl I was going to marry because she had the qualities I believed necessary to support me personally and professionally.

I went back to Philadelphia and made the decision to work for the Dutch Reformed Church in Patterson, New Jersey. Patterson was an upper-middle-class community, a nice place to live. And, if I were married, the Dutch Reformed Church would give us a house.

One day I called up Gladys and asked her to marry me. Gladys went to tell her parents. Her father was an alcoholic and didn't care. The first thing her mother asked was, "Is he saved?"

Gladys replied, "He's filled with the Holy Ghost."

That was the extent of my proposal, and she readily accepted. I was not yet ordained, but I had a job and we had a house. It seemed like enough for us at the time.

Marriage

When I was a little boy, my mother caught me touching my private parts. She yelled at me, "Don't ever let me see you do that again! Don't use that thing to do anything but pee-pee." By the time I got married, I had no experience with sex or sex education.

When I was in college, my friend Henry Ray took me out to meet girls. I'd hug them; I'd kiss them; but I would not have sex with them. Being raised in the Pentecostal church, I'd learned that sex is evil. Sex is bad. If you practiced sex and were not married, you'd go to hell. We didn't even mention the word.

We could fool around, but having sex was the unpardonable sin. This was the extent of my entire sex education.

Gladys and I were married in October 1950. We spent our first night as a married couple in the Hotel Theresa in Harlem. That was a big deal for me, because that was where Joe Louis and Dinah Washington used to stay.

We were both virgins and we knew nothing about sex. I was twenty-four years old at the time. We came back to the room and took off our clothes. We had both been raised with the same Pentecostal shame. Neither of us knew what to do. But we were married. It was expected. Even then, I felt like I was sinning. Neither of us knew anything about birth control, and Gladys got pregnant on our wedding night.

A little while after we returned from our honeymoon— which we spent at the home of a Pentecostal missionary in Buffalo, New York, when we were out running some errands, Gladys said she didn't feel well and that she hadn't had her period for six weeks.

I didn't learn what pregnancy was until I went to college. I remember sitting in the Milk Bar at Boston University with another student from the seminary when a girl came by and said, "See my rings? I just got married this weekend." When she left, my friend said, "Well, she's no longer a virgin."

I had no idea what he meant. Honest to God, I still thought that people went to the hospital to pick out babies, not giving a single thought to where they all came from.

I told Gladys she'd better see a doctor because it sounded like she might be really sick; that's how naïve I was. The doctor explained that she was pregnant, and our daughter, Renee Denise Callender, was born on July 15, 1951, almost nine months to the day after we got married.

Dutch Reformed Church

We were the first black family to live in Glen Rock, New Jersey. The ladies from the church redecorated the house for us and made sure we were supplied with more than enough household goods and furnishings. Walking into the house was one of the happiest moments of our marriage, and I still am grateful for the congregation's overwhelming welcome.

I was really excited to be embarking on this chapter of my life. I did a lot of good work there in a short amount of time and really began to reach the black community in the surrounding area. From my conversations with Adrian De Young and Mr. Vanderwegh, I believed that was my mission. I found out later that our visions for that objective were very different.

I always believed that the vitality of any church could be measured by the health of its youth ministry. Naturally, one of the goals I had for the Dutch Reformed Church was to reach the children, especially the black children of the area. I organized a vacation Bible school for hundreds of black kids. It was a weeklong session sponsored and led by our church, but we held the event at a local black church.

The white Dutch Reformed Church sponsored the program. We really connected with the kids, and that connection reached many of their parents, too—so much so that black families started to come to our church.

As the attendance started to swell, I met with many of the black families and prepared them for church membership, which was, I thought, the mutual vision for the church.

That mission was on the verge of being realized when I found out that there was a serious disconnect between me and the church's Dutch leadership. They accepted the idea of black people visiting the church, but there was no way they could become members of the church.

How could I have been so wrong about what I thought I was brought there to do? I was bewildered and heartbroken for all of those families that I connected with and counseled to become part of a new church family. I had been so captivated by the spirit and the love of those children from the church camp, and, through their leadership and energy, they brought their families into a journey that followed me to the Dutch Reformed Church.

I invited them, I welcomed them, I nurtured them, and I ended up crushing them because I set them up to be rejected. I was so embarrassed; I felt horrible. Not only did their hopes evaporate, but they were also abandoned. Instead of bringing the love of God to these people, we gave them the hate of man.

My bewilderment turned to anger. I could not work for or with the Dutch Reformed Church anymore. I reached out to Harold Dekker and asked if he still wanted me to help him with his Christian Reformed Church radio ministry, *The Back to God Hour.* Thankfully, he said yes. I left the Dutch Reformed Church the next day.

The Christian Reformed Church

Harold Dekker welcomed me to work in New York with open arms and an open heart. He was very happy that I came to follow through with his opportunity to understand the needs of the people in Harlem who responded to his radio ministry. I was the first non-Dutch member and black minister in the Christian Reformed Church. This was 1951.

I began poring through the mail from the listeners in Harlem. I noticed a few key profiles emerging from the letters. Most were from older people who were religious but found it difficult to get to a church due to sickness, immobility, and a lack of access.

The radio ministry served as a way for them to receive their religious experience on Sunday. So I hit the streets and began going door-to-door and meeting many of the people who wrote to see if or how I could connect with them. I learned that many people not only listened to the *Back to God Hour*, but they also listened to all the religious broadcasts on Sunday. They tuned into *The Lutheran Hour*, *The Catholic Hour*, *The Old-Fashioned Revival Hour*, and *The Back to God Hour*, and they wrote to all of them.

I also found out that a common reason they listened and wrote to these programs was that each program usually offered them something if they wrote to the radio ministry. They wrote because they might get a Bible, food, clothes, money, or help.

I prepared a report detailing my findings to the church leadership in Chicago. I explained that the people were not responding to the "unique" message of the Christian Reformed Church. They were just religious people who couldn't get to church on a Sunday and were hoping to get a handout or a hand up from the church.

I also told them I thought we could do something. After all, they were listening, and that was half the battle. Since we were at least getting the listeners' attention, I suggested we try to find out how best to really minister to them and build a connected community. I recommended that a first step should be to organize a Bible class and see if I could get them interested in that.

My idea got a warm reception from the church leadership in Chicago, and they gave me a small budget to take this first step. So, on Sunday afternoons at the Harlem YMCA, I organized a *Back to God Hour* Bible study class; as many as twenty people attended every Sunday.

While I was interested in ministering to these people, I was more interested in having a job so that I could attend the Union Theological Seminary in New York. I really poured myself into my work so that the Christian Reformed Church would give me a favorable evaluation.

I enthusiastically taught the Bible class and the Christian Reformed doctrine. As interest grew with my regular students, I offered them a Wednesday-night class at which they could learn about the Christian Reformed Church's theology. About six people came, most of them men. Much to my surprise, they all fully committed to the class and we were all enriched by our time together. God had a plan and was leading all of us. By the end of the class, they all wanted to become members of the Christian Reformed Church.

After they passed the examination for membership, all of them were allowed to become members of the church! *Black people* in the Christian Reformed Church! This was great news. The bad news was that no church would accept them. The closest church was located in New Jersey, and its parishioners were white, so we were not allowed to take them there. This was a bittersweet signal that progress was made, but there was still a long way to go with respect to social equality and acceptance in 1952.

There we were, a minister and his parishioners with no church home. So we all agreed that our Bible classes on Sunday and Wednesday at the Harlem YMCA would become our church. We were really pioneering a journey together; it was all sweat equity in the infancy of this ministry. It became *our* church that formally planted the seeds of my life in Harlem.

As we established a base for the Christian Reformed Church in Harlem, the church leadership agreed to sponsor my education at Union Seminary and to move my family and me to Harlem.

I loved my time at Union Seminary, and I learned so much from my experience there. I worked with some brilliant professors like Reinhold Niebuhr (still famous in international relations circles as one of the godfathers of political realism), John Bennett, Paul Tillich, and Bill Webber, a wonderful teacher who worked in East Harlem. I used to do "field work" with the East Harlem Protestant Parish. I liked what they were doing. They just weren't interested in Bible study. They were interested in social change!

All of this experience inspired my thesis at Union Seminary. The basis of my thesis was a belief that the Christian Reformed Church was in a unique position to partner with the East Harlem Protestant Parish to lead a revival in Harlem for the black community. They hired me as their missionary in Harlem, and the seeds of my future life had begun to take root.

Chapter 5:
Harlem Renaissance

Several hundred years ago, Dutch immigrants settled in an area of New York that they found good for farming. They called it Harlem, after the namesake community they had left behind in their homeland. They established a tight-knit community that was self-sufficient and economically viable for several generations. Through their economic sufficiency, an infrastructure emerged that gave birth to complementary businesses and opportunities for expansion. Harlem became a vital destination for many generations of Dutch immigrants. For the Dutch, Harlem transitioned from a homogeneous destination to a hub from which its native-born "American Colonist" generations began to safely and confidently migrate to other vocations and emerging city centers of the Northeast.

The migration from the predominantly Dutch hub of Harlem opened the door for a new cultural migration into Harlem by the British. Early British settlers to America found better opportunities for prosperity in Harlem than in the overpopulated hubs of other established British settlements in New York. They leveraged and transformed the solely agrarian roots of Harlem to a relatively stable balance of trade, commerce, and finance. This transformation engendered a shift in the cultural populace and influence from the Dutch to an era of British predominance.

Strivers' Row in Harlem was borne out of the remnant of the generations of British prosperity in Harlem to the next cultural transition of Harlem's infrastructure, in particular housing and businesses, to Jewish influence and ownership. It was at this time in the late 1890s that the seeds of migration of the black community to Harlem began to take shape.

By the turn of the twentieth century, there had already been a few generations of native-born black New Yorkers, with the population swelling on a daily basis from immigration and migration from other parts of the United States. In fact, there were more Barbadians in Brooklyn than in Barbados at this point.

While most immigrants from all cultures traded the desperate situations of their homelands for other sets of challenges here in the United States, they still found that they had a better chance for a better life. So a generational vision of hope still shone brightly through their lives.

To be sure, all immigrant cultures and races have authentic experiences of struggle, discrimination, and mistreatment. The plight for a culture of color was great, which was wholly evidenced by the obstacles and double standards that confronted the black community in Brooklyn and Manhattan, irrespective of whether its members were native-born Americans or first-generation immigrants. They had the most difficult and inequitable challenges in finding places to live, opportunities for work, and places to worship.

They had to pay more than a Caucasian for the same house or apartment. They received lower wages for the same job with little to no opportunity to advance in a career when a Caucasian—qualified or not—was available. The mark-up or "premium" a family of color had to endure in Manhattan in particular prompted a migration of the black population to Harlem.

Blacks had been moving to Harlem ever since the early 1900s, fleeing the congested and hostile West Side of New York City, the crowded tenements there, and the increasing eruptions of anti-Negro feelings. More housing became available in Harlem as the mantle of influence fully transitioned from the British residents to the Jewish owners. At this time, housing in Harlem was superior to any that blacks had access to in Manhattan.

By 1914, most blacks were moving to Harlem because they had nowhere else to go—not even Brooklyn, where only those of a higher income could afford to live. More than a few went there because the district was becoming a fashionable place for Negroes to live.

It was at this point that Saint James Presbyterian, a very large black church, decided, out of necessity, to join the migration.

Saint James's move from Manhattan to Harlem was not strictly symbolic. It was significant in that it legitimized the black community by rooting it in Harlem. It represented a commitment to a community and established a base from which the next cultural renaissance of Harlem's history would emerge.

The move was certainly met with resistance from many white residents and churches, but it happened. During the emergence, peak, and decline of what is known as the Harlem Renaissance, churches played a vital role. The churches kept the community of Harlem together and provided a fairly peaceful and loving haven to serve not only spiritual needs, but social, educational, and youth services, and aid to the underprivileged.

The Harlem Renaissance was born amid social and intellectual upheaval in the African-American community in the early twentieth century. It was an African-American cultural movement that thrived in the 1920s and 1930s, emerging toward the end of the Great War and blossoming from a literary movement and creative expression in African-American music, theater, art, and politics.

From that upheaval emerged a voice and a unity that was liberating for a growing black middle class comprised of the generations that stepped out of the bondage of slavery. They persevered by selflessly pouring themselves into education and employment opportunities following the Civil War. While technically free, the reality of society was far from it for these generations.

During a phenomenon known as the Great Migration, hundreds of thousands of black Americans moved from the economically depressed and socially fractured South to the industrial cities of the North to take advantage of the employment opportunities created by World War I.

As more and more educated and socially conscious blacks settled in Harlem, the neighborhood developed into a vibrant political and cultural center of black America. During the 1910s, a new political agenda advocating racial equality arose in the African-American community. The center of that universe in America was Harlem.

The juxtaposition of all colors enjoying, openly debating, and influencing the arts in a "neutral" environment made Harlem the equivalent of London's Hyde Park Speaker's Corner forum. One class and one race *owned* the infrastructure, the white Jewish community, and therefore benefited the most financially. But all *enjoyed* the environment.

A lot of ministers had done a great deal of work to improve black people's situation in New York City, particularly in Harlem. They were led principally by Adam Clayton Powell, Jr., a crusading preacher of well-known heritage. His father was Dr. Adam Clayton Powell, Sr., a man born of Virginia slaves who acquired considerable means and was the prominent pastor of the Abyssinian Baptist Church—the great gothic structure of New York bluestone—for thirty years.

Before the Abyssinian Church came to Harlem, it was located on West Fortieth Street downtown, opposite the site of the old *New York Herald Tribune.* In 1921, the church sold the site for $190,000 and erected the present edifice on 137th Street at a cost of $350,000.

Two other churches followed the Abyssinian to Harlem: Saint James Presbyterian, which moved from Wall Street, and Mother Zion AME—the African Methodist Episcopal— Church. AME was the mother church that broke away from the white Methodist church.

The leaders of these three churches, with A. Philip Randolph, then-president of the Brotherhood of the Sleeping Car Porters, formed the Greater New York Coordinating Committee for the Employment of Blacks. Before long, it had become a powerful organization. In the spring of 1938, Adam Powell led the committee in a "Black-Out Boycott" against the Consolidated Edison Company to force it to hire blacks in nonmenial capacities.

When the boycott tactic produced few gains, Powell geared this organization for sharper action. By means of intense agitation from the soapbox, the newspaper, and the pulpit, they assembled a group that fought with the Harlem Chamber of Commerce —which had consisted of all the white merchants in Harlem. This jobs-for-Negroes movement contributed to Harlem's fame.

There is no doubt in my mind that the black church has had a long and honorable history. Without it, life would have been bleak indeed for many of our black ancestors.

When I visited Harlem in 1944, the Harlem Renaissance was in its winter. Faith, love, and trust in the community were still the norm, but the weight of the second major migration to New York City during World War II brought stress to the infrastructure, the rhythm, and the comfort people enjoyed in Harlem.

Chapter 6:
Mid-Harlem Community Parish

When I started my ministry, my approach was different from that of the existing churches. For one thing, we did not start with Sunday services. We started with programs for alcoholics and drug addicts, and we organized rent strikes because the people who lived on Seventh and Eighth Avenues in Harlem didn't go to church. We also started a large youth program in the twenty-eighth precinct, blocking off the streets so we could have it for the whole summer.

Our church sought out the neediest at their point of need. They were not people who felt comfortable going to the established churches. They were very poor—most were on welfare. There was a great deal of alcoholism and drug addiction. I had to deal with these people's immediate needs. I felt compelled by the Lord to be a street minister, to go where Jesus called to lead. And so it began.

I graduated from my advanced work at the Union Seminary in 1952 and went out to work full-time for the Christian Reformed Church. I pleaded and finally convinced them that we needed a permanent location. We looked all over for a building. The Christian Reformed Church leaders brought in their lawyers and contractors from New Jersey, and the building that's still on the corner of Seventh Avenue and 122nd Street is the building they bought.

The paradox of this moment was that, while I was a minister wanting to care for his flock, I wasn't really interested in conducting religious services. I used the building to serve other critical needs in the community. We called it our church, but it was more of a missionary center than a place for Bible studies and services. In fact, our church services were still limited to our little Sunday *Back to God Hour* Bible study at the Y.

I look back and I can't believe it myself. I convinced the church leadership that we needed a church home and they gave it to us, but I still maintained the important function of ministering to the flock at the YMCA. For reasons I cannot explain beyond my God-given laser focus on my passions, I compartmentalized my functions as a minister and a missionary.

During this time, the missionary work was flourishing in the community. However, my work as a minister was simply limping along.

Through our missionary work in Harlem, I wanted to serve the drug-addicted, the homeless, and victims of the legal system. Through the combination of church, private funding, and rallying concerned citizens, we started a clinic to detoxify drug addicts, a housing clinic, a legal clinic, and several other community services.

While this was all part of the Christian Reformed Church, the primary leadership had no idea what was going on. They were in Grand Rapids, Michigan, and I was doing my thing in New York.

I had told Newell Booth back at Boston University that this was what I always wanted to do. Nobody watched over my shoulder. I could do anything I wanted. They sent me a check, and I would send them a monthly report telling them how many people were involved.

Hundreds of people were engaged in various ways. We were *being* the church, but we were not *doing* church. In terms of traditional religious services, we were limited in our ministry.

The missionary work we were doing in Harlem was making a big difference and getting noticed by church and secular media. The positive attention we received was far-reaching through local, regional, and national media outlets. It did not take long before the Missions Board in Grand Rapids heard about the coverage we were getting and decided that its members should come to Harlem to see what was going on. They were receiving regular updates from me, but they did not recognize or appreciate the impact and significance of what we were doing until they heard stories in the news media.

The visit was going well until they realized I was not formally conducting any religious services. It didn't help matters much when they noticed that I renamed our building and headlined our ministry as the "Mid-Harlem Community Parish" and parenthetically referenced "a Christian Reformed Church" underneath. They did not like my explanation that nobody in New York City knew of the Christian Reformed Church, so I had named it something with which people could identify. Having no religious services and changing the name certainly were obstacles but, by the grace of God, they were not insurmountable.

They did like that we were serving the youth in the area by conducting Sunday school and vacation Bible school. The church leaders sent me a crew from Grand Rapids to be on my staff. They insisted that I begin serving the whole community by conducting formal religious services because "our denomination believes in preaching the Word" and saving souls. I wanted to keep my job, so I complied.

Don't get me wrong; I understood the importance of church services to the parishioners, especially as a means to nourish them so that they were filled with God and energy to serve the community. But my passion was aimed at getting social action going. So, out of obedience, I held services in the church on Sunday mornings, but hardly anyone showed up.

Eventually, I gathered a team on Sunday evenings and we went out onto the street. We had an empty lot on 121st Street, so we moved the piano out there and had the choir perform. We went on the lot because that's where the people were—they weren't coming into the building. That's how we started formally telling people about God, by going out on the street and preaching.

We had to meet them wherever they were. They were happy to come into the church to get help for something (not realizing that any help we gave them was from God's love for them). But they did not want to be bothered by listening to some preacher or becoming a member of some church.

When we took our service to the streets, the community took notice. People would say, "This church must be something special if they come out on the street!" A full service it was: praise and worship, prayer, scripture reading, a sermon, and, of course, an invitation to be saved.

People became curious and we started growing a committed base of members. I started to enjoy this aspect of being a minister, and Grand Rapids was really happy with the results.

I had to train the new people who came to our church in fundamentals of Bible study and everything else. This was an area of mission work I never really considered, and I certainly did not envision the contribution it made to social reform. It is hard to stay committed to a cause if you do not have the love of

God and the belief in something greater than yourself and your circumstances.

I was just beginning to see how teaching could contribute to a community's vitality. With all of the knowledge I had gained through seminary, I never really learned or took notice of all that Jesus did by fervently teaching his flock. His teaching was nourishing the lives of everyone he touched. We began filling our church home with God and the love of Jesus, and then took our message to the streets.

Things were really starting to take off for me, the church, and our mission work in Harlem. I cultivated relationships that provided so much that I would have never had access to otherwise. Resources included money from the Taconic Foundation, which supported the integration of white hospitals so that they'd serve black patients as well.

Doctors, nurses, and psychologists from the hospitals became friends of mine and began to serve needs at the Mid-Harlem Community Parish clinics. We expanded our clinic for addicts; in fact, the entire fifth floor of our church was dedicated to this clinic. I knew I was doing what I was born to do. I even got the opportunity to speak on *The Back to God Hour* a few times as a guest minister. I was the first black minister ever interviewed on the program.

Chapter 7:
Jazz

It was because of the confluence of my ministry, missions, and public service work in the 1950s that I began working with Interdenominational Ministerial Alliance. This organization was made up of the clergy of Protestant churches not part of the Baptist Alliance (e.g., Pentecostal, Presbyterian, Lutheran, etc.). They did a lot of political work for the mayor of New York City to push social reform initiatives and garner votes in the black wards.

At one point they went to Mayor Robert F. Wagner, Jr. and pointed out that, while there were so many black people in prison, the Roman Catholics and Episcopalians had a monopoly on the prison chaplaincies, and none of them were black. The white ministers, they said, didn't know how to minister to our people, and there ought to be some black chaplaincies.

As a result, Mayor Wagner appointed three: One went to the president of the Alliance, one to the vice president, and the third—a part-time chaplaincy on Rikers Island—was mine.

I served as chaplain at Rikers Island prison for two years, and the prison work became an extension of the mission work we were doing at the Mid-Harlem Community Parish.

When I got to Rikers Island, a number of amazing jazz musicians were in jail on drug-related charges: J.J. Johnson, Walter Bishop, Chet Baker, Ike Quebec, Johnny Simmons, and Freddy Richmond among them. I thought, "Man, I've got all these guys on records at home, and here they are sitting in jail."

After they got out of prison, many of these jazz greats came to my church. They'd come to my Bible class, and they'd play worship music when I preached in the streets on Sunday mornings, just as they did when we'd meet while they were incarcerated at Rikers. What a worship band it was! I'd teach my class, then I'd say, "Come on, fellows, play some Bird for me." So I got to know a lot of the guys and I learned more about jazz.

One of the reasons that I connected with these jazz musicians was that I had a real interest in jazz. They also knew I was a clergyman in the community. Almost all of them had deep personal and emotional problems. Because many were alcoholics or drug addicts, their lives were filled with complexity and uncertainty.

And in our conversations, I tried to help them by directing them to our church's clinic to deal with their addictions. Here we had people who could help them to break through the negativity in their personalities and strengthen their self-esteem.

It was through my chaplaincy at Rikers Island and our addiction clinic at the Mid-Harlem Community Parish that we got to know all the guys in the Duke Ellington and Count Basie bands, and I began to get an insight into the epidemic of drug use among black musicians.

They were fantastic artists, but so many were tortured, exploited, and broken by their demons, race-based oppression, and the mistreatment or misdiagnosis of their sickness. Some never recovered, but anytime they were out of jail and were playing in the clubs in New York, they'd call me up and tell me to come listen to their gig.

I learned a lot about the art and soul of their music, but more importantly, I learned even more about addictions and numerous triggers of a broken human experience that can lead to disease and hopelessness. My experience at Rikers Island provided valuable insight into what we were doing in our clinic.

We brought hope to the hopeless and healing to the suffering, but most importantly, we were sharing the love God had for the lost. It was those who came to know God who were fully healed from their addictions. My time at Rikers Island really helped form the blueprint for our clinic's success and for the transformation of attitudes toward the drug problem in New York City.

Most of these guys never went to church priot to our paths crossing at Rikers. The closest they came to God was saying, "Goddammit." They were always curious, "What's up with this preacher?"

It turned into a relationship of trust and confidence. They knew that I liked them and their music, and this helped build trust. They trusted me because I met them where they were.

By using the depth of their feelings and their technical ability, these tremendously talented musicians were experiencing, in those artistic musical moments, their true selves. As soon as they put their horns down and came to the table, you wouldn't know you were sharing time with the same person.

Duke Ellington

Of course, the greatest of all of the jazz artists that I knew was Duke Ellington. In the language of the kids today, he was cool! Suave, good looking, and a great dresser, he was armed with a cute and clever vocabulary. I loved him. There was just something about him. Whatever *it* was, he had it.

He didn't know it, but in my opinion, he was the greatest. I got to know him when he was working with the New World Symphony, an all-black symphony orchestra in New York City. They played several times at the New York City Philharmonic and Carnegie Hall.

I learned that he grew up in Washington D.C. and was influenced greatly by James P. Johnson, a fantastic piano player who left the South to come north. Ellington wrote more songs than anyone else in the jazz world. He earned his success. He worked at it. He had class, talent, and variety. And his bands were always full of terrific stars. He liked to hang out with people like myself who were not musicians, but music lovers. Every now and then when he was in town we'd go out together, or we would just play cards.

He had the unusual ability to attract some of the greatest musicians in the world, such as Ben Webster, a saxophonist; Sonny Greer, a drummer; Rex Stewart, a trumpet player; and Johnny Hodges, the world's greatest alto saxophonist. Numerous other jazz musicians became famous both in the Ellington Orchestra and after they left. As a team, they were unbeatable.

The background accompaniment Duke wrote for individual talents not only showed them off, but also made them feel comfortable. He had tremendous influence in the music world and in the black community. His band became famous when it was the house band at Small's Paradise, a whites-only club in Harlem that had black waiters and a black orchestra.

A few years later, when I became involved with the Newport Jazz Festival and the National Civil Rights Movement, we'd talk more often. I was so impressed with Duke's knowledge of American history, black history, and jazz. We never really had a serious talk about the race issue because his band was so great that they could play venues that black bands never played and that black people couldn't patronize—the biggest being the Cotton Club in Harlem.

One time, when Duke was older, I asked him how he felt about more black orchestras not being able to play in the big clubs like the Cotton Club. He said to me, "I'm just cracking the wall." He never considered himself a militant civil rights activist. Duke Ellington was the greatest. He had an expression that I myself used many times: "I love you madly."

Billie Holiday

One of the more tragic stories from this time in my life was about Billie Holiday. I love her music. I would go listen to her perform in clubs around New York any chance I got. She was so gifted, but, like so many other artists, she was haunted by some demon in her life that was only pacified by heroin.

When she was arrested for using drugs, I finally had the courage to take a more aggressive stand in raising awareness that using was not a crime but a sickness that could not be treated by simply incarcerating the victim. I'm not saying that using was right (and I'm certainly not saying it was good, or that it should be overlooked), but that the way we responded to its use needed to be addressed and that addiction could be cured in a much different way.

When Billie Holiday was busted, I gathered volunteers from the Mid-Harlem Community Parish, from our clinic, from the neighborhood, and from the music scene in Harlem. We went to the precinct where she was being held and peacefully picketed with signs that read, "Let Lady Live." We preached a message of compassion for the sickness in an attempt to change attitudes toward the disease of addiction.

On July 17, 1959, I was standing in Billie Holiday's room at Metropolitan Hospital. She was under police guard as she began her last journey, traveling all alone. Her death was more than the conclusion of a troubled individual life. For me, it was the end of something that has not completely returned to American music or American life. A few days later, Bill Dufty, who co-wrote *Lady Sings the Blues* with Holiday, asked me to deliver the eulogy at her funeral; Billie had been living with Bill and his wife, Maely, at the time of her death.

While her life was in some ways tragic, Billie was special to our time. It was sad for me to see how race, class, sex, and politics were used to belittle even those whose lives have been enhanced by superior talent.

We hear so much about how terrible a life Billie Holiday lived because she was a drug-addicted black woman with a fifth-grade education. As a singer, she seemed to enjoy telling the tales of degradation that went with the troubles of race and drugs. But neither had much to do with her talent or her artistry. It was Holiday's singing that made her special to herself and to her listeners, who enjoyed treating her like royalty.

Billie Holiday was so unique that she cannot be completely defined by her color, gender, sparse education, or any other limits. Even though her sound was unusual, her voice small, and her range narrow, she expressed emotions so intimate and so pure that few can emulate her.

There was nothing cheap or obvious about Billie Holiday's art. She brought a harsh and vulnerable dignity to sorrow, but was far from lacking in the charm delivered by unsentimental joy. Holiday was a woman who knew what had happened to her and what she had to do, and who audibly reveled in the great gift she had received.

Our protest for Billie was held to expedite her release so that she could be cared for with dignity. The protest also generated some attention and momentum in our effort to transform the public perception of addiction as a criminal offense to a sickness to be treated.

Thelonious Monk

Thelonious Monk is perhaps the only jazz musician I knew who was Harlem-raised. Most believe he reached his peak during the bebop era. He was a contemporary of Miles Davis, Jackie McLean, and Horace Silver. He had one of the most original piano styles in jazz, but his genius was not recognized until relatively late in his life. Monk played jagged piano solos and tunes that allowed for space between phrases.

He was kind enough to do a benefit at my request for the Morningside Community Center, associated with the Church of the Master where I was minister at the time. The Morningside Community Center provided a range of social and recreational programs for disadvantaged youth in Harlem, reminiscent of the community center Thelonious grew up in. Monk didn't talk much to anybody; he was preoccupied with his music and his drugs. Because of his distinctive style, I was surprised at the warm reception he received at the church.

Monk and I saw each other from time to time in various clubs in New York City and occasionally at the church. (He'd attended our church every once in a while; he'd come in, sit in the back, and sleep in a pew.) I always wanted to have lengthy conversations with him about his style and his future.

He was a unique artist, but he was a poor conversationalist. I remember calling him on the phone in preparation for the concert at the church, and the conversation went something like this:

"Hey Monk, are you really working on the piano for the concert?"

"No, I'm not."

"Do you think we'll have a successful concert unless you do your best?"

"No, I don't."

Then I'd say, "Monk, this is important to me and the community. Would you like to come and visit at the church and talk about the good ol' days of jazz?"

"No, I wouldn't."

I guess I was lucky, because another friend told me, "At least you got sentences! To most people, he just says, 'No!'"

Thelonious was a very unusual human being and extremely good at what he did. I'm glad that I was able to know him and work with him.

I was humbled when I was referenced on page 336 of the recently published book, *The Life and Times of an American Original: Thelonious Monk,* by Robin D. G. Kelley:

> Monk did not let all the press go to his head. His commitments to his community remained a high priority, even if it meant performing in the house of the Lord. On April 7th, Monk and his quartet performed at the Presbyterian Church of the Master in Harlem as the featured artist in their Sunday evening Jazz Workshop Series. The Reverend Eugene Callender, a relatively young and dynamic minister, community activist, and consummate jazz lover had just inaugurated the series in hopes of reaching a younger, hipper generation. Monk had enormous respect for Rev. Callender because of his leadership in the Harlem Neighbor-

hood Association (HANA) and the Harlem Youth Opportunities Unlimited (HARYOU), but especially for his ongoing work with the Morningside Community Center.

Illinois Jacquet

Years later in my career, I developed a unique friendship with another great musician, Illinois Jacquet. I first heard him playing his sax in my room upstairs in the attic of 52 Pleasant Street, where my parents would let me listen to jazz. When he was only nineteen years old, Illinois Jacquet made a record with Lionel Hampton. He was sax soloist on the number "Flying Home."

We played golf together. We ate lunch together. We went out to clubs together. When Illinois Jacquet died in 2004, I was asked to conduct his memorial service at the Riverside Church, and I led his burial at Woodlawn Cemetery in the Bronx.

Lena Horne

When I started working for John Lindsay as the deputy commissioner of housing for New York City in the late 1960s, I was blessed to have inherited a wonderful gentleman on my staff named Ralph Horne. He was responsible for housing integration and was one of the few people I could really count on when I embarked on the critical changes necessary to reclaim the agency's mission. Ralph was trustworthy and really cared about making a difference for the citizens of New York. His value could not be measured. We became quite close professionally during the first three months I was in on the job. One Friday afternoon, I asked Ralph if he would like to get together for dinner. I wanted to thank him for his extreme professionalism and high character through the difficult organizational changes we needed to make to be more efficient and cost effective in serving the city's housing woes.

"I'd love to join you, Eugene. Do you mind if my niece joins us? We've been trying to get together for weeks, but our schedules never seemed to match until tonight."

"That would be great!"

Ralph and I left the office and headed over to *Frank's Restaurant* for cocktails and dinner. We were having our first relaxing moments in months while we began to unpack and share each other's lives outside of work. As we were settling into our next round of drinks, I noticed a striking woman crossing the threshold of Frank's. She looked so familiar but I could not place where I knew her from. As she strode across the bar searching for the person she came to meet, her grace and poise struck me like a lightning bolt.

In that charged moment, I grabbed Ralph's shoulder and exclaimed, "Oh my God, it's Lena Horne. Ralph, Lena Horne is here!"

Ralph looked as shocked and excited as I did. Lena Horne gazed in our direction, and suddenly her search appeared to be over.

"Ralph, she is looking right at us! She is coming toward us!"

"Indeed she is," Ralph replied.

Lena Horne, fully equipped with a beaming smile that could bring joy to any circumstance, rushed toward us, threw her arms around Ralph, and said, "Hi, Uncle Ralph! It is so good to see you."

I was stunned and felt so awkward, but Ralph calmly said, "Eugene, this is my niece Lena."

"It is great to meet you, Eugene. Thanks for letting me join the two of you for dinner. Uncle Ralph has spoken very highly of you and the work that the two of you are doing."

I stumbled with my reply. "The pleasure is ours, Ms. Horne."

"Please, call me Lena."

We had a remarkable evening. It was so peaceful, so genuine, and so—normal. I marveled at the lovely connection that Ralph had with his niece. It was the way I'd dreamed a family should be. As we departed Frank's, I reflected on my childhood and the peace I received from listening to a young Lena Horne on my record player.

While I was in high school, seeking refuge in the attic from my father's fury, I was allowed to listen to jazz records. One of the artists I enjoyed was a black musician named Jimmie Lunceford. He was a contemporary of Count Basie and Duke Ellington. Jimmie hired Lena to sing with the band, and I loved to listen to their music. It was such a great escape for me.

I credit Jimmie, Lena, Count Basie, Duke Ellington, and so many other jazz artists with helping me survive the last difficult years as a teenager in my family's home. While Lena did not have as powerful a voice as Billie Holiday or Ella Fitzgerald, she did sing with a uniquely heartfelt expression that evoked a singular connection with the listener. Lena was so expressive with her singing that I felt as if she were singing just to me.

The following Monday, I cornered Ralph to give him a hard time for letting me embarrass myself like a star-struck teenager when I recognized Lena.

"Why didn't you tell me your niece was Lena Horne?"

"I was Ralph Horne before she was Lena Horne," he replied with a smile. "Truthfully, aside from her being preciously humble, we are simply family first and always, and we want folks to know us as family. We think that is more important and infinitely more special. Family is what defines us."

"I experienced that firsthand Friday night, Ralph. You are blessed, and you both blessed me."

While I did not stay in my role as deputy commissioner of housing for long, I remained friends with Ralph for the rest of his life. Ralph, Lena, and I would get together for cocktails and dinner to stay connected throughout the years. I made every possible effort to go see Lena perform around the city—not only because I loved her artistry, but also because I loved her family. I felt connected to them.

Lena's personal assistant was a member of the Church of the Master in Harlem where I was Minister at the time, so Lena became connected with the church and contributed to many of its programs, such as detoxification and the street academies. She once found out that we needed a stove for the church's community hall, so she bought one and had it delivered. Lena had a great and giving heart.

In 1992, Ralph Horne passed away. His funeral was at Riverside Church, and, when the family proceeded into the sanctuary, Lena noticed me in the back of the church and called out to me, "Eugene, please join the family. You belong to us and with us."

A Chance to Heal

My relationships with such musicians and artists, along with my street ministry, brought into harmony my greatest passion in life, social justice. The plight of artists with drug addictions was a very natural progression for me as a mission for social reform.

Drugs and drug addicts were pariahs in the city, and most people were terrified of them. I wasn't scared to be doing what I was doing in Harlem. There was no reason to be afraid. When we first began our clinic at Mid-Harlem Community Parish, we let the drug addicts sleep in the church.

We needed to establish a presence, a trusted environment, and unconditional love before they would feel comfortable letting us help treat their addictions. But these people were so sick and committed to getting their fix that they would resort to stealing from the church to pay for their drugs.

One day in the middle of a cold December, my beautiful black cashmere coat—a gift from Earl Brown, a councilman with whom I had done a lot of work—was missing. When the word got out that somebody had stolen my coat, three of the girls, addicts—I remember one was named Joyce, another Juanita—said, "Rev, they shouldn't do that to you. You're the only one that cares about us. You provide a shelter. You feed us. They shouldn't do that to you. Don't you leave this building until we come back."

I don't know where they went. They asked me the size and color of the coat, and in less than three hours they came back with three black cashmere coats in my size! Later, they found out that one of the guys we let sleep in the church stole my coat. He pawned it, a typewriter, and a radio from the church. They found it all at a pawn shop.

I understood the problem. Drugs were their life. Of course I got mad, but they couldn't help themselves. They had to have drugs, even though we were trying to help them detoxify. They'd go upstairs to the clinic and endure seventy-two hours of withdrawal.

We had doctors and nurses who would give them Ritalin and Thorazine to help with the sleeping and the pain, but it was basic cold turkey. They'd clean themselves out and then go get high again because the high is much better after you've cleaned yourself out. When you're hooked, you get high to keep from getting sick.

I understood all this. My aim was to change New York City's attitude toward and policies addressing drug addiction. Prior to our activity in that community, all users were criminals and all addictions were crimes. It was a crime to use heroin, a crime to use marijuana. We helped shift the community's understanding of drug addiction, transforming it from a criminal activity to a health problem.

We organized the parents. We started a drug education group. I had all these volunteers who came from Lenox Hill Hospital and from Americans for Democratic Action. We became a lobby for understanding, addressing, and healing those suffering from addictive diseases. We started a program called Addicts Rehabilitation Center, which became the largest drug and alcohol program in the city.

I went on a crusade about drug addiction because I was incensed over how society, legal and law enforcement system protocols, and attitudes dealt with drug addiction. Treatment of the users was criminal! The pushers were criminals, but the users were sick and needed help. Clinical help, detoxification, and, in many cases, psychological support were the only way to heal an addict.

Heal the addiction and you take major steps toward curbing the demand. Curb the demand and you have less supply. With less demand and supply, you have fewer addicts. Like any other kind of sickness, if you can identify root causes and find ways to prevent the sickness, you stand a much better chance of truly healing the sickness.

Chapter 8:
Social Injustice

One of my very best friends is Mark Lane. We worked on so many projects together. He was a prominent Jewish lawyer in New York who dedicated much of his time and legal service to the clinic we set up at the Mid-Harlem Community Parish.

Mark was instrumental in helping me establish our detox clinic for drug addicts, the first of its kind anywhere. We made its existence known in the community and the jazz world, and the press helped us get the word out that its services were free. We had a force of volunteers from Lenox Hill Hospital, Saint Mary's Hospital, and Presbyterian Hospital. The volunteer doctors and nurses were instrumental in helping us aid these kids and adults both medically and emotionally.

Mark and I were heavily involved in New York City and Harlem community service activities. We were everywhere taking on every institution we thought was a purveyor of social injustice.

We organized the first rent strikes. We took on the absentee landlords. We took on everyone. Mark and I took on Warwick House, the worst of the mental institutions in the state of New York, which was known to mistreat mentally challenged black children of the Harlem community.

Although Mark was a white Jewish lawyer and I was a black Christian minister, we shared similar passions. Mark was a born leader. He was elected to the New York State Assembly in 1960. Mark and I worked together in the civil rights movement, and Mark was once arrested for opposing segregation as a Freedom Rider in 1961.

Mark wrote several wonderful books, and one his most compelling was called *Rush to Judgment.* Written after John F. Kennedy was assassinated, *Rush to Judgment* questioned the War-ren Commission's conclusion that three shots were fired from the Texas School Book Depository. It remains one of the most famous pieces of Kennedy assassination conspiracy literature.

In the 1968 presidential election, Mark appeared on the ballot as a third-party vice-presidential candidate, running on the Freedom and Peace Party ticket with Dick Gregory. He is such a dynamic and interesting guy.

A Catalyst to Change

I often went door-to-door, looking forward to meet-ing more and more people in the neighborhood. I wanted to meet them and I wanted them to know me. I also wanted to invite them to our church. In 1955, while canvassing the com-munity in Harlem, I met the Rowes, a family of nine living in one little room.

Their apartment was part of a single-room-occupancy (SRO) unit created by absentee landlords who owned several brownstones in Harlem. These landlords made more money by having more tenants. All of the families who lived in that build-ing had to share one community bathroom and one community kitchen.

I was appalled by their horrendous living conditions. There were two little beds in the Rowes' apartment. The kids had to sleep sideways to fit. The parents slept on a mattress on the floor. The pain that I felt for them touched me so deeply that I decided I had to do something about it.

The Rowe family's experience—squeezing too many bodies into too small of a space—was not unique in New York City at the time. It was typical of all of the people who lived in those SROs and others who did not live in the SROs. This really opened my eyes to the horrible conditions that many were experiencing—not only in Harlem, but in other communities in New York City.

At that same time, the Christian Reformed Church was in the process of buying the five-story building at 122nd Street and Seventh Avenue. This location was selected to be the center of Christian Reformed missionary activity in Harlem.

The leadership from the Mission Board in Grand Rapids selected a group of lawyers, architects, and interior designers to convert that old building into a beautiful new center. The first floor was made into the main worship center. The second floor was designed to be a recreation center. The third floor was a dormitory for the staff assigned to work with me in Harlem.

I selected the fourth floor as the location for a residential apartment for the Rowe family; we converted the entire floor into a five-bedroom apartment. Mr. Rowe became the building's custodian, and the Rowes lived in that building until all of their children had finished high school. Their oldest daughter, Carolyn, went on to become the first black female graduate of Calvin College.

I established a network of skilled and influential business, political, spiritual, and social power brokers throughout New York City. Doors opened for me professionally and socially through the network that spanned all colors, classes, creeds, and political proclivities. One of the great things about New York City is that it is not only the pulse of America, but that it serves as a global hub that draws people who want to satisfy their taste for a better life, either for themselves or in service to others.

Sugar Ray Robinson

One of the pleasures of my life is golf. While golf was a game at its roots, in the 1950s and 1960s in America, it was also a platform used to perpetuate a chartered environment for segregation, a haven for the entitled that enabled social inequalities spanning the bases of race, creed, and sex. Exclusive country clubs were social-, business-, and class-conscious organizations whose existence served to protect the self-selected elite and make evident the chasm between those included and those excluded.

While at that time, my color would have prevented me from joining a country club, some of the elite constituents of *the network* could invite me to play as a guest. Even so, it was a sport I enjoyed and a time of fellowship that I cherished. I have many wonderful memories and stories from my days on the course. However, the first step of my journey was to learn how to play.

I frequented Sugar Ray Robinson's barbershop in Harlem at 123rd Street and Seventh Avenue. I had always heard that Sugar Ray was an avid golfer in addition to being pound-for-pound one of the world's greatest boxers. One day when I was getting my weekly trim and fellowship—hanging out at the barbershop was less about grooming and more about talking and solving the ills of the world with a band of self-proclaimed experts on everything—I asked Sugar Ray if he had any tips to get me started on my quest to play golf.

He said, "I've got the best tip of all: my friend Charlie Brown. In fact, he should be here in a few minutes."

Charlie Brown was a black pro. Although he was never allowed on the PGA circuit, he played in and won in many black-only tournaments. Sugar Ray and Charlie played every chance they could, and Charlie developed Sugar Ray's game to a very low handicap. While Sugar Ray was well known for his excellence in the ring, outside of the ring he was still a colored man, especially when it came to finding places to play golf in the 1950s and 1960s. He was invited to play at country clubs, but not able to become a member of any of them. Even with all of his star power, he still occasionally struggled with abuse and social disdain simply because he was colored.

Sugar Ray introduced me to Charlie when he came to the barbershop. Charlie and I chatted for awhile, and then he took me to a back room in the shop, where Sugar Ray had a collection of fifteen full sets of clubs. Charlie took a good look at me and picked out a set and he said, "I think these will work best for you. Are you ready to go?"

The clubs Charlie chose for me were perfect and became my first and favorite set of golf clubs! I took lessons from Charlie on and off for about three years and developed a pretty good game. He was a very nice guy. I enjoyed being with him and learning from him. I asked him how he learned, and he said it was through years of observation when the pros were giving lessons to the members. During his many years as a caddy at several county clubs around the New York metropolitan area, he would steal moments to play when the courses were closed. He was a self-made scratch golfer.

Joe Louis

After a couple of weeks of lessons, Charlie said, "Hey Eugene, there is an opening in a foursome this weekend at Orchard Hills Country Club in New Jersey. Are you interested in filling the spot?"

I was hesitant. "Do you think I'm ready?"

"Absolutely! I taught you, didn't I?"

"I'll do it. Who are we going to be playing with?" I asked.

He said, "I can't make it, Rev. It will be you with Joe Louis and two of his friends."

I was engulfed in more than a hint of terror at the thought of taking my untested golf game to a new level of embarrassment in the presence of my hero, the former heavyweight champion of the world.

When I was growing up, I only discovered the aura of American sports icons through my friends and classmates. My brother, Leland, and I grew up idolizing Red Sox players like Jimmie Foxx, Lefty Grove, and Billy Werber, who were our childhood heroes. These great ballplayers were all white, and because we were the only family of color in our immigrant neighborhood, we were only exposed to the white world of mainstream sports. Therefore, at the time when we were young teens, our family had no knowledge of the Negro leagues and the all its great players.

My Pentecostal parents knew nothing of this phenomenon of idolizing sports heroes, save for one—Joe Louis, the first sports hero for people of color of my generation. This was particularly true with my family. We built our days around a Joe Louis fight. We gathered as a family, listening intently to each broadcast of a Louis bout, and when he won, we'd throw open the window and celebrate with shouts of joy, "Hot-cha dynamite! Joe Louis won the fight!" I could not believe I was going to be playing golf with Joe Louis!

The weekend came, and I rehearsed introducing myself to Joe Louis in my mind a thousand times driving to the club. I pulled up, and it was like another world. I did not know what to expect. I was surprised to see other colored men at the club, but disappointed to find that they were all working and serving the members.

My surprise became a stark reminder of the racial gap in America. I parked and began to unload my car when a caddy approached me and said, "You must be with the Louis foursome. Please allow me to take your clubs."

Two things struck me. The first was the reminder of what was about to happen: I was about to play golf with Joe Louis! The second was that I clearly stuck out. It was obvious to them that one colored man would only be playing golf with another colored man, and because of that they expected me and planned for *us*.

I stewed on the second revelation for years, but in the moment I focused on the personal magnitude of the first. I was about to meet Joe Louis. The caddy escorted me directly to the first tee box area, where Joe and his two friends were waiting for me. I awkwardly approached him, like a child trying to contain his excitement on Christmas morning. I extended my hand and simply said, "It is a pleasure and honor to meet you, Mr. Louis. Thanks for letting me join you today."

Joe looked at me sternly and said, "Nobody calls me Mr. Louis. Call me Joe."

His two friends in the foursome were from his boxing days and started to tease Joe—and me for that matter—by calling him "Mr. Louis" throughout the round. It really started to agitate Joe and took him off his game a bit. Fortunately for me, Joe did not let his friends' chiding take away the pleasure of the round. I was overwhelmed with excitement and joy; I became a golfing buddy of Joe Louis.

Most of his golfing buddies were big-time promoters and gamblers from his boxing days. They were all colorful characters, and I enjoyed my time with them.

We played golf about six times a year for four years. Joe was a genuinely nice and good person and I really enjoyed getting to know him. As great and famous as he was, during the time we played golf together, he was only allowed to play at the country clubs as an invited guest. He and I could not become club members because we were colored.

The staff treated Joe Louis and his guests pretty well, but it was very clear that he, and we, did not *belong*. We were not welcome in the clubhouse. We couldn't take showers like the white golfers. That was, and is, hard for me to believe, given his international stature and accomplishments.

Ralph Bunche

This discrimination played out over and over again. People of color who were openly accepted outside the United States were constantly struggling for acceptance and battling hatred within many sectors and institutions in their home country.

Ralph Bunche, for example, was the number two man in the United Nations from its birth. He designed Israel's current geopolitical structure and was recognized as a great mind and person internationally, independent of his color. He was a Nobel Peace Prize winner, the first person of color to achieve this distinction. He was a brilliant, peaceful, and wonderful man. He was welcome to walk through nearly any door of virtually any institution in the world, but, because he was a man of color, he could not gain membership at Forest Hills Tennis Club in New York City. He loved to play tennis.

Ralph and I played tennis a few times, and he worked me over pretty good, but we had a good time. Ralph was invited to play everywhere in the world, but he could not gain an invitation to become a member of the best private tennis club in his backyard of Queens, New York, all because he was colored.

I found these oppressive inequalities unbelievable, and I began to fall hopelessly into the belief that if Joe Louis, Ralph Bunche, Sugar Ray Robinson, and countless other world-renowned people of color could not break through, then we never would.

This belief was already commonplace among the majority of black America. There was no real outrage about this kind of inequality and mistreatment because all of the pain and focus of our common effort was aimed at the essentials. If the basics of life were a constant and at times a life-threatening struggle, then surely privileged entitlements could never be achieved and would never become real.

Jackie Robinson

This story played out for another American hero of color who I admired from afar for many years for what he did, a man I was blessed to call a friend, and who I admired most for what he did beyond the baseball diamond: Jackie Robinson.

At the end of the 1956 season, Jackie Robinson announced his shocking retirement from Major League Baseball. He was tired of being on the road and wanted to be with his family. He came to work in New York as the vice president of personnel for Chock Full o'Nuts, a unique chain of diners.

I met Jackie Robinson for the first time when he invited me to a meeting that he was spearheading in Harlem. He was attempting to form the Freedom National Bank (FNB), with a charter to be managed by people of color for people of color. I was then the chairman of HARYOU at the time, a Harlem anti-poverty and social reform public service organization. Given Jackie's persona, there were several financial and political New York powerbrokers in attendance.

When asked why he thought forming the FNB was necessary, Jackie replied, "This needs to be done because the white banks are not giving lines of credit and significant loans to blacks. White bankers are prejudiced and see blacks as poor risks and not capable of managing money. Something must be done to give all Americans, and that includes people of color, an equal opportunity and equal access to assets to bring their ideas and dreams to life, if they qualify."

I listened intently and was very impressed by his passion. I completely agreed with his objective. After the meeting, Jackie approached me and said, "Eugene, you were awfully quiet during the meeting. I am interested in your thoughts. You have a much better understanding of the community, the people, and the politics of this city than I do—especially Harlem. I was told that you would be the best person to help us navigate through this process, given all of your experience. So what do you think?"

I replied, "We can do this, but we will need to get the 'hustlers' out of the process."

"I will," Jackie said.

"Harlem is a complex political environment," I told him, "but it is the right place to establish this kind of institution."

Jackie leveraged his relationship with Chock Full o'Nuts founder William Black, a Russian immigrant, who committed to providing technical help in developing the plan and to help find investors. One of the people to whom he introduced the concept was George Champion, the president of Chase Bank. Champion found the project so compelling and necessary that he provided a substantial investment. He also agreed to lead a campaign of investment from larger banks. Champion had a philosophy of making the biggest entity the biggest contributor of any project requiring investment.

It was during this project that he mentored me on establishing a win-win scenario for all investor and project stakeholders. In order for the project to be successfully funded, the largest company needed to have the largest contribution because all others base their investment on what the biggest player does. I adopted what I learned from this project and applied it going forward to all future projects requiring funding. This philosophy transformed each of the initiatives for which I worked. The funding process led by George Champion certainly worked for establishing the FNB.

Most of the investors and the project team asked Jackie to be the first president of FNB, but he did not want to do it. He did accept a board position and served for two years. Instead, the group named William Hutchins. Hutchins was a successful businessman who had made a lot of money through a chain of liquor stores. He actually did a fine job of managing the bank responsibly and meeting the community's needs. I really enjoyed being a part of this important project for Harlem.

After Jackie and I worked together on the FNB project, we built a good professional and personal relationship and found pleasure in each other's company for the next several years. We especially enjoyed our golf outings. Although I loved baseball and most assuredly followed Jackie's career with the Dodgers, we hardly spoke about it. I think that had a lot to do with why we got along so well.

He seemed to be glad that I was happy just to know him as Jackie Robinson the husband, father, friend, working-class professional, and golfing buddy, and not Jackie Robinson the first black baseball player in the major leagues. In fact, he was really interested in what I was doing about social reform, so, when it came to work topics, Jackie led the conversations with questions about progress in the social issues in which I was involved.

Truthfully, especially in the beginning, I just wanted to figure out how to hit a golf ball like Jackie; I did not really want to talk about work when we played golf together. But he was tenacious. One of the real downsides to his historic baseball persona was the towering shadow that was cast over his excellent record and his commitment to social reform and the civil rights movement.

As you could imagine, Jackie was constantly hounded by people asking him about baseball, and since our relationship was born out of the convergence of our current professional lives, I consciously made an effort to not talk with him about his life in baseball unless he opened the door. One of those "opened door" moments occurred during one of our golf outings. So I asked him how he endured the transition in crossing the racial barrier into Major League Baseball.

Jackie said, "Branch Rickey's (the Brooklyn Dodger General Manager) transparency and understanding of what I would encounter gave me the perspective that I needed to do it, as did knowing that I was not just doing this for me. He told me that there might have been a few others who were better or more seasoned talents from a pure baseball perspective in the Negro Leagues, but that I was the best combination of ability, personality, education, and service, which is why he picked me over others. He believed I would be able to endure the constant scorn and have the best chance at successfully playing well through the transition. I respected him for that and since he committed to me, I committed to the mission and him."

Jackie elaborated, "Branch Rickey was all about winning, and that was his primary motivation to bring me, or any of the other great ballplayers from the Negro Leagues, to play for the Brooklyn Dodgers. The rest of it was a nice byproduct of the experiment, but would not have really meant much if we did not win. At the end of the day, though, it came down to the fact that someone was giving me a chance to do something because I was qualified, so I had to do it, and I wanted to do it."

Jackie further shared with me that the person who aided him most in his struggle to endure the belittling treatment he received on a daily basis—from within the Dodgers organization, throughout the league, and from the white Major League fan base—was Pee Wee Reese, a white teammate. I will never forget when Jackie looked me in the eye and said, "God sent me Pee Wee Reese. He protected me in the locker room and on the road. When we traveled to other cities, I usually had to stay in hotels that were in black-only neighborhoods, and Pee Wee always made sure I was never alone. I can't tell how many times Pee Wee helped me maintain composure in the face of so much hate. He deserves so much credit for the racial barrier successfully being broken because there were more than a few times I wanted to walk away. Pee Wee helped me continue on."

I wept when Jackie told me this. For the first time, I felt the weight of his pain. I suppose I imagined what it must have been like to be Jackie Robinson before I met him; he was a hero of mine, after all. As with most heroes, society—myself included—tends to focus on the glorification of what Jackie represented, rather than considering the personal struggle he endured for all of us, not just people of color.

I was raw from the hate he suffered simply because of the color of his skin, but soothed by the grace and inspired by the hope of one taking a bold step for the good of all and one coming alongside him to protect and comfort him in his constant suffering. I'm humbled by the magnitude of what the spirit of two unlikely teammates has done for the face of a nation and the mindset of its people. I never met Pee Wee Reese, but if I could I would hug him and thank him for loving my friend, Jackie Robinson.

Martin Luther King, Jr. said that Jackie was "a legend and a symbol in his own time" and that he "challenged the dark skies of intolerance and frustration." Jackie carried this challenge well beyond his years in baseball, and I am grateful to have walked with him on our journey to make a difference and serve those who needed a hand and a voice.

By the spring of 1958, Jackie and I were playing golf about every two weeks—I finally reached peace with my Creator and accepted the fact that I was never going to hit a golf ball like Jackie Robinson—and it was during this time that I realized social reform was a great passion in his life, and he was looking to me for ideas and experience so that he could make even more of a difference. We turned out to be a good match for where we both were at that moment. I had the experience, connections, and good reputation for social reform and civil rights; he possessed an iconic reputation and worked for a company that was committed to providing opportunity for those who might not otherwise be given it.

I know it was not a coincidence that Jackie went to work for Chock Full o'Nuts and that we became golfing buddies. Chock Full o'Nuts was one of the first companies to emphasize hiring black employees from an equal opportunity perspective. Jackie initially focused on the problems the company was having with absenteeism and its high turnover rate. He wanted to instill a sense of pride, commitment, and satisfaction in working hard and doing a good job.

Jackie liked this part of his job because he did not want to be a mere figurehead. Instead, he wanted to be challenged, and to be given meaningful responsibilities. He was determined to roll up his sleeves and make a difference. He would go to the office in the morning to manage his corporate executive responsibilities, and then he would visit the different Chock restaurants in the afternoon to talk to employees. He encouraged them to work hard and succeed because, he told them, they all had the ability to improve their lives.

One day he called me at work and asked, "Gene, with all the stuff you are into with your ministry and public service, is there anything that we could do together?" I told him I would think about it and offer some ideas the next time we played golf.

At the Mid-Harlem Community Parish, we had been ministering to a group of twelve single mothers and their kids. Some were homeless, some were addicts, and all were destitute. We were able to help them with their pain and meet them where they were. But we were lacking a mechanism to help them get beyond their circumstances. Most would spend a period of time at the Parish, get some rest, get detoxified, and then disappear for months at a time. Upon their return they would usually be in worse condition than before.

Another thing these women shared was that their total income consisted of a welfare check. Given their inability to keep jobs, the lack of employment opportunities, and the fact that they would lose the "income" from their welfare checks if they got a job (almost always temporary at best), they stopped looking for work. While the welfare program was born out of good intentions to help—and it did help in the beginning—its perceived permanence became an entitlement recipients could count on. That is how entitlement from welfare became entrenched in the culture.

Shortly after Jackie asked me if there was something we could do together, Francine, one of the single mothers in our Parish ministry, approached me. She had just completed her second detoxification at the Parish. I asked her how she was feeling and she said, "Rev, I'm lost. I'm killing myself and my baby. I want to stop, but I don't know how. I want a better life for both of us."

"What do you think would be a good first step toward a fresh start?"

Without hesitation, Francine said, "A job. But nobody is going to hire me. Never have, and never will."

That is when I realized Jackie and I could help these women.

I couldn't wait to get to my next tee time with Jackie. I told him that we had twelve single mothers we were helping out at the Parish and that while we were offering them shelter and compassion, we needed to be doing more to help them rise above their circumstances. I asked him if there was any way we could set up an internship program in his chain of restaurants, and he immediately saw the opportunity. By the time we hit the eighteenth green, we had a business model that only had to overcome one potential obstacle: the welfare offices of New York City.

Our plan was to schedule the women to assist as servers and cleaners at the various Chock restaurants around the city during the usual midday rush, noon to three. In order to get around the wage issue threatening their welfare checks, we planned to arrange for monthly milestone gifts, or bonuses, and to cover their transportation to and from the restaurants. The Parish staff and volunteers would care for their toddlers not in school and support the older ones with tutoring, help with homework, and other fun after-school activities until their mothers returned from work. The goal was to run this plan for a year, and if the women consistently met their responsibilities, they could earn full-time jobs. The key to pulling off this plan required one last critical participant, my friend Jim Dumpson, the commissioner of welfare in New York City. Our relationship developed during my years of public services and ministry.

Jackie and I described our plan to Jim and told him that our primary aim was to help these women rise above their current conditions, to aid them in becoming self-sufficient, and, in doing so, permanently get them off of dependence on their welfare checks. In order for the plan to work, we needed Jim to give us the opportunity to use the milestone "gift" incentive without it threatening their welfare checks during the first year. He loved the idea and fully supported it.

And so it began. This was a pretty big leap of faith that we were taking, but our excitement and anticipation of what could happen far surpassed any trepidation we might have had. The women seemed overjoyed when we told them about the opportunity. All of them were completely committed to their responsibilities because they believed that they had a chance to succeed if they did their jobs. They had never had the opportunity to test their belief before. That was the difference.

Jackie was blown away with their quality of work. With the exception of two of the women, they were all high-school dropouts, but each exhibited a work ethic, a commitment, and an aptitude for growth that brought tremendous benefit to Chock Full o'Nuts. What was even more astounding to both of us was that after the first six months, each woman voluntarily got off welfare and went to work for Chock Full time. They wanted to do it! What an answer to a prayer.

Chock's restaurant business was growing. We had more single women coming off the streets and into the Parish, so at our plan's six-month mark, we brought forth another wave of opportunity. As our experiment was drawing to a conclusion, Jackie told me that outside of his family, this was one of the most satisfying and life-changing things he had ever been a part of—even more meaningful than baseball.

As Francine and her baby were about to leave the Parish, she pulled me aside and said, "Rev, I want to thank you for saving mine and my baby's life."

I said, "God's love saved your life, and you accepting that love has given you the peace that you are now feeling."

Jackie and I continued this program for one more year. James Dumpson was amazed with the results we were getting. Midway through the following year, James Dumpson was offered another position, which was a great career move for him. Unfortunately, his replacement was a "by-the-book" kind of guy, and did not approve of the methods we used in the milestone gift portion of our program. He claimed it circumvented the rules of the welfare program, and that if we continued "paying" these ladies, they would have to immediately forfeit their welfare checks. This pretty much shut down our project.

It was very sad. We tried to change his mind. We explored alternatives, but we quickly lost the momentum we had built. I wish it had never ended, but I still found joy each Sunday when Francine and her daughter came to church.

Jackie and I still played golf together, were very active in civil rights, social reform, and politics, and remained friends in the years following our welfare-reform experiment. Several times after our golf games, he would come back to Harlem with me to have lunch, and on three of those occasions, his clubs were stolen. Instead of getting outraged, he would always offer the same response to me, "The guy probably needed the money for something." That was the kind of guy Jackie was. He was a great and gifted athlete, but he was an even greater man.

Challenges can arise in any friendship, and ours was no different. He and I had weathered many healthy debates from opposing perspectives, and all were issue-based, not personal. That is, until we took different sides on the actions of Paul Robeson. Paul was a lovely and abundantly talented man who had a huge heart for equality for all people, as he believed we were all God's children. He was an All-American student-athlete at Rutgers, as well as a gifted singer and actor. To date, I've never witnessed a more magnificent portrayal of Othello than the version of the character Paul evoked. He sang at my church a few times and I still get chills from the anointing of his voice worshiping God.

While Jackie had never really met Paul, the only significant difference between the two of them was their political philosophies—Jackie was on the conservative right and Paul on the liberal left. They both loved America, and both wanted to help improve the lives of Americans—especially those suffering from social injustice. It was from this context that I was so bewildered by Jackie contributing to the prosecution, if not the persecution, of Paul in the Republican hearings in Washington DC.

Paul was constantly being watched for his political activism and advocacy for socialism and anticolonialism, which he saw as a means to bring about social reform and equality here and abroad. The U.S. government took further issue with Paul because of his friendly association with people from the Soviet Union, where he was welcomed to perform (unlike numerous places in the United States). He was regarded as a true and celebrated talent, irrespective of his color; consequently, he was in high demand to perform throughout the USSR and he was treated royally. It was because of his activism and professional relationships through the arts in the Soviet Union that Paul became one of the prime targets in the second wave of the Red

Scare from the late forties to the fifties. In essence, Paul Robeson embodied what I called the "Disciplined Left," which actively pursued social reform and equality through policy and public responsibility. In fact, the Disciplined Left in America was really most productive in actively supporting major peaceful movements for social reform and civil rights.

Jackie was a staunch conservative who, like Robeson, really cared about social reform and civil rights in America, but it was a matter of political ideology that drove Jackie to testify against Paul in the hearings.

I asked Jackie, "Why are you doing this? What is the basis of your participation in prosecuting Paul? Have you ever met him?"

He responded sternly, "Paul's activism is anti-American, so I believe it is my duty to respond when called."

I said, "That is your right, but from my experience with Paul, he loves America and is only trying to make it better for everyone that is an American to live free, and have an equal opportunity to make a living. In so many ways, I see him pursuing solutions to the same broken conditions in our country that you and I talk about all the time. I can't help but think that you are being exploited to testify without taking the time to really know Paul and draw your own conclusion."

Jackie was upset with me. He stuck to his assertion that Paul's actions were anti-American and that his associations were potentially threatening. Jackie and I hardly saw each other socially for some time after this encounter.

Our work never stopped; we pressed on with trying to impact our city and our nation. About two years after our conversation about Paul, Jackie and I were taking a break from a meeting when he said, "Hey Gene, I want to apologize to you. You were right to call me out on my motivations and lack of really knowing the full scope of what Paul was doing. We both wanted the same things. It was just from different perspectives. I just wanted you to know that."

Jackie and Paul were both wonderful men and I was so glad that Jackie and I were able to come to terms on the strength of our friendship and the model of forgiveness from God. I was also glad to have my golfing buddy back, even though I still could not come close to hitting a golf ball like Jackie. That was just fine with me.

Chapter 9:
Politics

My interest in political and governmental activities began when I was six years old. My mother took me to Central Square in Cambridge where there was going to be a large parade to welcome Franklin D. Roosevelt, who had just been elected president of the United States. He was in Cambridge to celebrate the three-hundredth anniversary of the founding of Harvard University, of which he was an alumnus.

My mother held me tightly by the hand and said, "Pay attention. This is very important." And as the open-air vehicle with President Roosevelt in the back seat waving his top hat passed by, my little heart was bouncing with the excitement and joy of the crowd.

"Mama, why are we doing this?" I asked.

"This is very important. This man, President Roosevelt, is going to save the country."

The people in Central Square started to sing, "Here comes Mr. Roosevelt, liquor, liquor, liquor!"

I said to my Pentecostal mother, "What does that mean? Liquor, liquor, liquor."

"That's the only thing I don't like about Mr. Roosevelt. He's going to remove the prohibition laws of the United States."

"Why is that bad?"

"Because then everyone will be drinking whiskey again and they'll all start behaving like Uncle Fred."

I remember that scene very well. I was taken by the warm and genuine smile on the president-elect's face. I followed his career very closely through my childhood and into my young adult life.

He remained the president until he died in 1945. I was standing on the steps of a little store owned by a black West Indian woman on Howard Street in Cambridge because my mother sent me to that store that day to buy a hundred-pound bag of brown rice. As I was preparing for the purchase of groceries, somebody ran up the street yelling, "President Roosevelt just died." This was April 12, 1945.

I said, "What?"

I stood there on those steps and cried. I was in college at the time. I collected myself, arranged the groceries in my cart, and pulled the cart home faster than I ever had before. The whole family was sitting around the radio listening to the news of the president's death. Everyone was crying. Whether you voted for him or not, he was our president and our leader. It was a time when we were all involved as citizens, and he navigated the citizens of America through all manner of adversity during his unprecedented four terms. I grew up through the years of his presidency, so all I knew was to care and to participate. My passion to make a difference in the world was certainly influenced by the times we lived through and FDR's leadership during those times.

Marietta Tree

This passion naturally led me to my first major involvement in the political process during Adlai Stevenson's 1952 presidential campaign. This was a great experience for me, as I got to bridge my ministry and role as a minister in the city with social reform in a political platform. It was during this campaign that I met Marietta Tree.

She was on the campaign committee to elect Adlai Stevenson for President. She recruited me because she had heard of my work in the community. We used to go out on the street corners of New York making speeches about Stevenson. Marietta had a major impact on my life and provided a blueprint for many of the missions and public service programs I was a part of.

She was the daughter of the Episcopal bishop of Massachusetts. Her maiden name was Peabody, a very well-known name in Massachusetts. One brother was an All-American football player at Harvard and former governor of Massachusetts; another brother, Sam, and his wife were extremely generous and socially well-connected in New York City. The entire family gave a lot of time and a lot of money to various charitable organizations, especially to the missionary services we were providing to the addicts, the homeless, and the disenfranchised in Harlem in the early to mid-1950s.

Marietta was married to a member of the British Parliament named Sir Ronald Tree. They had beautiful homes in Manhattan, London, and Barbados. She was a real lady, a patrician. Irrespective of her social or power standing in society, she had a heart for doing what was right. Marietta Tree not only had the means, but also used her resources and time to do what she could to make life better for those who were struggling. She once lent us her Manhattan apartment for an event to raise money for the Morningside Community Center.

Marietta facilitated my invitation to join the Presidential Democratic Campaign Committee for New York. I was blessed to meet and work with a lot of powerful people in the Democratic Party, including Eleanor Roosevelt, throughout the primary and general elections. I was the only black on this committee, which actually gave me greater access and importance to the campaign and party leaders, because I was their gateway to the black vote in the elections. We delivered our voter segment for New York City in the 1952 elections. Being a minister also helped, by giving me another platform for a voice and influence beyond race.

The success I had in 1952 enabled me to have an even greater role in the 1956 campaign for Adlai Stevenson in New York. It was a fascinating and exciting time for me. I was selected to be on the executive committee of the Reform Democratic Movement of New York City (also known as the New York Committee for Democratic Voters). Again, I was the only person of color on the committee. The purpose was to elect more liberal candidates who shared the philosophy of the Reform Democratic Movement and to expand the interest and knowledge of the electorate of New York City. Our intention was to serve the communities, rather than the pockets of politicians. I learned and leveraged a lot from that experience. My role on the committee was to meet with churches, civic groups, and other organizations or associations that served minority populations to communicate the platform of Adlai Stevenson.

NAACP

In 1957, the nominating committee of the New York Chapter of the National Association for the Advancement of Colored People—the NAACP— said they wanted to nominate me for its president.

I had been working in Harlem for several years, and my name had often been in the paper. I was not a fiery orator, but I was engaging and credible. I led by doing good, solid work, but I did not feel I had enough experience to be considered for the post. The committee asked me to reconsider because they thought they needed a change. One of the women to whom I was close was on the nominating committee, so finally I said I'd do it. We ran a good campaign. I lost the election by forty-three votes.

Afterward, Percy Sutton, a friend of mine, admitted that the election committee appointed by the chapter had fixed the ballots so I would lose. He told me that the rationale was that they didn't want me to become president because I would bring in new people and they would lose control of the organization. This would not be my last experience of political manipulation.

New York Family Politics

After my initial foray into politics, an emerging movement was really gaining momentum and was starting to rival the stranglehold of the old-guard leadership that Tammany Hall had on Democratic Party politics in New York.

Tammany Hall political leadership emerged in the very early days of New York City to help immigrants, particularly the Irish immigrants. It had several rises and falls over the centuries, but in the 1950s it was in the middle of a powerful rise with Carmine DeSapio at the helm. Neither the Tammany Hall leadership nor the emerging reform movement had been able to deliver New York for Stevenson, but in both elections, the minority vote was deemed large enough for Stevenson to suggest I had done a good job.

I became pretty active in supporting elected officials and participating in social reform aspects of Harlem community politics. The first politician for whom I did a lot of work was a black man and graduate of Harvard, Earl Brown. He succeeded Adam Clayton Powell as city councilman when Powell was elected to Congress. Earl was very much interested in bringing about change in the political structure of Harlem. He wanted to challenge a group of five district leaders in Harlem politics who he thought were interested in serving their own needs more than those of the community.

I supported him and helped him win his election. Once elected, we worked to bring the public sector and the church together to serve the most needy of Harlem through my street ministries and the Mid-Harlem Community Parish.

Early in 1957, a group of black New York City politicians came to my office to encourage me to run for City Council for the Harlem district. The most powerful of the black politicians in the city was Hulan Jack, the borough president of Manhattan. Hulan appeared to control the five Harlem district leaders, and his family, like mine, had immigrated to America from the West Indies.

I had very little interaction with Hulan Jack and his associates prior to their meeting me in my office. Hulan cut directly to his agenda and said, "Reverend Callender, we think you should run for Earl Brown's seat on the City Council."

I was shocked. "Why?" I asked. "He does good work."

Hulan replied, "Not really, and besides, he's not from the West Indies like you and me. *Our kind* is the best to serve in leadership. Besides, Earl doesn't like people from the West Indies."

At that time, several black elected officials in Harlem were from the West Indies; Earl Brown and Lloyd Dinkins, the other two Harlem district leaders, were not. It always made me so angry that not only were people of color discriminated against, but there was blatant discrimination within the community of colored people as well. Those who emigrated from the West Indies considered themselves a higher class than those whose heritage was from the South. A kernel of this hypocrisy, beyond pure nationalism, was very evident growing up in my Barbadian American home at 52 Pleasant Street.

"But Earl likes me. He and I get along real well, and we work real well together," I said.

"He doesn't like you; he's just using you," Hulan Jack angrily responded.

The five district leaders in Harlem were career politicians. Earl Brown was becoming pretty powerful, and Hulan Jack wanted to cut him out of the scene. Dinkins would be next. Not only did Hulan and the West Indies political network control elections through voting "clubs" that manipulated votes with the promise of important jobs to those who supported them, but, as with all struggles for power, there was also a darker, more threatening way that the West Indies district voting "clubs" coerced votes from those who did not appear to support their objectives. The coercion came in the form of threats to make life harder for you or someone you love by impacting a job, damaging personal property, or threatening lives.

Hulan Jack said, "We will support you if you work with us, Reverend, and with our support, you cannot lose this election."

I purposefully attempted to put them off and said, "I'm just not sure it's something I want to do to Earl." Hulan told me to call the next day with my decision.

Hulan tried to encourage me: "All you have to do is say yes, Rev, and we will take care of everything. You don't have to do a thing; we'll provide the money for the campaign and guarantee that you'll win."

I just couldn't do that to Earl because he had been good to me, and because I believed we supported each other to make a difference in his district. We were better together because we complemented each other: I had a vision, passion, and people committed to our mission with the belief they could make a difference; he had access to resources and infrastructure that accelerated our success in serving the community where it was needed most.

After I collected my thoughts and emotions from Hulan Jack's unexpected visit, I called Earl Brown.

"Earl, you're not going to believe what just happened to me. I need to see you in person. Can we meet today?"

"You don't sound good, Eugene. Are you all right?"

"Not really. Can you come to my office so that we can talk?"

"I'll be right there, Eugene."

It had been less than two hours since Hulan Jack and his cronies left my office when Earl walked in. My head was in my hands, just staring at my desk.

Earl exclaimed with great concern, "Reverend, are you all right? What's happened to you?"

"It's really about what is happening to *us*. Actually, it's what others want to use me to do to you. Hulan Jack stopped by my office today to coerce me into running against you in the council elections."

Earl was furious. "Hulan Jack is corrupt and doesn't give a shit about the people in this city. He only cares about himself. What did you tell him, Eugene?"

"I told them that you and I work well together, that you were doing a good job in the community, and that I just didn't feel comfortable doing what they asked me to do to you. They gave me a night to sleep on it before I told them my decision. Earl, they said they could guarantee I would win."

"If we sit back and let it happen, they'll find a way to beat me with you or someone else."

"What do you think we should do?"

Earl paused for a minute and said, "I have an idea. Tell them you'll run so that we can keep them close and learn about their plans. There are others who are much more powerful than they are who can stop them."

"Earl, this is all sounding pretty serious, and it seems like we are getting caught in a dangerous web of power that has little to do with a government for the people."

"Welcome to the games people play in the name of politics and power. Good and bad people play the game, but in the end, everyone plays if they want to survive. I wouldn't blame you if you decided to walk away from this, but I will guarantee you this: Hulan Jack will not allow your life to be the way it was the moment before he encroached on it. He will attempt to control you unless you do something about it."

"That sounds ominous, Earl," I said. "How do you propose we get my life back from something I never asked for in the first place?"

"Call Hulan tomorrow and let him know that you will run against me. Then let me know as soon as you know what their plans are to not only guarantee that you will win, but what they plan for you once you are in."

"What happens after that?" I asked.

"You will have to trust me, but I'll take care of every-thing," Earl said.

What a day. My head was spinning. Things were taking on a life of their own—a life I did not ask for. I did not like anything that I heard in my office that day, but the only difference was that I knew Earl—and barely knew Hulan. I just wanted all of it to go away, and it seemed to me that, given the choice between my uninvited options, I would stand a better chance of reaching a result that I could live with if I worked with Earl. I had trusted him up to this point in my life, so I decided to stick by him this time. He seemed to have both of our best interests in mind.

The next morning, I called Hulan Jack and told him that I was in. Even though I was on the phone, I was very nervous about engaging in something that I had no control over and knew that I did not intend to do. Perspiration began to bead on my forehead.

Hulan said, "That is great news, Reverend. You are making a great choice for your career. Let's meet tomorrow afternoon so that we can brief you on our plans for you."

Those two sentences hit me like a bolt of lightning. *They* were choosing a career for me, and *they* had plans for me. It truly was all about them, their control, and their power; it had nothing to do with serving the good of the community. Though I had been semi-aware of this from the beginning, hearing his words and tone over the phone brought clarity to what they were doing. They were the beginning, I believe, of a rapid deterioration in Harlem politics. In my opinion, it was during their reign that the community of Harlem lost its voice in New York City, because many of its elected officials only cared about the money and entitlements they received, instead of caring for the people they were elected to represent.

I met Hulan Jack the next afternoon as planned. This is how I understood what they were doing: Hulan Jack and his associates told me they wanted to control the communities and the businesses in sections of the boroughs that were heavily populated with people of color but owned by white people. They needed to remove Earl Brown from office because he was making it difficult for them to manage all policy, legislation, and budget for their needs. My role in their grand plan, once elected, was to vote the way they needed me to.

Hulan said, "Reverend Callender, focus on your church. We'll give you all the support you need to help it grow in the community and we'll give you the details on how to vote. Together, we will build up and serve the community."

It was after midnight when I returned home. I immediately called Earl and told him everything, He was intrigued by their plans and said, "Eugene, don't go to sleep. I'm going to make a few calls, and then I'll come over to your place."

At about two in the morning, Earl called me up and told me to be downstairs in fifteen minutes. He said, "We are going to meet with some people who are very interested in what you shared with me from your meeting today. I think they can help us."

Earl picked me up, but didn't tell me where we were going. We drove close to an hour, out to Rockaway Beach. We went into a little beach house, and there was Carmine DeSapio, the head of Tammany Hall, the most powerful politician in New York State and one of the most influential leaders in the country. He was the head of the Democratic Party in New York. This was the first time I'd ever met Carmine. I had heard rumors that he had connections with influential and notorious families, which helped build his political power base. It was three thirty in the morning and he was in a bathing suit. I thought that was odd. He was playing poker when Earl and I walked in.

Earl introduced me, "Hi, Carmine. This is Reverend Callender."

Carmine greeted me: "Reverend Callender, Earl has told me lots of good things about you. I've also heard about the great things you are doing for people at the Mid-Harlem Community Parish."

I said, "Thank you, Carmine. There are a lot of really great people at my church serving the community."

Carmine introduced us to the other poker players. "Reverend Callender and Earl, this is Tommy Lucchese, Johnny Merli, Lucky Luciano, and Tony Salerno. We get together once in a while to play some cards and catch up on life."

I knew they all belonged to the prominent families and they were there playing poker with the head of the Democratic Party of New York State! I began to realize that this was not just a random occurrence, that Carmine DeSapio just happened to be playing cards with a few of his buddies at Rockaway Beach at three thirty in the morning. It was planned.

Earl Brown said to me, "Tell them what you have told me."

I was scared. Carmine said reassuringly, "That's all right, Reverend, you just tell me."

Apparently Earl had called them, and they hadn't wanted to hear what had happened just from him. They wanted to hear it from the preacher, himself. I shared the details of the plan.

Carmine paused. "Thank you for your honesty, Reverend Callender. I appreciate it. I recommend that you stick with the plan to run against Earl for the council seat in Harlem. I'll take care of the rest."

I responded, "But I neither sought nor have a desire to take Earl's seat on City Council. He is doing a great job!"

"Don't worry about that, Reverend Callender," Carmine said. "You will not have to run. I just need you to stick to your intention to run for City Council, no matter what. Can you do that?"

I inquired, "I think so, but I do not understand, what is going to happen?"

"I will take care of it. You do not have to worry about a thing as long as you stick to your plan to run for Earl's council seat. Oh, by the way, this meeting never happened. Can you handle that, Reverend?"

"I can."

Earl and I left the beach house and got back in the car to drive home. We drove in silence for about ten minutes, when I finally said, "What have you gotten us into, Earl? What is going to happen? What were those other guys doing there, and why is a councilman seat in Harlem so interesting to them?"

Earl calmly responded, "Everything will be fine. I've suspected that the other guys and their families had an interest in Harlem because they saw a real economic opportunity in the area for both legal and illegal opportunities. For instance, I think they have their plan to replace and remove the Jewish slumlords and business owners in Harlem. They are also interested in moving in on Bumpy Johnson's numbers-running action in Harlem. The only interest they could have in the council seat is to just see whom they might be dealing with on the legislative and business side of their interests. Hang in there, Eugene. It will all be fine."

Earl's reassurance was short lived. Hulan Jack called me minutes after I arrived in my apartment, and he was furious. I barely got the word "Hello" out before he initiated his tirade, "You backstabbing motherfucker, you told Carmine DeSapio about our plans to get you elected!"

I responded in a quite surprised tone, "What are you talking about, Hulan? I don't know what you are talking about."

"I'll tell you what I'm talking about you two-faced bastard. I just got my black ass handed to me by Carmine DeSapio. I just got off the phone with him two minutes ago telling me that he knew all about my plan to get you elected to Earl Brown's council seat. How did he know about this if you didn't tell him, you rotten piece of shit!" I don't feel great about these lies, but this is what I did. Somehow I had allowed myself to be sucked into the hustle of Harlem politics.

I don't feel great about these lies, but this is what I did. Somehow I had allowed myself to be sucked into the hustle of Harlem politics.

"Calm down, Hulan," I said. "First of all, I have never met Carmine DeSapio, so it would be impossible for me to tell him anything. Secondly, we finished your planning meeting late last night, and I'm still trying to get a grasp on it all because it has all happened so fast. I went straight to bed when I got home so I did not have time to tell anyone about the plans that you shared with me last night."

Hulan screamed, "Who did?"

"I don't know, Hulan, but it wasn't me. I'm still getting my head around running for councilman, which you asked me to do. I committed to do this according to your plan and have every intention to follow through."

"I don't not believe you, and if I can prove that you did it I'm going to bomb your church with you in it, you double-crossing piece of shit!"

"Hulan, I understand that you're very upset, but I didn't do the things you're accusing me of. You invited me into your plans. I committed to you, and I intend to keep my promise. What do you want me to do now?"

Hulan bristled, "I'll get to the bottom of this and I'll tell you what will happen next!" He hung up and I never heard from him again. I do not know what Carmine DeSapio did to make them stop their plan to unseat Earl Brown. But I never ran for Earl's City Council seat. However, this immersion into the power bases and power struggles of New York politics proved useful to me in the years that followed.

While my first personal experience with Carmine De-Sapio (and friends) put me on his good side, I was still very active with the reform movement of the Democratic Party of New York. Ironically, the group formed years earlier during the Stevenson campaigns to initiate a major change in the party politics that Carmine and his Tammany Hall power network wielded in New York. Most of us in the movement didn't like Carmine DeSapio's politics, connections, and what we felt was a lack of focus on the citizens of New York. However, having just experienced the reach of his formidable power firsthand and having personally benefited from that power, I treaded wisely on my course for opposition.

I chose a safe course of opposition: one based on diplomacy and a strong focus on issues. I made sure I was respectful to those entrenched in the political scene of New York. I found this approach to be very useful throughout my career in public service and participation in local, regional, and national politics.

The education I received through my whirlwind experience of *not* running for Earl Brown's councilman seat ended up being one of the most useful events of my career in public service. I was grateful to have learned early enough in my career how to relate to and work through people on all sides—mostly opposing sides—of a complex human network of power. Having the ability to recognize these power struggles and navigate through them served me well in the years to come.

Percy Sutton

Percy Sutton was a good friend of mine. He was born in Texas and he was the last of fifteen children. His father, Samuel, was born during the time of slavery and was an early civil rights activist. Samuel was the principal of a segregated high school in San Antonio and Percy's mother was a teacher there. In addition to being a full-time educator, Samuel farmed, sold real estate, and was an active businessman who owned a mattress factory, funeral home, and skating rink. All of Percy's siblings were college educated. A dynamic black man, Percy started a political club organized in the basement of my church, the Mid-Harlem Community Parish. He called it the Mid-Harlem Democratic Club.

Percy was an ambitious and courageous leader of the minority community in New York City. He also had the support of the liberal white community. Percy decided to run for mayor. He embraced a strategy of appealing to whites by taking a strong anti-crime stance and championing strong white-ethnic neighborhoods. While he was considered a legitimate candidate, he placed fourth in the Democratic primary in 1977 behind Ed Koch, Mario Cuomo, and incumbent Ed Beame. After his defeat, there was a lot of talk that New Yorkers saw the color of his skin instead of the potential of his leadership. This was a very disheartening experience for Percy.

We often talked at our local hangout—Frank's on 125th Street, and Percy always felt that his rejection by the Democratic Party was based in racism, pure and simple. Years later Koch, who succeeded Beame as mayor, called Percy "one of the smartest people I have met inside or outside of politics."

Percy went on to be a very successful businessman, and he continued to influence politics in Harlem. Some of his political achievements in and out of office include establishing the New York City Marathon, backing Herman D. Farrell Jr. for mayor, and helping Charles Rangel unseat Representative Adam Clayton Powell Jr.

Powell had been embraced by the New York black community because of his frequent attacks on white America, so Percy's decision to actively support a campaign against him was unpopular among a majority of his race. I was one of the few black ministers who supported Percy because I believed that that he focused on who could best serve the needs of all the district's constituents.

Percy's successful business ventures included the purchase of New York's leading black newspaper, *The New York Amsterdam News*, as well as WLIB (the first black-owned radio station in New York City), the rebuilding of the Apollo Theater, and the production of *Showtime at the Apollo*.

Percy often shared stories and lessons he learned from his father growing up. One story really stuck with Percy, and he used the lesson from it as a guiding principle in his life. He related to me how his father would not let him and his siblings play in a segregated San Antonio park on the one day of the year that they were allowed in. That day was June 19, the anniversary of Texas's implementation of the Emancipation Proclamation. His father would say, "Suffer the hurts, but don't show the anger. Because if you do, it will block you from being able to effectively do anything to remove the hurts."

Percy shared a lot of great wisdom and personal experiences over the many decades of our relationship. At my eightieth birthday celebration at City College of New York, he related to the large audience how much he valued my advice and friendship. He proclaimed, "Eugene and I were always close brothers and always would be."

Percy Sutton died on December 26, 2009. Ironically, he passed away while I was writing this section of this book honoring his life and our friendship together.

me, at about 3.

1929

My father, Arthur Callender   My mother, Eva Callender

family

Above: I'm seated in the front row, left; Leland is standing in the back row, center.
Left: Back row: my brother, Leland and my sister, Thelma; front row: mother, me.

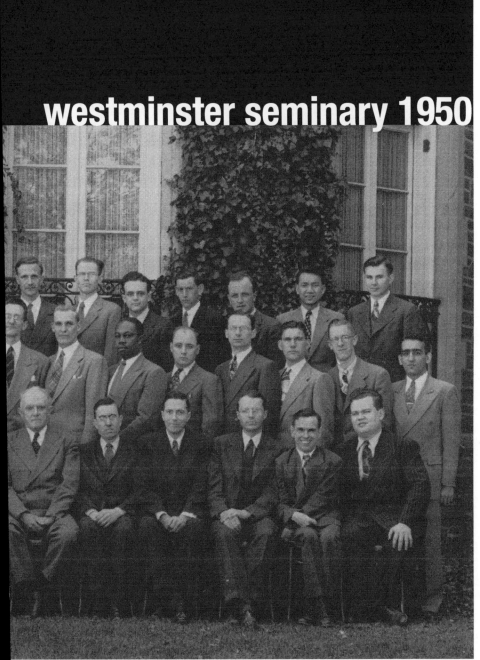

westminster seminary 1950

Class of 1950. I was class president and Westminster's first black student. Photograph used with the permission of the Archives of the Montgomery Library at Westminister Theological Seminary, Philadelphia, PA..

harlem
neighborhood
association
1961

Founding Meeting of the HNA. I was voted chairman for its bi-racial constituency.
Photographer: Unknown. Photo source: Reverend Callender's personal collection.

Me with swing jazz guitarist, Freddie Green, from the Count Basie Orchestra at the Newport Jazz Festival, 1962. Photographer: Unknown. Photo source: Reverend Callender's personal collection.

new port

jazz

festival

1962

To me, jazz is

the manifestion of the

pulse and soul of

the black community.

United States Senate
WASHINGTON, D.C.

January 19, 1961

Dear Reverend Callender:

Now that our campaign has been brought to
a successful conclusion, I want to thank you for
your good work with the Citizens for Kennedy and
Johnson.

I am very grateful for your contribution to
our victory. We now have the opportunity of con-
tinuing to work together for our country's welfare
during the next four years. Please accept my
personal gratitude for your help.

Sincerely yours,

John F. Kennedy

JFK/ba

Above: It was a thrill to receive this letter from JFK.

Right: My first of six presidential inaugural invitations.

The Inaugural Committee

requests the honor of your presence

to attend and participate in the Inauguration of

John Fitzgerald Kennedy

as President of the United States of America

and

Lyndon Baines Johnson

as Vice President of the United States of America

on Friday the twentieth of January

one thousand nine hundred and sixty-one

in the City of Washington

Edward H. Foley

Chairman

ALEX HALEY
P. O. BOX 2907
SAN FRANCISCO, CALIF. 94126

December 13, 1969

Dear Gene and Lee:

Before I even get into an appalling stack of waiting
mail, I want to say how really great it was to see you
two again. Often I reflect to myself about how one of
the prices that seems to have to be paid in the kind of
driving after a dream in which I'm engaged is that you
see so little of those dear ones whom you love. I keep
telling myself that when the dream is realized, as I
have every confidence that it will be, that then all
this can be rectified -- and I hope so.

And also I want to convey another thought that I've had
since I've been back here, this specifically to you, Gene:
at the table, I mentioned to you how over the years it has
remained fresh in my mind, from a professional perspective,
the accounts you long ago told me of your entry into the
big city, first working right out there in the streets with
those among us who have been the really greatest losers among
us. I always have remembered your stories' graphic quality,
and I know how meaningful and effective they could be in a
book's beginning.

I say "beginning," for what I have been reflecting upon
since night before last there is that you, Gene Callender,
have an important book to write. You really do: a book of
your own chronology of ascension in social endeavors and
contributions in New York City. I imagine thatx really few
individuals have functioned in quite as many key capacities
of real social contribution as you have, with the exposures,
the insights, the experiences that you have had in the course
of this. And I see the need of your reminiscings and commentary
in book form as two-fold. One is that what you could say, out
of valid experience, would help so many people better understand
the depth and nature of the problem. Another is that we so
badly need more, more books which will collectively comprise
a record of this transitional phase that black society is in.

Think seriously of this. You should start putting down notes
of things that come back to your mind when you think back.
Whenever you have time, expand the notes into more detailed
material, and put it into a folder, to grow. When it has grown
enough, you let me know, and let me quick-read through it,
however rough, and I can, and will, most happily, give you the
very best development advice that I can. I know you have not
the time. Who does? But, the point is, make it! For you
really do have in you a needed book, my friend.

Ain't I right, Lee? YOU tell him!   Love,

WHO: ALEX HALEY
WHAT: THE AUTOBIOGR
APHY OF MALCOLM X
WHERE: MY HARLEM APT
WHEN: 1963-65
WHY: BLACK ADVOCACY
HOW MUCH: $5,000 UP-
FRONT TO GROVE PRESS

Alex and I fought hard in NYC to find a publisher for The Autobiography of Malcolm X. He was my dearest friend and stood up as the best man when Lemoine (Lee) and I got married back in 1962. In 1969, Alex wrote us this letter suggesting that I turn my story into a book.

Above: **A** one and only. This picture represents the first and *only* time these two men—Martin Luther King, Jr. and Malcolm X—ever posed together for a public photo. Photograph used with permission from the Associated Press.

Left: **M**arching with Martin Luther King, Jr. in Selma, Alabama, 1965.That's me directly behind Coretta Scott King. Photographer: Unknown. Photo source: Reverend Callender's personal collection.

JOHN V. LINDSAY

MAYOR OF THE CITY OF NEW YORK

TO ALL TO WHOM THESE PRESENTS SHALL COME – GREETINGS:

Know ye, That reposing special trust and confidence in the integrity, diligence and discretion of

REVEREND EUGENE ST. CLAIR CALLENDER

I have appointed him
MEMBER OF THE NEW YORK CITY YOUTH BOARD
FOR A TERM OF OFFICE EXPIRING April 6, 1972.
and do authorize and empower him to execute and fulfill the duties of that office according to the law; and
to have and to hold the said office with all the rights and emoluments thereunto legally appertaining unto him

In testimony whereof, I have caused these Letters to be made patent
and the Seal of the City of New York be hereunto affixed.
Done in the City of New York this 7th day of April in the year of

1968

This was my second appointment from Mayor Lindsay of NYC. My first was in 1966 when I served as Deputy Administrator of Housing for the City of New York. I loved working for him.

Secretary George P. Shultz
Department of Labor
14th Street and Constitution Avenue
Washington, D. C. 20201

Dear George:

I don't know when I've had to make such a difficult decision. Your offer of an opportunity to serve as Assistant Secretary for Labor Standards presents an important and exciting challenge, but after careful thought and consideration I have decided that I must decline your invitation.

As you must know, 1969 is a crucial year in the life of our city. New York is in the throes of a crisis on almost every front. Citizens who have long been denied the opportunity to participate in the processes of government and in the formulation of programs and plans affecting their personal lives and their communities are responding to the efforts of the present city administration to give them a meaningful "piece of the action" as never before.

The goals of Mayor Lindsay and his administration to maintain the present high standard of living for the majority of New York City's citizens and to drastically improve the quality of life for those who have been described as disadvantaged will be challenged in the political arena this year. What is to happen in this city this year will prove a beacon and set the pace for cities across the nation.

I feel strongly that those of us who are a part of this city administration have a personal duty and a professional responsibility to strengthen and advance Mayor Lindsay's courageous thrust. There is a serious need to communicate to the voting public of New York the tremendous progress we have made in the last three and a half years, and to assist the Mayor in defining publicly the critical distance we have yet to travel in the interest of meaningful social change. I therefore feel compelled to remain in the city.

You know of my faith in you and my appreciation of your ability to involve the Department of Labor in the crucial domestic issues that concern the disinherited of our urban communities. Your wisdom will be of immense value in aiding the President to unite our country and heal some of our national ills.

I trust that you will understand and accept my decision. If I can be any assistance to you in either a personal or a professional capacity, you know that you may call on me.

Sincerely,

Eugene S. Callender

U. S.
DEPARTMENT
OF LABOR

OFFICE OF THE SECRETARY

WASHINGTON

U. S. DEPARTMENT OF LABOR

OFFICE OF THE SECRETARY

WASHINGTON

FEB 2 6 1969

Mr. Eugene S. Callender
40 West 135th Street
New York, New York 10037

Dear Gene:

    While I was sorry to receive your decision I
appreciate the warm tone of your February 21 letter. I
was particularly interested in your last sentence and we
hope we can call on you as consultant on our various
programs.

    Best personal wishes.

Sincerely yours,

George

Secretary of Labor

**federal government
appointment in wdc
1969**

Harlem Prep Graduation Ceremony #2 in front of the famous Hotel Theresa on 125 Street, 1968. Photographer: Unknown. Photo source: Reverend Callender's personal collection.

harlem prep graduation

ny urban coalition, 1969

AUG 23 1970

The Urban Coalition

1819 H Street, N.W.
Washington, D.C. 2000(
Telephone: (202) 223-950(

CHAIRMAN: John W. Gardner
CO-CHAIRMEN: Andrew Heiskell / A. Philip Randolph

August 25, 1969

Dr. Eugene S. Callender
40 West 135th Street
New York, New York

Dear Dr. Callender:

On behalf of the National Urban Coalition staff and Board of
Directors, may we welcome you as a new member to the team of
local executive officers.

As the Northeast Area Director responsible for New York City,
I would like to meet with you in the very near future to discuss
at length the kinds of things that the National office can do to
help strengthen your operation on a local level. Perhaps you
can contact me at Area Code 202/659-4855 to let me know the
exact date that you will be coming aboard and I can arrange to
meet with you in New York to discuss the aforementioned.

Again, congratulations. We at the National office look forward
to a warm and lasting association with you and your staff in the
many months ahead.

Very truly yours,

Earl Phillips
Associate Director

cc: John Buggs

Received upon my appointment to the NY Urban Coalition.

1995

White House Conference on Aging

Eugene S. Callender

In recognition of your outstanding contributions
toward the success of The 1995 White House
Conference on Aging

May 5, 1995

Over the course of my career I served, in total, on five presidential councils (under
five separate presidents).

THE WHITE HOUSE

WASHINGTON

October 2, 2000

The Reverend Eugene S. Callender
New York, New York

Dear Reverend Callender:

Congratulations on marking 50 years of
dedicated religious leadership.

Through your many years of devotion, you have
enriched the lives of countless others and served
as an example of faith to those in your community.
You have worked tirelessly to help the people of
your church, tending to their spiritual needs
as well as fostering an atmosphere of compassion
and fellowship. Your efforts make a positive
difference to our world and our future.

Hillary joins me in sending best wishes for
every future success.

Sincerely,

Bill Clinton

From President Clinton congratulating me on 50 years of ministerial service, 2000.

Powell Center Foundation Grant Already Paying Dividends

THE NEW YORK LIFE Foundation's record-breaking $10 million grant last year to The City College of New York's Colin Powell Center for Policy Studies is already having a powerful impact.

The award, the Foundation's largest ever, established the New York Life Endowment for Emerging African-American Issues.

"We expose students who might not have had the opportunity, because of the focus of their studies or financial constraints, to the real world of policymaking and its practitioners," says Vincent Boudreau, director of the Colin Powell Center.

"Being a New York Life graduate fellow has been a career-changing experience," says DeShaunta Johnson, a fifth-year doctoral candidate in clinical psychology. "It has forced me to consider how public policy relates to the poor and the mentally handicapped," she explains.

first Colin Powell Center New York Life leader-in-residence, Dr. Eugene Callender. Dr. Callender headed the New York State Office of Aging under former Gov. Mario Cuomo and established several social service organizations in Harlem.

"After what I've heard in our sessions with Dr. Callender, it is clear that what happens in the political and policymaking arenas has a direct impact on the lives of my clients," Johnson says. "That fact has motivated me to be more involved in how health policy is made."

Melissa Frakman, an undergraduate majoring in economics and international relations, says her studies have been enhanced immeasurably by her participation in the program. "What I've learned from other New York Life fellows and our guest speakers, specifically about the impact of globalization on minority communities, has been eye-opening," she explains. "I would like to

Rolston, a fourth-year student at City College's Sophie Davis School of Biomedical Education. Rolston intends to become a primary care physician in an underserved community.

"As a New York Life scholar I am learning a great deal about public health issues. I am honing my skills to be an advocate for minority communities in the policymaking process," she says. Rolston is a volunteer nurse at a Harlem elementary school.

New York Life fellow Kanene Holder teaches social studies and science at the Harlem Children's Zone, a social services organization serving more than 10,000 at-risk children. She is also a writer/actress who has performed her one-woman satire in New York City. "I had little exposure to the political process before the Powell Center Program," says Holder, who expects to complete her graduate degree in childhood education this May.

ate studies, Tsikiwa is a member of the AIDS ministry at the Abyssinian Baptist Church in Harlem. "I'd like to use what I learn as a fellow to help me advance the cause of bringing HIV education and treatment to underserved communities in the U.S. and around the world," says the native of Zimbabwe.

The New York Life Foundation grant is also supporting a distinguished speakers program on African-American issues. The first event took place last month. Derrick Bell, Jr., a visiting professor of constitutional law at New York University and one of the nation's most influential civil rights scholars, and Rev. Dr. James Forbes, Jr., the first African-American senior minister of the Riverside Church and current president and founder of the Healing Nations Foundation, were the colloquium's featured speakers.

Between the support of the Colin Powell fellows and the special programs

Practical Advice: Dr. Eugene Callender, who ran the NYS Department of Aging under Gov. Mario Cuomo, shares insights with some NYL fellows.

Open Forum: City College students and staff swap ideas at a NYL-sponsored Powell Center program on African-American issues.

it has sponsored through the grant, New York Life has already touched the lives of hundreds of students, according to Andrew Rich, an associate professor of political science and the associate director of the Colin Powell Center.

The grant provides scholarships and internships for City College students and promotes the study and understanding of African-American perspectives on public policy.

It also helps develop networks and relationships between prominent opinion-makers and the Colin Powell Center; strengthens connections between communities in need and at risk and the Powell Center and City College, and, through the New York Life Leader-in-Residence program, brings a proven leader active in African-American issues to the Powell Center each year to teach, mentor, and participate in workshops.

Johnson works as a consultant and counselor at several social service agencies serving the homeless, substance abusers, and the mentally ill.

Eight undergraduate and five graduate fellows are being supported by the grant during the current academic year. In addition to their coursework, each group of fellows meets every week for two hours to discuss policymaking and political issues, as well as their own research.

The weekly sessions are led by the

learn more about how international trade and investment have changed the economic dynamic for small businesses in minority communities," adds the City College junior. Frakman will be interning this winter in New Dehli, India, with the Confederation of Indian Industry.

"Among the biggest challenges advocates for the poor face, at least from a policymaking perspective, is securing better access to health care," says New York Life fellow Renee

"I now have a much better understanding of what it takes to get an idea enacted into law," adds the Howard University graduate. "My goal is to become a college professor and to motivate young people, particularly minorities, to be involved in the policymaking process."

New York Life fellow Felicity Tsikiwa transferred to City College after Hurricane Katrina forced the temporary closure of Xavier University in New Orleans. In addition to her undergradu-

obama inauguration, 2009. it was a cold, chilly day in washington d.c.; but i wouldn't have missed this day for the world.

The Presidential Inaugural Committee
requests the honor of your presence
to attend and participate
in the
Inauguration of
Barack H. Obama
as President of the United States of America
and
Joseph R. Biden, Jr.
as Vice President of the United States of America
on Tuesday, the twentieth of January
two thousand and nine
in the City of Washington

renee and me

Receiving the Pioneer Award in 2009 from the National Black Theatre. I enjoyed the evening in the warm company of my one-and-only, dear daughter, Renee Callender-Williams.

It was an honor and joy to be the keynote speaker in Albany for the 2010, State of New York event celebrating Martin Lurther King's birthday. Photograph used with the permission of NYS Office of General Services. Photographer: Michael Joyce.

Chapter 10:
Martin Luther King, Jr.

In 1957, at the age of thirty-one, I got involved in the national civil rights movement as part of a project team preparing for and participating in the Prayer Pilgrimage for Freedom to Washington D.C. Through the confluence of my ministries and public service, I became active on the civil rights and social reform fronts.

A. Phillip Randolph and Bayard Rustin were key members of the civil rights movement in New York City at this time, and they asked me to be on the fundraising committee for the Prayer Pilgrimage. I became the chairman of the Prayer Pilgrimage Committee in New York because of my connections in the city.

One of these connections was my Jewish friend Mark Lane, whom knew I could raise money. The Jewish community in America contributed a lot of money to efforts associated with the Civil Rights Movement and was extremely supportive of Dr. Martin Luther King, Jr.

Bayard Rustin had asked Dr. King to speak at the prayer pilgrimage, and he agreed. Rustin had four main objectives:

- a demonstration of unity of the Negro people,

- a protest against violence directed at Negros in the South,

- a thanksgiving for the Supreme Court decision on integration, and

- a demonstration to let Congress know that we expected the civil right program to pass.

Dr. King and Bayard Rustin planned to set up a conference with congressional leadership the morning of May 17, 1957, followed by the pilgrimage culminating at noon with a rally on the mall at the Lincoln Memorial. It was at noon on May 17, 1954, that the Supreme Court rendered its decision on integration in the public schools.

Two key fundraising events had taken place in New York City on May 3, 1957, to create awareness of the civil rights movement in advance of the pilgrimage. These were Dr. King's speaking engagements at a luncheon at the Abyssinian Baptist Church in Harlem and at the Stephen Wise Free Synagogue in Manhattan. Rabbi Klein and the members of the synagogue were progressive and active in the community. Rabbi Klein extended a heart of compassion and outreach to the needy and oppressed. He and the members of Stephen Wise Free Synagogue were passionate in the battle to end social injustice.

Mark Lane was active in the synagogue and close to Rabbi Klein. In early February 1957, I was having a breakfast meeting with Mark and Jeannie Rosoff, another friend of ours from the synagogue, to plan for Dr. King's visit to Manhattan, when it occurred to me that Martin Luther King had never been to Harlem. I said, "Mark, we need to get Dr. King to Harlem, and I think the event at the synagogue is a perfect opportunity. What do you think?"

Both he and Jeannie simultaneously exclaimed, "That's a great idea!"

Mark said, "I'll coordinate the schedule with Rabbi Klein's team so that we can plan for an event in Harlem."

Jeannie added, "I'll work with Dr. King's team to see if they can extend his trip to include a rally to meet the people of Harlem the night of May third."

"Great," I said, "I'll organize the event in Harlem."

Rabbi Klein was on board and excited with our idea. Jeannie received confirmation from Dr. King that he would love to come to Harlem for a rally.

Now I needed to plan and mobilize our Harlem event. I met with the owners of the Hotel Theresa and the surrounding businesses on the block because I wanted to set up a stage in front of the hotel. All of the owners were not only on board, but were excited about the event. I planned to have a jazz band play while people congregated in the streets prior to Martin Luther King being introduced. While I was searching for a band, I discovered that Duke Ellington's orchestra was in town and would be playing at the Apollo during the week of the event. "How perfect!" I exclaimed to myself.

I was able to reach Ellington to see if he was interested in participating in the event, and he said, "I'd be happy to do it, Rev, but I'm under contract with the Apollo, and you'll need to get permission from them." I told him I would work on it and get back to him.

I was pretty good friends with Robert Schiffman, Sr., the owner of the Apollo, and we used to help each other out in Harlem over the years. We had worked on several projects together through HANA, the Harlem Neighborhood Association, focused on social reform. His son, Bobby, had recently taken over day-to-day responsibility of running the Apollo Theater.

I met with Bobby in his office so that I could explain why the event we were planning for Dr. King in Harlem was so important. At first, Bobby gave me all sorts of reasons why it wasn't a good idea. It was a Friday night, one of the busiest nights at the Apollo, and he couldn't afford to lose the business with Duke not performing at the Apollo.

I said, "Bobby, first of all, this event has potential to bring even more business to the Apollo for the weekend. Secondly, this is the right thing to do, and your dad would jump at the opportunity to do this. Shall I call him or will you?"

I called his dad and I explained that this was the first time King was going to be addressing the people of Harlem and that it was a great opportunity for the community. I knew we'd get a great crowd.

He said, 'OK. We'll do it!" And Bobby agreed, too.

I called Duke with the good news, and he said, "I'll see you there, Rev."

As plans firmed up and the reality of Dr. King coming to Harlem took shape, I asked Larry Gerosa, a friend of mine, for some help. He was comptroller of the City of New York, so our paths crossed many times through various projects and initiatives. He also owned a large construction company.

I asked him if he could lend us a flatbed truck that we could use as a stage in front of the Hotel Theresa. He said, "It sounds like a great event, Eugene. I'd be happy to help."

Everything was coming together: I scheduled a local jazz band from Harlem to perform prior to Duke Ellington, and on the day of the event, as they were setting up on the flatbed, their pianist called me and asked if we'd have a piano there.

It had never occurred to me that I'd have to provide anything for the musicians, but, fortunately, we had some practice moving a piano around from our days of taking the church to the streets in the early 1950s. I scrambled and rounded up a few of the winos who were hanging out at the Mid-Harlem Community Parish to help me push the piano from my church at 122nd Street up to the Hotel Theresa on 125th Street. We recruited a few more winos who were standing on the corner to help us get the piano up the ramp and onto the flatbed. I took them all to lunch for helping me, and I encouraged them to come listen to Dr. King that night. All six of them did.

At about nine that evening, the jazz band started to play on the platform, and there was already a large crowd of people on the streets and sidewalks around the Hotel Theresa, anticipating Martin Luther King's arrival. When Duke Ellington and his Orchestra took the stage by nine thirty, the crowd had swelled.

The vibe of the crowd was joyful, and they loved the music wafting from the loudspeakers. There was a multitude of people in the streets surrounding the Hotel Theresa within the range of our loudspeakers. When Martin Luther King arrived, I caught Duke Ellington's eye, and he winked at me to acknowledge that he would wrap the set up.

As the crowd cheered at the close of the song, they became aware that Dr. King had arrived and grew silent. Duke and Dr. King shook hands and briefly hugged as Martin made his way to the podium and microphone we had set up for him at the front of the stage. He paused for a moment to collect his thoughts, and every soul there paused in anticipation with him.

Martin's message to Harlem was one of hope, dreams, and love. The streets erupted with joy and hope. He gave us all a clear message of peace in the non-violent movement for change. He inspired us as a community to rise above all circumstances to make a difference for our children. He spoke with hope and anticipation for the Prayer Pilgrimage as an event to appeal to the conscience of the nation on integration and civil rights for all persons in America.

Dr. King and I embraced for a moment on the stage, and then I said, "You spoke God's truth to Harlem tonight."

He replied, "Eugene, Harlem has blessed us all tonight. Thank you for making this happen and I'll see you soon."

Prayer Pilgrimage for Freedom

A. Phillip Randolph and Bayard Rustin planned the Prayer Pilgrimage for Freedom in Washington as an event to mark the third anniversary of *Brown v. Board of Education*, a landmark U.S. Supreme Court decision striking down segregation in public schools. The purpose and timing of the demonstration was to urge America, especially the government, to abide by the decision, as the process of desegregation was being obstructed at local and state levels.

We worked hard to prepare for the event, and the day finally arrived on May 17, 1957. Tens of thousands of us congregated in front of the Lincoln Memorial for the March on Washington. The three-hour demonstration included several celebrities, including Mahalia Jackson, Harry Belafonte, and Paul Robeson. Among the speakers were Roy Wilkins, a journalist, executive member of the NAACP, and civil rights activist; Mordecai Johnson, a son of former slaves, preacher, educator, and the first African American president of Howard University; and Dr. Martin Luther King, Jr.

Martin was the last and most anticipated speaker. His speech on this day not only planted the seeds but also set the agenda for voting rights as an important part of the civil rights struggle.

Dr. King's oratory that day is named the "Give Us the Ballot" speech, as it eloquently implored America to bring about the changes necessary to make the charter from our founding fathers real, that all people are created equal and have the same fundamental rights, such as the right to vote. He expressed what America could be by the changes that voting rights for people of color would bring about. Here are some of the memorable calls for action from his speech:

> Give us the ballot and we will no longer have to worry the federal government about our basic rights.

> Give us the ballot and we will no longer plead to the federal government for passage of an anti-lynching law.

> Give us the ballot and we will fill our legislative halls with men of good will.

> Give us the ballot and we will place judges on the benches of the South who will do justly and love mercy.

Dr. King brilliantly tied the Prayer Pilgrimage for Freedom to what is morally right, as well as to a call for change for a better America. He broadened the civil rights movement by charging that leadership is required from the government, from white liberals in the North, from white moderates in the South, and from all people of color who live and work in all diverse communities of America. King urged everyone at the Prayer Pilgrimage and all those active in the struggle for civil rights across the nation to "show love, understanding, and abstinence from violence in pursuit of liberty and justice for all."

The Prayer Pilgrimage for Freedom gave stimulus and support to Dr. King's movement that began in the South. It was a great experience for all of us who organized this event. We gained insight from the march, which laid the foundation for future demonstrations across the nation for the civil rights movement. Dr. King graciously thanked us for our work.

Soon after the success of the Prayer Pilgrimage, I became more and more involved in the marches for civil rights, marches for restaurant integration, marches for job opportunities, and marches against segregation in the South. I truly believed in what we were marching for, but the more that I marched, the angrier I became. I began to struggle with our approach to the mission.

Increasingly, through the abuses I witnessed, I realized non-violent resistance did not come easily to me. I believed in fighting for what I believed in. I believed in fighting back if somebody hits you. I struggled with the biblical principle of loving your enemy and turning the other cheek. I was unable to accept those principles until much later in life.

In 1961, I was corresponding with Dr. King, expressing my internal struggles and growing anger with each hateful transgression perpetrated against our race.

He admonished me, "I can see how you would feel this way, Eugene; it is human nature. God's nature is not always easy, but His way is the way of love through all things. I will continue to pray for continued strength for all of us, Eugene."

He recommended that I consider coming to Jackson, Mississippi, to work with a group of people who had been working with him in the civil rights movement in the South. The group was called the Student Nonviolent Coordinating Committee (SNCC). Two of the leaders of the group in Mississippi at that time were H. Rap Brown and Stokely Carmichael. I welcomed his guidance and decided to visit Mississippi.

I met with Rap and Stokely so that they could better prepare me for the marches by teaching survival techniques. It seemed so absurd that they would have a curriculum to teach nonviolent techniques to avoid getting hurt while your head was being beaten.

I was really struggling not to strike out when someone was beating me, especially in the head. I had suppressed rage from the legacy of my father's brutality for all of my adult life, but my growing anger from the hatred against our marches and my human nature released an impulse to react violently. The few weeks I spent with Rap and Stokely were tough for me, but at that time they were committed to nonviolent responses to the hateful resistance we would receive on our marches. Their self-protection techniques proved to be invaluable.

After my training in Mississippi, I joined Martin Luther King in the marches in Albany, Georgia, and Birmingham and Selma, Alabama. The Albany campaign was largely focused on desegregation. There was so much hatred aimed at us. Most of it was verbal abuse, and unjust incarceration coordinated by the Chief of Police, Laurie Pritchett.

The physical violence mostly took place beyond the public eye and often in isolation. The approach most often used was a beating with a shovel and shouts of "We're going to beat you first, then bury you if you don't leave." As tough, hateful, and painful as Selma was, Birmingham in 1963 was even worse.

The Albany campaign proved to be a real educational process for the Southern Christian Leadership Conference (SCLC), in that they discovered a need to be more focused on the purpose of our protest. The strategy for the Birmingham movement was planned and executed by Wyatt Tee Walker, who was chief of staff for Dr. King and the executive director of the SCLC. Wyatt and I also spent a lot of time together once he became the senior pastor at the Canaan Baptist Church of Christ in Harlem in 1967.

Reverend Walker's strategy for the campaign focused on one goal, the desegregation of Birmingham's downtown merchants, rather than total desegregation, as in Albany. Our objective for Birmingham was simply the establishment of a human rights commission, with the sole purpose of providing an equal opportunity for blacks to be interviewed for jobs in the stores in which they shopped. There was nothing radical about our objective, but those who opposed us met us with vicious hate.

The Birmingham campaign used a variety of nonviolent methods of confrontation, including sit-ins, kneel-ins at local churches, and a march to the county building to mark the beginning of a voter-registration drive. Regardless of the method, we were met with aggressive resistance from several white citizens of Birmingham, including the Ku Klux Klan.

Bull Connor

Birmingham's version of Laurie Pritchett was Eugene "Bull" Connor. He was the commissioner of public safety in Birmingham and the leader of the authorities' brutal response to our mission. Connor's exploits of abuse were many. During the Freedom Rides, Connor gave Ku Klux Klan members fifteen minutes to attack an incoming group of Freedom Riders before having police '*protect*' them.

The Riders were severely beaten '*until it looked like a bulldog had got a hold of them.*' James Peck, a white activist, was beaten so hard he required fifty stitches to his head. Connor used this approach for our marches as well. Those who resisted and hated us because of the color of our skin would look us in the eyes and scream at us, "Hey nigger, you might get killed if you keep this up!"

Bull Connor and the people of Birmingham also pricked us with cattle prods, stoned us, and sent dogs to attack us. They would mock us, abuse us, and do all that they could to try and break us. Truthfully, for the most part, they did—if not on the outside, certainly, for many of us, on the inside.

But not Martin Luther King. While I admired Dr. King, I actually got mad at him. As the confluence of rage and fear inside of me boiled over, I asked Dr. King, "How can you just sit there a take this abuse? And how can you ask us to just take it?"

"There is nothing worth living for if it's not worth dying for," he replied.

Many people were killed during our struggles to overcome social injustice. Those fallen heroes became the foundation on which our current generations can boldly stand today. Intellectually, I understood what Martin was saying and that we were doing the right thing. But I was still struggling to have my heart match my head.

The city of Birmingham started to take action and obtained an injunction barring all protests. The SCLC was convinced, and rightly so, that the order was unconstitutional. The Birmingham campaign defied the court order and prepared for mass arrests. King elected to be among those arrested on April 12, 1963.

While in jail, Martin Luther King wrote his famous "Letter from Birmingham Jail" on the margins of a newspaper, since he had not been allowed any writing paper while held in solitary confinement. Dr. King's letter is a response to a statement made by eight white Alabama clergymen on April 12, 1963. The clergymen, including ministers, priests, and rabbis, agreed that social injustices existed but argued that the battle against racial segregation should be fought solely in the courts, not in the streets.

Martin Luther King responded, arguing "that without nonviolent forceful direct actions such as his, true civil rights could never be achieved." Martin added, "This 'Wait' has always meant 'Never.'" He asserted that not only was civil disobedience justified in the face of unjust laws, but that "one has a moral responsibility to disobey unjust laws." The letter was extraordinarily powerful, and his message to all of America still applies. Key thoughts related to the necessary action of the Birmingham Movement include the following excerpts:

> "Injustice anywhere is a threat to justice everywhere."

> "We know through painful experiences that freedom is never voluntarily given by the oppressor, it must be demanded by the oppressed."

> "Justice too long delayed is justice denied."

During Dr. King's incarceration, many of his supporters appealed to the Kennedy administration, which intervened to obtain his release. Martin was allowed to call his wife, who was recuperating at home after the birth of their fourth child, and was released early on April 19.

Unfortunately, the court injunction and the beatings were starting to have an impact on the movement in Birmingham. The campaign was faltering because the movement was running out of demonstrators willing to risk arrest.

James Bevel, SCLC's director of direct action and nonviolent education, came up with a bold and controversial alternative: to train high school students to take part in the demonstrations. As a result, more than one thousand students skipped school on May 2 to meet at the Sixteenth Street Baptist Church to join the demonstrations, in what would come to be called the Children's Crusade. More than six hundred ended up in jail. This was newsworthy, but in this first encounter, the police acted with unusual restraint.

On the next day, however, another one thousand students gathered at the church. When they started marching, Bull

Connor unleashed police dogs on them, then turned the city's fire hoses on the children, washing them down the street as if they were trash to be disposed of. Television cameras broadcast to the nation the scenes of schoolchildren being knocked down by fire hoses and attacked by dogs.

That night, we met back at the Baptist church like we always did after a demonstration. Martin Luther King would come back to the church every night and lift our spirits up with his beautiful, eloquent rhetoric. But this night was different. He could tell that we were so shaken by what had happened during the day, and now our children were involved.

He addressed us, "We had a tough day out there, and there is no denying that. But you can't hate Bull Connor. Bull Connor is God's child, too. You can despise what he did to us today, but you can't hate Bull Connor." He continued, "Hatred hurts the person who hates, not the person we hate. God has a plan and purpose for what happened today, and Bull Connor is part of that plan."

It took me a long time to understand the wisdom of his ways, which were, in so many ways, acting as Jesus did. It wasn't until I finally understood the scripture that meekness was power under control, not weakness, as I always thought it to be. This fundamental misunderstanding of meekness was my disconnect during these marches of passive nonresistance. I obeyed, but I neither liked it nor understood it. It was through Dr. King's life example that God's Word was revealed to me so many years later.

Martin Luther King was right about Bull Connor being part of God's plan, because widespread public outrage from what he did was seen by millions of people. As a result, the Kennedy administration intervened more forcefully in negotiations between the white business community and the SCLC.

On May 10, the parties announced an agreement to de-segregate the lunch counters and other public accommodations downtown, to create a committee to eliminate discriminatory hiring practices, to arrange for the release of jailed protesters, and to establish regular means of communication between black and white leaders.

After a few years of working with the Civil Rights Movement, I was appointed New York spokesman for the SCLC, and the scope of the focus of my life took on a much greater scale, from a local to a national level. We were raising money so that we could do Prayer Pilgrimages and peace marches, especially in the racially divided South.

One case that hit home occurred in Birmingham in May of 1963: There was a horrifying bombing of kids in church in Sunday school. One of the members of my church was related to one of the families whose child was murdered. We had them come to New York, and we conducted a prayer vigil and big service for them. We gave them a place to stay and supported them through their loss and time of grieving. We also raised money for the families of the victims and for the rebuilding of the structures damaged by the bombings.

On August 28, 1963, Martin Luther King gave his famous "I Have a Dream" speech at the March on Washington D.C. The newspapers claimed this was the most-attended political rally ever. I just know that we were there to promote jobs and freedom.

I arrived two weeks early and stayed with three other friends and organizers, John Heyman, David Barry, and Bryant George. We stayed at John Heyman's house. The day of the event, the three of us marched together to the Lincoln Memorial. On the way there, I noticed that John was wearing open-toed sandals. I asked him, "Aren't you afraid of someone stepping on your feet?"

He replied, "If a black man steps on my feet, I'll say, 'Excuse me.' If a white man steps on me, I'll tell him, 'Get the hell off my foot!'"

The four of us deliberately stayed with the crowds during the event. Like everyone else there that day, we were moved to tears.

Later that year, SNCC undertook an ambitious voter registration program in Selma, Alabama. By 1965, the Selma movement had made little headway in the face of opposition from Selma's sheriff, Jim Clark.

After local residents asked the SCLC for assistance, Dr. Martin Luther King came to Selma to lead several marches, at which time he was arrested along with 250 other demonstrators. I joined him and other SCLC leaders in Selma. The marchers continued to meet violent resistance from police.

It was like Birmingham all over again. Jimmie Lee Jackson, a resident of nearby Marion, was killed by police at a march in February 1965. Jackson's death prompted James Bevel, director of the Selma Voting Rights Movement, to initiate a plan to march from Selma to Montgomery.

On March 7, 1965, acting on Bevel's plan, Hosea Williams of the SCLC and John Lewis of SNCC led a march of six hundred people fifty-four miles from Selma to the state capital in Montgomery. Only six blocks into the march, however, at the Edmund Pettus Bridge, state troopers and local law enforcement, some mounted on horseback, attacked the peaceful demonstrators with billy clubs, tear gas, rubber tubes wrapped in barbed wire, and bullwhips.

They drove the marchers back into Selma. John Lewis, who eventually became a congressman from Alabama, was knocked unconscious. He nearly lost an eye. He was dragged to safety by the rest of us. At least sixteen other marchers were hospitalized. Among those gassed and beaten was Amelia Boynton Robinson, who was at the center of civil rights activity at the time.

Once again, the national broadcast of the news footage of lawmen attacking marchers seeking the right to vote provoked a national response just as scenes from Birmingham did two years earlier. The marchers were able to obtain a court order permitting them to make the march without incident two weeks later. So we did.

After a second march to the site of Bloody Sunday on March 9, however, local whites murdered Reverend James Reeb, another voting rights supporter. He died in a Birmingham hospital on March 11. On March 25, four Klansmen shot and killed Detroit homemaker Viola Liuzzo as she drove marchers back to Selma at night after a successful march to Montgomery. We were all upset by Viola's senseless murder.

Eight days after the first march, President Johnson delivered a televised address in support of the voting rights bill he had sent to Congress. This bill was being formulated during the Kennedy administration, with Bobby Kennedy taking the charge and seeing it through to completion under the Johnson administration.

In the address, President Johnson told the country: "But even if we pass this bill, the battle will not be over. What happened in Selma is part of a far larger movement, which reaches into every section and state of America. It is the effort of American Negroes to secure for themselves the full blessings of American life."

Later, he said, "Their cause must be our cause, too. Because it is not just Negroes, but really it is all of us, who must overcome the crippling legacy of bigotry and injustice. And we shall overcome."

Johnson signed the Voting Rights Act of 1965 on August 6. The 1965 act suspended poll taxes, literacy tests, and other subjective voter tests. It authorized federal supervision of voter registration in states and individual voting districts where such tests were being used.

People of color who had been barred from registering to vote finally had an alternative to taking suits to local or state courts. If voting discrimination occurred, the 1965 act authorized the attorney general of the United States to send federal examiners to replace local registrars. Johnson reportedly told associates that signing the bill had lost the white South for the Democratic Party for the foreseeable future.

Upon the signing of the Voting Rights Act, several of us joined with Martin when he went to go register. When we approached the county building in Georgia, there were hundreds of white men with baseball bats and other blunt weapons standing in front of the doors chanting hateful threats to Martin's life and hateful slurs toward our color. It was actually terrifying, and most of us there told Martin that he did not have to go in and register, that this moment seemed too dangerous.

He replied, "I appreciate your concern, but if I do not go it will invalidate all that we have worked for and all that I have professed and believe in. I am going."

As he took his first step toward the mob, there was silence—with the exception of the leather from Martin's shoes on the pavement as he strode forth. We were frozen on our side of the driveway and Martin boldly stepped into the chasm that separated white and black America.

When he approached his oppressors, neither bat nor voice was raised; the sea of hate parted as he continued his march forward. He made it to the doors and the parted, white sea reformed, this time facing the doors that Martin had just entered. After what seemed like hours, but was only minutes, the white sea quietly parted again to clear the way for Martin to walk safely back to us. A terrifying moment had never been more beautifully fulfilled. I was blessed to have witnessed it.

The Voting Rights Act of 1965 had an immediate and positive impact for African Americans. Within months of its passage, two hundred fifty thousand new black voters had been registered, one third of them by federal examiners. Within four years, voter registration in the South had more than doubled. In 1965, Mississippi had the highest black voter turnout at 74 percent and led the nation in the number of black public officials elected. In 1969, Tennessee had a 92 percent turnout; Arkansas, 78 percent; and Texas, 73 percent.

Several whites who had opposed the Voting Rights Act paid a big price. In 1966, Sheriff Jim Clark of Alabama, infamous for using cattle prods against civil rights marchers, was up for re-election. Although he took off the notorious "Never" pin on his uniform, he was defeated. Clark lost as blacks voted to get him out of office. Clark later served a prison term for drug dealing.

Blacks' being granted the power to vote changed the political landscape of the South. When Congress passed the Voting Rights Act, only about one hundred African Americans held elective office, all in northern states. By 1989, there were more than seventy-two hundred African Americans in office, including more than forty-eight hundred in the South.

Nearly every Black Belt county (where the majority of the populations were black) in Alabama had a black sheriff. Southern blacks held top positions within city, county, and state governments. Atlanta elected a black mayor, Andrew Young, as did Jackson, Mississippi, with Harvey Johnson, and New Orleans, with Ernest Morial.

Black politicians on the national level included Barbara Jordan, who represented Texas in Congress, and Andrew Young, who was appointed United States Ambassador to the United Nations during the Carter administration. Julian Bond was elected to the Georgia Legislature in 1965, although political reaction to his public opposition to U.S. involvement in Vietnam prevented him from taking his seat until 1967. John Lewis represents Georgia's fifth congressional district in the U.S. House of Representatives, where he has served since 1987.

Chapter 11:
Separation

From the moment I had moved to New York with my family, I had poured myself into work and life in the City. I was not the best father. When I found out Gladys was pregnant, I knew I was not ready to be a father. I was not really mature enough. Within two months of the wedding, I knew I'd gotten married for all of the wrong reasons.

Gladys and I eventually separated, and later we finally agreed that it would be best to divorce. I met with the elders of the Christian Reformed Church in New Jersey, where I had been ordained. I told them that my wife and I were separated and that we were thinking of getting a divorce. That was unheard of in the Christian Reformed Church. They tried to get us together but I knew that it just was not going to work for me, and it was completely unfair to Gladys to keep her in a troubled marriage. So they said, "Well, then, you have to leave the church."

I said OK, I would leave. But I didn't want to leave. This was my flock, and every one of those folks there were people I ministered to, recruited, and trained. I had been with them for several great years. I also didn't want to lose the house they bought for us, but I had to go.

The church severed its ties with me and I was no longer able to be its minister, its missionary in Harlem, or have any affiliation with the Mid-Harlem Community Parish. I deserved the professional consequences for my indiscretions. My failure as a family man and the destruction of the lives of Gladys and Renee are a great regret in my life.

Farewell

The parish people decided to have a farewell party for me including people from the community—winos, drug addicts, and ex-drug addicts. People got up to say things about me. As the program was closing, the most prominent wino in the neighborhood, Skinny, got there at the last minute.

I said, "Let Skinny speak."

"Rev was the only one on Seventh Avenue who paid any attention to me," he said. "When I heard Rev was leaving, I went around and collected this gift from all of my friends." He'd collected twenty-nine cents, just enough to buy me a bottle of Thunderbird, Skinny's favorite wine.

I remember the time that Skinny came to see me with a bottle of Thunderbird in his back pocket. As he left, he tripped on the sidewalk and fell down. He turned around and saw all of this red juice on the sidewalk and he said, "Oh my God. I hope that's blood!"

Every summer and fall, Skinny would roll his pants up to his knees. In the winter, he'd roll them back down. As soon as the weather got really cold, Skinny would walk in front of a car on Seventh Avenue. He'd intentionally get hit by the car so he would be taken to Harlem Hospital and taken care of during the winter months.

Changes

After I divorced Gladys, I lived by myself for a while. That was, until I met a woman called Lemoine Pierce. In early 1960, I was running a meeting. I was so struck by the beauty of the guidance counselor, that I had to focus extra hard on the meeting's agenda. At the end of the meeting I said to her, "Mrs. Pierce, would you stay for a few minutes? I would like to talk to you." She agreed. Over the weeks and months that followed, we gradually got to know each other. I was in love, and eventually Lemoine and I were married.

Chapter 12:
The Church of the Master

After I left the Christian Reformed Church, the Reverend James H. Robinson, founder and pastor of the Church of the Master, invited me to come and see him. I had met him in mid 1950s, when he ran for borough presidency. He said he wanted me to consider coming to Church of the Master as his assistant pastor. I was dumbfounded at both the opportunity and the timing. God's grace and plans are amazing. So without hesitation, I went for it.

The Church of the Master, as I found it in 1959, had come a long way from its humble beginnings, built by the sweat of a young senior student at Union Theological Seminary, James H. Robinson. To fully understand this accomplishment, you first have to understand the neighborhood. From the mid-1920s through the early 1940s, Harlem had substantial constituency of white middle class Americans owning and living in the community. By the mid-1940s, Harlem was a predominantly black community.

The health of the Presbyterian Church suffered when the whites moved out. Churches were abandoned and left to rot. The newly elected moderator of the New York Presbytery, Henry Sloane Coffin, minister of Madison Avenue Presbyterian

Church, preached in his moderatorial sermon saying, "I have not accepted this position to preside over the death of the Presbyterian Church in Harlem."

Reverend Coffin hired James Robinson, a senior seminary student, to create the Harlem Mission of Madison Avenue Church out of an old, empty, abandoned building. In 1948 that church was officially renamed Church of the Master, which became an international model of Christian worship and outreach.

I sadly said good-bye to the Mid-Harlem Community Parish in August 1959, and joyfully became the assistant minister of the Church of the Master, which was located three blocks west of where I had been working, on 122nd Street and Morningside Avenue.

The next year, 1961, Reverend James Robinson left the church to work full time with Operation Crossroads Africa, and I was chosen by the congregation to be his successor.

Around the time I joined the Church of the Master, there was a dramatic rise in substance abuse in Harlem, which coincided with the accelerated rate of truancy and dropouts in the borough schools.

I knew these kids because I used to spend a lot of time on the streets. They were smoking pot and some were into heroin. So we started our own program at Church of the Master for high school dropouts. The church had already created a separate institution known as the Morningside Community Center, founded by Jim Robinson, which was affiliated with the Church of the Master. It had two camps in New Hampshire, a social group work program, and a mental hygiene clinic. When I arrived, the church kept and expanded those programs.

We were given a farm that had 396 acres in Chatham, New York. The congregation, mostly middle-class blacks, approved of my missionary work at the camp facilities. But they were not keen on my participating in community social reform work in the main church building, itself. They were especially resistant to my trying to do anything that resembled the Mid-Harlem Community Parish. I was new, I was happy to have a job, and I had the camps at my disposal to use as I saw fit. While their attitude bothered me, I believed that with some results, they would open their minds and hearts to reaching out.

Chapter 13:
Malcolm X

Through the 1950s and most of the 1960s, several movements and organizations focused on raising the collective consciousness of the black race in America.

While Martin Luther King, Jr. was a voice of inclusion and equality for all people, several prominent figures and emerging ideologies actively sought separation. They called for segregation of a black-only sovereignty to overcome the abuses, oppression, and suffering associated with white America.

One of the most prominent black segregationist figures emerged in Harlem in the mid-1950s and attained a global reach by the mid-1960s. He went by the name of Malcolm X. While he and I were at odds over how to overcome the ravages of racism in America, we did agree that it was an epidemic that had only one dire conclusion, not only for people of color, but for America, if not addressed.

Malcolm X and I had very different childhoods. But, when we consider his young life experience, we can begin to understand the sources of his ideology.

Malcolm X was born in Nebraska, in the town of Omaha, on May 19, 1925. His parents, outspoken father Earl Little and mother Louise Little, named their child Malcolm. Young Malcolm Little was influenced by his father's ideas and words. Earl Little was a Baptist minister and spoke at various events and venues. His father unabashedly supported Marcus Garvey, the well-known pan-African activist. Earl also led the local Omaha chapter of the Universal Negro Improvement Association, which is most often referred to as UNIA. Earl, along with other UNIA leaders, encouraged their audiences to take pride in being black and to be self-reliant. Malcolm was influenced by these teachings as well as tragic events, such as the murder of his uncle by white supremacists.

White supremacists also threatened and harassed Malcolm's immediate family. They moved to Lansing, Michigan, because Klansmen threatened Louise during her pregnancy with Malcolm. Unfortunately, the harassment intensified for the Littles once they were in Lansing. Supremacists burned their house in 1929. Fortunately, none of the Littles were injured in that assault, but Malcolm's father was struck and killed by a streetcar two years later. Many in Lansing's black community suspected Earl was murdered and blamed the Black Legion for his death.

The police ruled that Earl had slipped and fallen under the streetcar. Like many, Malcolm did not believe the police and their "official" account and wrote about this tragic incident years later. He asked, "How could my father bash himself in the head, then get down across the streetcar tracks to be run over?"

Malcolm's hardships, which were mostly the product of others' cruelty, did not prevent him from being an excellent student, especially in junior high school. What did derail Malcolm's academic career was an eighth grade teacher who told Malcolm his goal of being a lawyer was not a realistic aspiration for a man of color. Soon after this setback, Malcolm's mother had a nervous breakdown and was judged to be legally insane. She was institutionalized and her children, including Malcolm, were each sent to different foster homes. One thing all of these foster homes had in common was the fact that white families operated them.

After Malcolm's domestic stability vanished, he began to descend into the darkness and despair of crime. While in Harlem, Malcolm began to dabble in dealing drugs, racketeering, robbery, and other criminal pursuits. After spending two years in Harlem, Malcolm moved back to Boston, where he began a series of burglaries that specifically targeted white, wealthy families. He was caught and sent to state prison for eight years.

Once in prison, Malcolm quickly earned a reputation for his hostility toward religion. This hostility earned him the nickname "Satan." Even so, he retained a desire for social contact. Another prisoner, John Elton Bembry (whom Malcolm later called "Bimbi"), commanded Malcolm's total respect. After the two had established a friendship, Bembry persuaded Malcolm to self-educate. Malcolm acted on the advice and soon developed a passion for reading. Even after the prison lights had been turned off for the night, Malcolm would read by scant illumination from outside lights shining through his tiny cell window.

Malcolm changed in other significant ways while he was in prison, most notably, joining the Nation of Islam. Malcolm's brothers visited him at prison and told him about the philosophies of the Nation of Islam. These tenets, especially ones that depicted white people as evil, resonated with Malcolm. The Nation of Islam also preached black unity and self-reliance, ideas that Malcolm first heard from his father and UNIA. After considering all of the injustice he, his mother, father, and uncles had suffered at the hands of white supremacists, Malcolm decided to write a letter to Elijah Muhammad, the leader of the Nation of Islam. Muhammad replied and instructed Malcolm to repent, renounce his past transgressions, and pray to Allah.

Malcolm did as Muhammad instructed him and he became a member of the Nation of Islam.

Malcolm emerged from prison in 1952 a changed man. He demonstrated his transformation by changing his surname from "Little" to "X." He would later explain in his autobiography that the "X" denoted a true African name he could never learn. Malcolm quickly grew into his new identity. He soon became a temple leader and eventually was chosen to lead Temple Number Seven in Harlem. He rapidly enlarged its membership and became entrenched in the community. He took his message to the streets and the airways whenever he could. One of his favorite places to speak in the streets of New York was at Michaux's National Memorial Bookstore in Harlem Bookstore.

Michaux's was an important Harlem institution for nearly fifty years. It was Harlem's literary center. Lewis Michaux founded the bookstore and, like Malcolm's father, Rev. Earl Little, was heavily influenced by Marcus Garvey. The people of Harlem called Lewis "The Professor." The Professor stocked his bookstore with a huge inventory that included many books on the Negro experience. Michaux's hosted African leaders, and was a gathering point for rallies and street corner speeches. Malcolm developed a friendship with The Professor and sought advice from him.

Many black speakers at Michaux's would climb stepladders so that they could have a platform on which they could preach. Those who focused on African nationalist agendas would wave flags or other national symbols to dramatically present their messages.

It was in front of Michaux's where I first heard and met Malcolm X in the late 1950s. He and other outspoken orators, such as Edward "Pork Chop" Davis and Ensign Cook, were frequent speakers at Michaux's pulpit. Malcolm X's message had a fire that burned with anti-white, anti-Jewish, and anti-

Christian themes of hate. His messages really bothered me, but I never confronted him at Michaux's venue.

During this time, a restaurant called Frank's became a popular place in Harlem to go for after-work networking, power brokering, and cocktails. On one occasion, I became engaged in a conversation with a black journalist who was considering an article covering the speakers at Michaux's Bookstore. I described the impact Michaux's had on the community and argued that the speaker forum was relevant to social, cultural, and nationalist perspectives on important issues for all people of color.

The reported asked, "I've heard about this guy named Malcolm X. Do you know much about him?"

I said, "We've met and I've heard him speak at Michaux's. I don't really like his message very much."

"Do you think you could introduce me to him?"

"Sure. In fact, he's probably speaking at Michaux's now. Would you like to head over?"

We walked a few blocks over to Michaux's, and Malcolm was indeed about to speak. Malcolm was eloquent, as usual, as he delivered his consistent theme of segregation and aggression against oppressors. When he finished, I introduced the journalist to Malcolm X. Articles featuring the speakers at Michaux's, including Malcolm X, were published soon after they met.

I would frequently run into Malcolm X at various places around Harlem, but one of our mutual favorite places, one of the few things we ever agreed upon, was a barbershop at on 126th Street and Eighth Avenue. We had great conversations in that old barbershop. We debated politics in Harlem, the church, and his anti-white, anti-American, anti-Christian, and anti-

Jewish concepts and ideas. Malcolm followed Elijah Muhammad's teachings that all white people were devils. He would laugh at me and he said I was one of those "Uncle Tom niggers."

He thought I was one of those black Christian ministers who had sold out our race. Malcolm X was also very critical of my efforts and associations with white power, white money, and white corporate America to organize programs for the schools in Harlem or the unions to advance working opportunities and conditions for all people, including people of color. Malcolm would say, "'Aw, these Uncle Tom niggers and Christian ministers who hustle the people of Harlem are silencing our voice." He was talking to everyone in the shop and about everyone who did not follow his rhetoric. But in the barbershop, he was primarily talking about me to get a response.

I finally took the bait and said, "Malcolm, you seem to know so much about me, my faith, and my church. Why don't we have a debate in my church?"

He said, "Anytime."

I smiled with confidence and said, "I'll set it up and get back to you."

So I invited him and all of the guys in the barbershop to the Church of the Master for a "meaningful debate" on Christianity. I thought I was so smart. I had a theological doctorate, I was a Christian minister, and I was bringing him into my domain. I was so full of myself, there was no way Malcolm X, or anybody else for that matter, was going to be able to come into *my* house and compete with my intellect, my experience, and my book knowledge about the Bible. No way.

Within the first five minutes, I was in a state of shock. Malcolm X knew so much about Christianity, the life of Jesus, and the Bible. He did an outstanding job interpreting the Word of God in a personal and contemporary way. He did a better job than most ministers, including me at that point in my life, in making the Bible relevant to our lives in the moment we were in. He gained so much credibility with his knowledge of Christianity that it made his transition to expressing his ideology and the tenets of the Nation of Islam in a language all could understand. He completely blew me away in our debate about my topic of choice. He was so eloquent.

I discovered that he was a great debater, but what I did not expect was his ability and capacity to know so much about my supposed expertise. He clearly knew more about Christianity than I knew about the Nation of Islam; and during our debate, I — and I'm sure others — felt that he quite possibly knew more about the importance of a personal relationship that truly embodies Christianity than I and they did. I admired his tenacity and his preparedness. He had an answer for everything and I was exposed. That was his secret weapon and gift, and it is what made everyone so interested in what he had to say, regardless of which side you were on. He made sure he knew topics from multiple perspectives and he was always well prepared. Additionally, he took the time to research and know about his opponent in a debate.

I learned a lot from that experience, and even with my pride deflated by the whooping I took from him, I still managed to have fun in our debate at the Church of the Master. I realized from this that, at this time in my life, while I had a great knowledge of history and a scholarly understanding of biblical interpretation and Christianity, I lacked the ability and desire to personally live God's Word. That meant I had not established a personal relationship with God through His Son, Jesus. I don't know if Malcolm X knew this about me; I would not be surprised if he did. But I now know that God sent him into my life to enlighten me about, if not convince me of, this need.

Chapter 14:
Alex Haley

In the fall of 1960, I saw a man sitting on the sidewalk with an orange crate full of books and a typewriter sitting on top of it. He also had several suitcases surrounding him. I glanced at him and I noticed that he was very despondent. He was sitting there as if he was going nowhere. Something attracted me to him.

I asked him, "Hey, brother, what's happening?"

He paused, and actually seemed startled by my question. With despair he finally responded, "I don't know what to do. I just got evicted from my apartment."

"Why?" I asked.

"I owe my landlord nine months' rent."

"Nine months' rent! How could this happen? What do you do?" I asked.

He responded with conviction, "I'm a writer."

That turned me off right away. I remembered my uncle had a vacant apartment in Cambridge and once a man came to rent it and said he was a singer. My uncle said, "The only thing I know that sings for a living is a canary." My uncle wouldn't rent the apartment to the man. I ascribed my uncle's principle to all artistic endeavors. They could write from passion or write for a hobby, but rarely for a living. This guy only further confirmed my belief.

I asked, "What are you going to do?"

"Well, I'm trying to decide if I should jump in front of the next car or just go and jump straight into the Hudson River."

"Don't do that," I said, "I've got a one-bedroom apartment in Harlem. I've got a sofa in the living room that you can sleep on for a couple of days until you get yourself together."

He got into my car and on the ride uptown he told me he was in such despair because he had this great story to tell. But with this latest setback, he was consumed with thoughts of suicide. He was afraid the story was going to die with him.

At this point in the ride, I was having some really serious doubts about this man and my lack of judgment in letting him in my car, let alone into my apartment!

As we continued to drive, I asked him what his story was about. He told me that this story had been passed down through his family generation after generation. The story started with the patriarch of his family, Kunta Kinte, who was kidnapped in Gambia and transported to Maryland to be sold as a slave. He tried to run away three times and each time he was captured and returned to his master. On the third attempt, the master cut off his leg. This meant that the man had to stay on the plantation, and this gave him a chance to raise a family. The story of each generation stemming from Kunta Kinte was passed down through his family until it reached him.

I was captivated as we drove to my apartment.

I asked him, "What's your name?"

He answered, "Alex Haley."

As a youth, Alex Haley moved between his birthplace of Ithaca, New York, and Henning, Tennessee, a couple of times. Alex was the first born to his parents, Simon Alexander Haley and Bertha Palmer. Bertha gave birth to Alex on the August 11, 1921. His mother and father would later have three more children, two additional boys and a girl. A decorated veteran of the First World War, Alex's father, Simon, was a Cornell University professor of agriculture. I know that Alex was proud of his father and respected his triumphs over obstacles imposed by extreme racism.

He once told me, "My father is my inspiration to counter the hate of racism with dignity and with words of truth and love. He is the reason I write."

His father urged him to enlist in the military when he turned eighteen. Alex had been able to enroll at Hawthorne College when he was only fifteen. Although supremely intelligent, Alex's age prevented him from establishing a sense of belonging at the university. His father believed that a military experience would give his eldest son the discipline needed to succeed in a career. Obviously, Simon judged correctly because Alex successfully served in the Coast Guard for twenty years. He began as a mess attendant then achieved the rank of Petty Officer Third Class. That's about as far as Negroes could go in the Coast Guard at that time.

Alex was serving in the Coast Guard when the United States entered World War II. He served in the Pacific theater, and began to write while serving in the Pacific. In addition to providing an escape from boredom—an enemy greater than the Japanese, according to Alex—his writing earned him some spending money. His shipmates recognized his talent and paid him to pen love letters to their girlfriends back home.

Alex incorporated his writing into his military career. He petitioned the Coast Guard for a transfer, and they allowed him to enter into the field of journalism, where he soon advanced to the rank of Petty Officer First Class in the rating of Journalist. His continued successes eventually earned him the rank of Chief Petty Officer, a rank he held until he retired from the Coast Guard in 1959. Alex has the distinction of being the first Chief Journalist in the U.S. Coast Guard, which was a remarkable accomplishment for a Negro during the fifties. Alex had recently left his military career and was beginning the process of penning narratives of personal and family history. It was at this stage of his life that our paths crossed on a street corner in Harlem.

As I continued driving Alex toward my apartment, I finally I asked, "Is this really a true story?"

"As far as I know. My grandmother used to tell it to my mother all the time and I loved to listen to her. It means so much to me."

"Do you have any documentation? Can anyone else substantiate this story?"

"All that I have is in that orange crate. You can ask anyone in my family. We all know the story."

I said, "Look, I'll let you stay in my apartment. You write this story and I'll take you to *Reader's Digest*. I'll bet they'll print it."

Later, after he got settled, Alex gave me the name and number of his brother, George, in Kansas.

The first time Alex left the apartment, I called George Haley. I said that I was a minister in New York and that someone had told me the story about his family ancestor from Africa.

George proceeded to corroborate everything Alex had shared with me about Kunta Kinte and beyond, even to the point of emphasizing that his grandmother told the story to his mother and then again to him.

I shared with George that I had found his brother Alex in a desperate situation and that I was letting him live with me for a while until he got back on his feet. George was relieved and grateful; they had been trying to track Alex down for months. George and I kept in touch during Alex's time with me and well beyond. We met a few years later and remained friends. He was a good and bright man. (George worked with Robert Dole when he started running for public office in Kansas.)

With a place to stay, Alex went to work writing the Kunta Kinte story. We took it to *Reader's Digest*. They accepted the story to be published, and *Reader's Digest* paid Alex for the account of his family.

Soon after, I got a call in my apartment from *Playboy* magazine asking if Alex would interview Dr. Martin Luther King. They would arrange for him to meet Dr. King while he was in India. *Playboy* paid Alex several thousand dollars plus expenses for the interview, which was a lot of money in the early 1960s. *Playboy* was satisfied with Alex's interview of Martin Luther King—so satisfied it they asked him to do an interview with Malcolm X.

Alex didn't know Malcolm X when *Playboy* called. I did. While Malcolm X and I disagreed on many things, especially our religious beliefs, we ultimately grew to respect each other. From what I knew of Malcolm at this point in his life, he was devout and principled in his beliefs. I thought it would be highly unlikely that he would agree to an interview in a magazine like *Playboy*. I introduced Alex and Malcolm and we floated the idea for an interview. As I suspected, he was opposed to doing it.

I said, "Malcolm, if you do this interview, it will generate worldwide attention to the Nation of Islam."

Reluctantly, he agreed that he would at least pass the idea by Elijah Muhammad, the head of the Nation of Islam. Much to Malcolm's surprise, Elijah Muhammad approved of the article because it would be good publicity.

I made arrangements for Alex and Malcolm X to meet at my apartment, and they began the interview. Sometimes they would meet at the restaurant at Malcolm's mosque, but mostly they met in my apartment.

The article was a great success and so, the concept of writing an autobiography of Malcolm X was born. The focus of the book project was to provide a more comprehensive, explicit, and detailed recounting of Malcolm's life and the foundation of his ideological perspectives. Most of the interviews for the book were held in my apartment, where Alex did most of the writing as well.

During this time, I was still actively involved with my public service work. My office was located at 55th Street and Fifth Avenue. An agent in this building came to my office and asked if he could meet with Alex and Malcolm. I got the three of them together, but really was not involved beyond that. Alex told me that the agent obtained a $50,000 advance from Doubleday Publishing, split equally between them. That's nothing today, but in the early to mid-1960s, that was big money. Malcolm X gave his entire share to Elijah Muhammad and the Nation of Islam. Alex paid off most of his bills and had about $6,000 left.

Malcolm X filled the book with a lot of anger. When the book was completed, the book was delivered to Doubleday.

The editor who read it said, "Look, I think the book will sell, it is provocative, and is a fascinating read, but I won't approve it. Malcolm is too controversial, so full of hate, and his expression of conflict is too dangerous to promote."

The editor sent the book to Nelson Doubleday, the head of the company. Mr. Doubleday read the manuscript and said, "This book will never be published by my company!"

We had hit a dead-end. We asked for the manuscript back and the editor said, "No, we paid for this, it's ours now."

We were outraged. We fought back. We wrote letters to Doubleday's lawyers, and threatened to go to court. We went to the *Amsterdam News,* which ran a series of stories about how Doubleday, a big, white publishing company, was discriminating against blacks, violating the constitutional rights of Malcolm X, and illegally seizing the property of Alex Haley and Malcolm X. The stories were generating a lot of interest and bad press for Doubleday, and they worked. Doubleday gave the manuscript back to us and didn't ask Malcolm and Alex to return the advance.

Unfortunately, when we tried to sell the manuscript at other publishers, we were turned away. Some rejected the manuscript for the same reasons as Doubleday did, and others would not even take the time meet with us. We felt as if we were blacklisted. It was very frustrating and difficult to experience. One day Alex and I were down in Greenwich Village and we saw a sign that caught our eye, "Evergreen Publishing Company." I suggested we should talk to that company about the book.

We met with an editor who asked to see the manuscript. After reviewing it, he said, "This is great. Give me $5,000 and I'll publish the book."

So Alex took his last five thousand and gave it to him. Our hope was renewed and we were so excited. Three weeks later, the Evergreen Publishing Company went bankrupt. We were stunned and could not believe that we were back to square one. Alex was broke again. It seemed hopeless.

A couple of weeks later we got a call from somebody who said, "I was the guy at Evergreen who was originally assigned to your book. I like this story, but it will cost you five thousand dollars for me to work freelance and get this book published."

We protested, "But we just paid Evergreen our last $5,000."

He replied, "If you want me to find a publisher for this book, then I'm going to need $5,000."

By this time the three of us were jaded and highly suspicious, but we believed in this project, so I encouraged Alex and Malcolm X to press forward. Alex scraped up $2,500 and I took out a loan for $2,500 and gave it to Alex and Malcolm. We were now running on faith alone. The gentleman turned out to be honorable and worked with Grove Press to publish the *Autobiography of Malcolm X*.

Shortly before the book was published, Malcolm separated himself from the Nation of Islam. In his public announcement, Malcolm complained that the Nation had "gone as far as it can." Malcolm desired to work with a variety of civil rights leaders, and he said that Elijah Muhammad had forbidden him to do so. As a result, Malcolm felt constrained by Muhammad's strict religious doctrine. Malcolm quickly established a religious organization, Muslim Mosque Inc., and a secular group to advance the ideas of black nationalism. Malcolm made his announcement of his split from The Nation of Islam in the beginning of March 1964. Later that month he met Martin Luther King Jr. in Washington DC. The two leaders were there to observe a Senate debate on the civil rights bill. This March 26 meeting was to be the only time these two civil rights legends would be together in person.

Next, Malcolm traveled to Mecca. The purpose of his April visit to this holy city was the completion of his Hajj, the holiest of all Muslim rituals. While he was there, he had a culture shock. He saw white people who were also Muslim. He'd been taught that only black people were Muslim. It opened his eyes that color wasn't the issue. The experience completely changed his racial and religious perspectives. He was no longer totally anti-white, anti-Jewish, and anti-Christian—and he even had good things to say about me.

The following excerpts are from a letter Malcolm X wrote to his loyal assistants in Harlem during his Hajj experience. The letter was printed in *The Autobiography of Malcolm X: As Told to Alex Haley*. It captures the essence of his awakening and transformation and provides context for his leaving the Nation of Islam, explaining why he rejected his venomous attitude of blind hate.

> Never have I witnessed such sincere hospitality and overwhelming spirit of true brotherhood as is practiced by people of all colors and races here in this ancient Holy Land, the home of Abraham, Muhammad and all the other prophets of the Holy Scriptures. For the past week, I have been utterly speechless and spellbound by the graciousness I see displayed all around me by people of all colors.
>
> There were tens of thousands of pilgrims, from all over the world. They were of all colors, from blue-eyed blondes to black-skinned Africans. But we were all participating in the same ritual, displaying a spirit of unity and brotherhood that

my experiences in America had led me to believe never could exist between the white and non-white.

We were truly all the same (brothers)—because their belief in one God had removed the white from their minds, the white from their behavior, and the white from their attitude.

I could see from this, that perhaps if white Americans could accept the Oneness of God, then perhaps, too, they could accept in reality the Oneness of Man—and cease to measure, and hinder, and harm others in terms of their "differences" in color.

With racism plaguing America like an incurable cancer, the so-called "Christian" white American heart should be more receptive to a proven solution to such a destructive problem. Perhaps it could be in time to save America from imminent disaster—the same destruction brought upon Germany by racism that eventually destroyed the Germans themselves.

Grove Press was ready to publish the original manuscript when Alex and Malcolm X said they wanted to add an appendix that included some new things—especially the recent and significant changes in Malcolm's life preceding and since his trip to Mecca. Alex and Malcolm believed the changes to be profound and necessary for the book; they needed more time to write. Grove Press agreed. Alex and Malcolm X were finished with their edits by the end of 1964 and turned the manuscript over to Grove to do final editorial review and prepare for publishing.

The book depicting Malcolm X's life story was to be hugely successful. Sadly, Malcolm X would not live to enjoy its success. He was assassinated on February 21, 1965, while addressing the four hundred attendees at the meeting of the Organization of Afro-American Unity in the Audubon Ballroom in Manhattan. He was just beginning to speak when a disturbance broke out in the crowd. Malcolm, accompanied by his bodyguards, moved toward the ruckus. Suddenly, a man charged at him and shot him in the chest with a sawed-off shotgun. He was rushed to Columbia Presbyterian Hospital, but he died soon after arriving there at three thirty that afternoon.

Thousands of mourners came to the public viewing, which was held in Harlem at the Unity Funeral Home February 23–26. Alex and I went to the public viewing as well as to his funeral. The ceremony was held at the Faith Temple, Church of God in Christ, in Harlem. The church building seated about one thousand people, and it was full. Loudspeakers had been set up outside so that those who could not get in would still be able to hear Ossie Davis's eulogy. Local television broadcast the service. Many civil rights leaders attended the funeral, including John Lewis, James Farmer, Bayard Rustin, James Forman, Andrew Young, and Jessie Gray. Although Martin Luther King Jr. was not able to attend, he did send a telegram to Malcolm X's wife, Betty Shabazz. He wrote:

> While we did not always see eye to eye on methods to solve the race problem, I always had a deep affection for Malcolm and felt that he had a great ability to put his finger on the existence and the root of the problem. He was an eloquent spokesman for his point of view and no one can honestly doubt that Malcolm had a great concern for the problems we face as a race.

Alex was quite shaken by Malcolm's assassination. Alex and Malcolm X had become close during the nearly two years they were together. I was saddened by Malcolm's death as well. We came to know each other on a more personal level through the work he and Alex did together, and I got to witness his life transformation from his Hajj experience. Through it all, he was a man who was committed to what he believed in, and I respected him for that.

Indeed, Malcolm X and I read the riot act to each other many times. I could not tolerate Malcolm's idea of black superiority and that white people were the devils. This was one of the cardinal teachings of Elijah Muhammad and the Nation of Islam. Before his Hajj, Malcolm X could not accept the idea that God created all people, or as the Bible says, "God made of one blood, all nations to draw on the face of the earth."

While Malcolm X and I saw things differently, an area we both cared about was the youth of Harlem. He had a powerful impact on the young blacks there. Malcolm X emphasized black supremacy, segregation, and a message that being black is all they needed. I wanted black people to realize that being black was not enough; it was necessary to connect culturally, but it was not sufficient to live completely. Knowing you are black will not get you a good education, a good job, a family.

Whether we were debating life, religion, or the New York Giants, I will always remember my times with Malcolm X. He challenged me to be a better-prepared man, and he planted the seed of a relationship with God that I did not yet have at the time. I saw the work that God was doing in him, and in some ways, it helped prepare me for the work God had yet to do with me. I do miss him.

Percy Sutton, my longtime friend, became the attorney who represented Malcolm X and the Shabbaz family after Malcolm's assassination in 1965. When several New York City cemeteries refused to bury Malcolm X, Percy arranged for his burial in Westchester County. I remember David Dinkins (who later became mayor of New York City) saying to me at the time,

"If it had not been for Percy Sutton, I don't know where Malcolm would have been buried."

Through the combination of the changes in Malcolm's life from 1964 and because of his assassination in February 1965, the early spring of '65 release of the *Autobiography of Malcolm X* was a financial and critical success. The book was an instant and automatic best seller. I can see Doubleday kicking itself to this day because the *Autobiography of Malcolm X* now appears in nearly every language and every country in the world. There was a period of time for many decades that the book was the most read book in the world next to the Bible.

Alex wrote most of the book in my house and rang up an eight hundred dollar telephone bill. He offered to pay me several times but I wouldn't take the money because, as I said to him, "Alex, it's better for me to tell people that you owe me eight hundred dollars than it is for me to take this money. I get more mileage out of it." We had fun with that for many years. Alex certainly repaid me by giving generous public credit for my role in starting him on his journey. In the Appendix added to the final publication of the *Autobiography of Malcolm X*, Alex wrote:

Malcolm X had very little good to say of any Negro ministers, very possibly because most of them had attacked the Black Muslims. Excepting grudging admiration of Dr. Martin Luther King, I heard him speak well of only one other, The Reverend Eugene Callender of Harlem's large Presbyterian Church of the Master. "He's a preacher, but he's a fighter for the black man," said Malcolm X. I later learned that somewhere the direct, forthright Reverend Callender had privately cornered Malcolm X and had read him the riot act about his general attacks upon the Negro clergy.

Alex also gave me, as a gift, a galley copy of the manuscript we presented to Grove Press. That meant a lot to me and it was prominently displayed on my shelves for over four decades. I recently gave it to a dear friend of mine who supported me through my years of ministry, public service, and life in Harlem. Alex also signed the first book off the presses, writing, "To Gene, in whose apartment most of this book was written."

Alex experienced life from a very unique perspective. He was consumed with writing. To become a better writer he shared with me that he read the dictionary from cover to cover to know as many words as he could. He also loved the written word. Alex would volunteer at military bases to read and write letters for soldiers wives who couldn't do it for themselves. He found all things, great and small, worth capturing in words. In fact, he is the one who encouraged me write my memoirs.

Alex was a great storyteller who just loved life. He would see things differently from how I or others would. One time I took him to a soul food restaurant I liked called Obie's, which was famous for stewed tomatoes. We sat down and I said, "Alex, you need to try Obie's stewed tomatoes."

"No way, Eugene."

"Try them."

Reluctantly, he got a side order. Our waitress brought our dinner and I watched him inspect his bowl of stewed tomatoes, slowly rowing his fork through the food while intently smelling the flavors. He paused, looked up from the table toward me and said, "They don't look good, but they sure do smell good."

"Will you just try them already?"

He did, and he savored the first bite and then quickened his pace for the second, and a third before he exclaimed, "This is the best food I've ever tasted. If I were a tomato and I knew my destination were Obie's restaurant, I would voluntarily jump off the vine to get there as soon as I could."

Alex Haley expressed himself like no one else I've ever met.

For many years Alex maintained a longstanding role with *Reader's Digest* as a contributing writer. In 1966, *Reader's Digest* financed Alex's research and travel for ten years. Alex believed he was a seventh generation descendant of Kunta Kinte, and he traveled abroad and researched as he wrote for a number of years. One of the many places he visited was Juffure, the village that was home to young Kunta. There he heard the story of Kunta Kinte's capture as told by the village historian. This oral history provided the details he used for his account of his family's origins. Alex also traced the records of the ship, *The Lord Ligonier*, which he learned carried Kunta Kinte to America. The result of this historic collaboration was *Roots*, the Pulitzer Prize-winning book.

Alex Haley made millions of dollars through the publication of the *Autobiography of Malcolm X*. The book made more money than *Roots* and is still selling today. *Roots*, made into a series of TV programs, captured a huge television audience and sold a lot of copies. But to this day, the *Autobiography of Malcolm X* is used in schools all over the world and was used heavily as a basic source for Spike Lee's 1992 movie, *Malcolm X*.

Alex Haley stumbled into my life, or mine into his. But either way, we were blessed to have been brought together. He was a great friend and we enriched each other's lives. Alex was best man at my wedding with Lemoine. It was a small wedding in a little house on 145th Street. Other friends of mine, Dr. Kenneth Clark, and John Heyman, were groomsmen alongside Alex. My daughter, Renee, was there, too. I was so happy that we could be together.

Chapter 15:
Count Basie

Jazz and gospel music continued to be two of my most serious interests beyond community service. In 1962, I was invited to go to the Newport Jazz Festival in Newport, Rhode Island, to give lectures on jazz and gospel. I got to know quite a few of the great musicians from the Newport experience, men from the Count Basie Band, such as Joe Williams and Freddie Green. Freddie once said, "You've got to come and hear us in Las Vegas. We are going to do a big show with Frank Sinatra and Quincy Jones at the Sands Hotel."

I told him, "I would love that!"

My wife, Lemoine, and I accepted their offer and we stayed in the Sands Hotel for one week. It was one of the most exciting experiences of my life—to hear the Basie Band every night, two performances, led by Quincy Jones. They also accompanied Frank Sinatra. I remember saying to Freddie Green on the golf course one morning, "I've never heard the Basie Band play with such power and strength as they've been playing at the Sands. And more importantly, I've never heard Frank Sinatra sing so exceptionally great as he's sung with the Basie Band."

Freddie's response was, "Doc, when the Basie Band plays, we put a sound in their head and they can't help it—they've just gotta sing. We feed off of each other and make each other better. Frank can't help but sing with joy when he feels our music in his soul, and joy liberates the voice."

As Minister of the Church of the Master, I also became the executive director of the Morningside Community Center. We had an annual benefit each year to raise money for staff, programs, and growth for the center. With the help of Marietta Tree, whom I'd met on the Adlai Stevenson campaign, we created a memorable event that raised an extraordinary amount of money for our work in Harlem. Marietta's brother, Samuel Peabody, had become a very good friend of mine and he served on the board of directors of the Morningside Community Center. Sam and his wife, Virginia, found us a roof on an apartment building on Park Avenue to hold our event. It was really some evening.

We called it a "Brown Bag Party." The invitations were made out of little brown bags that when you blew them up, you'd "pop" them at the party once you contributed to the fundraiser. We mailed them to influential people who could make a contribution, taken from the list of names provided by Marietta Tree and her brother, Sam Peabody. The party made all of the society columns of the New York papers. Everyone wanted to come. The event was free. We placed blank checks all along the walls and on the cocktail tables. The purpose was for people who came to this unusual festive affair to make contributions to the Morningside Community Center, and in this we were very successful.

Two bands played that evening. It was a battle between the Count Basie Band and Maynard Ferguson's band. Maynard Ferguson was a white trumpet player who became one of the great leaders of an ensemble that produced some of the best-selling recordings in the jazz field.

Maynard Ferguson's piano player did not arrive on time, so Count Basie played the piano for the first set of Maynard Ferguson's band. I was standing next to Freddie Green and a couple of the other Basie boys. I said, "You guys better be good tonight. Those guys are going to give you some competition."

Freddie's response, while holding a bottle of beer in his hand was, "Rev, don't worry. Wait until we get up on the stand."

It seemed to me nobody could outplay Maynard Ferguson that night. When the Ferguson band had finished its first set, the Basie Band took the stage. They were very casual, very funny, and very easygoing. Then, suddenly, Count got on the piano. He must have played about a dozen jazz chords. And the trumpet section of his band stood up and blasted. The rest of the orchestra put the piece together and Maynard Ferguson might as well have gone home. In fact, Maynard said to Basie, "Look, man, this is your night. We'll stay, but we won't play any more."

And Basie said, "Oh yes, you will stay. This is a battle. You know how to play in this arena!"

It was one of the most wonderful and exciting evenings. I was just getting started as pastor of the Church of the Master and this night made it possible for the Morningside Community Center to gain extensive awareness in the New York City social work community, in addition to much-needed financial support.

Chapter 16:
Reformed Democratic Movement

I became active in 1959 with the Citizens for Kennedy campaign through my participation in the Reformed Democratic Movement of New York City. I was co-chairman of the movement's executive committee and my active role was to go to churches and civic groups affiliated with blacks and other minorities to talk about John F. Kennedy and why he should be elected the next President of the United States. Oddly, our biggest obstacles early on in the campaign did not come directly from the Republican Party, but from leaders of the Democratic Party, who were divided between the traditional group led by Carmine DeSapio and our emerging Reformed Democratic Movement.

The relationships and struggle for power between the two factions was contentious. Both factions wanted to run the Kennedy campaign in New York, and it got nasty. Our reform group finally took the position that if the National Democratic Campaign Committee gave the responsibility of New York to the DeSapio group, then we would not be able to support John F. Kennedy. The division and petty politics were destructive and caught the attention of John F. Kennedy's campaign manager, his brother, Bobby. Our "ultimatum" initiated a boiling point with the national committee, which brought a call to action. Bobby Kennedy came to town. While I had never met him prior to his visit, I was aware of him and his family. We were both thirty-five when we finally met.

Bobby called a strategy meeting in February 1959 for all sides vying for the Democratic Party and campaign leadership in New York City. The primary participants from New York included Carmine DeSapio and his old-line political lieutenant, John Merli on one side and Eleanor Roosevelt, Eleanor Clark French, Averell Harriman, Herbert Lehman, Tom Finletter, and me on the other. Bobby brought everyone together to get his brother's campaign back on course. The meeting was held in a conference room at the Roosevelt Hotel on 43rd Street and Madison Avenue.

We were all gathered in the conference room waiting for Bobby. There was incredible tension while we waited for what seemed like hours. This was the first time I had seen Carmine since our initial encounter at Rockaway Beach. We made eye contact, but nothing more. I was still trying to carry on the charade that I had neither known him nor spoken to him during the whole Hulan Jack/Earl Brown drama. He seemed to be honoring our agreement. Bobby finally entered the room and in a matter of seconds, displaced our self-imposed tensions with his fury.

Bobby stormed in with his sleeves already rolled up, and before he reached his seat proclaimed, "I don't give a shit about you, Eleanor Roosevelt, or you, Carmine DeSapio, or you, Herbert Lehman, or you, John Merli! I just want to get my brother elected! If that is not your number one priority in life, then this meeting is officially over for you. You guys get your asses together and get this fucking campaign going! You either work together and unify our objectives or I'll do it for you. Is there anything that I just said that is not clear?"

There was complete silence. There was no expression on anyone's face but mine, which was a smile of disbelief. A disbelief that ranged from, "I can't believe this brash skinny guy was so rude to the *saints of the Democratic Party*" to "I can't believe that this guy had the guts to say what we all needed to hear." It is nearly impossible to succeed in any mission from a divided position, and we were clearly divided. I would have never thought that Eleanor Roosevelt and Carmine DeSapio would be able to put aside their considerable differences to rally for this specific goal of getting JFK elected.

Bobby broke the silence after one minute. "I'm not hearing anything so I'll assume that this is now one team and *the* team to deliver New York for John Kennedy." He sat in his chair for the first time and set out the plan and tasks for the primary and the general election.

Bobby began giving out assignments to the team, "Eleanor Roosevelt, you will be in charge of corporate fundraising, alliances, and John's campaign platform to build support and ensure votes from the middle- and upper-class segments of New York City. Carmine, you will be in charge of mobilizing all the precincts statewide and driving all state campaign events, staffing, and canvassing communities to drive votes for John. Eugene, you will be in charge of mobilizing the minority-affiliated associations, including churches, and strategizing for reaching minority segments of New York City."

I looked at Bobby, smiled, and said, "Now *that's* what I call being task-oriented." It seemed as if in an instant he had unified a seemingly hopeless fracture in the political structure of the New York Democratic Party. He had never met me, spoken to me, and yet he knew what he wanted me to do. He definitely did his homework and he had a plan.

"There is no other way, Reverend; now go do your job." Bobby stood up. "If there are no further comments or questions, let's get to work." He looked intently into the eyes of each person in the room, and nobody responded. He walked out of the room as quickly and purposefully as he had entered it. When the doors closed behind him, we stared at each other in silence for about two minutes, not with the tension that we had before Bobby Kennedy stormed into our lives, but with wonderment of what had just happened. It was like experiencing an earthquake and being still in the aftermath, just to make sure it was over, before determining if everything was all right.

Eleanor Roosevelt broke the silence with a dignified call to arms, "You heard the young man. We are the team to get this work done. Let's get our man elected." Her words seemed to comfort the sting of Bobby's lashing, as everyone around the table acknowledged their agreement of not only being on the team but with the team. We went to work.

I left the meeting and replayed the whole experience of meeting Bobby Kennedy for the first time in my mind. I was excited that he was able to unify this warring group of the New York Democratic Party, if only to get his brother elected. However, I was initially shocked by how brash and rude he was toward these party titans. Nevertheless, I remained committed to doing my job within the team. I cannot speak to how the others felt personally about Bobby, because none of us ever spoke about him or about that meeting in general. I will tell you that each one of us did do our jobs with one focus in mind and within the context of the team. He turned us into a successful team in a twenty-three minute meeting. The united team delivered New York for John F. Kennedy in 1960, and Bobby delivered him for America.

When John F. Kennedy became President of the United States, Adlai Stevenson became the United Nations representative and Marietta Tree became part of the United Nations staff. Bobby Kennedy was appointed to the position of special assistant to the president. One of the projects that fell under Bobby's responsibilities was heading up a task force to understand and abate juvenile delinquency in the United States. The net cast by this project covered New York and coincided with both my public service and youth ministry responsibilities.

Chapter 17:
HARYOU - ACT

Back in the early 1960s, when the Harlem Neighborhood Association (HANA) was formed and was comprised of all the social work agencies in Harlem, I worked with and through HANA as the platform for different activities and social change inside Harlem.

In 1961, I was co-chairman of HANA's board. I read an article in the newspaper saying that the New York City Youth Board was going to give the Jewish Board of Guardians a $50,000 grant to start a mental hygiene youth program in Harlem. At that time, the Church of the Master had a mental hygiene clinic that served adults. Ken and Mamie Clark, of the Northside Center on 110th Street and Fifth Avenue, had a mental hygiene program for children and adolescents. I called up Ken Clark that afternoon and asked him if he had seen the article, which he had. I asked why the New York City Youth Board hadn't consulted him or me? He didn't know either.

We met the next day. I was furious. Since HANA was made up of all the social agencies in Central Harlem—the Salvation Army, Community Service Society, YMCA, YWCA, and the Board of Education—I called a meeting of the board. I said we needed to fight what I described as "social welfare colonialism." I felt that the city wanted to impose a program on our community though we already had two existing programs. They could have given us each $25,000 and we could have done the work. We decided to fight.

I preached a sermon the Sunday following the meeting titled "Social Welfare Colonialism." It made the *New York Times*. I got a call from Mayor Robert Wagner's office saying he wanted to see me about my statement. I would meet with him, but I wanted to have the whole executive committee of HANA with me. When we met, the mayor asked what he should do and I told him to give the money to Church of the Master and Northside Center for our existing programs. He turned to the deputy mayor and asked, "Can we do that? Maybe we can do both."

"No, we're not doing both," I responded. "If you're going to put a mental health program in Harlem, it's going to come to Church of the Master and Northside. We can do it."

The deputy mayor, Henry Cohen, took us in an anteroom in his office and asked us what HANA was all about, and we told him. He asked if we knew about the president's anti-juvenile-delinquency committee headed by Bobby Kennedy. I told him that I did.

He said, "Forget the $50,000. I've got a better plan. Why don't we go and get some big money and perform some real work in Harlem?"

Cohen told us to trust him. While it sounded promising, the HANA team came away from the meeting skeptical that anything would happen. To our surprise, and delight, Henry Cohen called me within a week and invited HANA to meet with David Hackett, Bobby Kennedy's number one man. I brought Milton Yale, who was white, Jewish, and the executive director of HANA. Cohen told Hackett about our association.

David said he thought he could get us a $250,000 planning grant from the president's anti-juvenile-delinquency office. This would allow HANA to fund much more than just a mental hygiene youth program. We could organize a major youth program in Harlem!

After the grant award was announced, we encountered opposition. A group led by the Reverend Adam Clayton Powell, a U.S. congressman from Harlem, and Ray Jones, a leader of the Democratic Party in NYC and a powerful politician in Harlem, complained that HANA shouldn't get the money because it had a white executive director. They asserted, "What could Milton Yale possibly know about what to do to help the black youth of Harlem?"

We had a meeting in the house of the borough president, Edward Dudley, a black lawyer, along with several black leaders who jumped on me, saying HANA was "a white organization." I told them it wasn't a white organization. Sure we had white people on the board, because the Salvation Army, Community Services Society, and the Board of Education were run by white people, but I was there and there were others, and we weren't looking at it from a racial point of view. We were unified in our mission and efforts to get a job done that could really benefit the community! I told them this was not a race or culture issue, but rather, it was a community improvement program. How could that be bad and who better to implement a plan than the community's neighborhood association? I could not believe that we were even having these conversations.

At that time, Adam Powell was then chairman of one of the most powerful committees in Congress, the Education and Labor Committee. His committee had to approve our grant, and Powell said he would stop it.

I asked, "What do we need to do?"

Ray Jones said, "Get rid of Milton Yale."

I loved Milton. He was a dedicated soul. He worked hard and did good things. But I said, "OK, the community is worth more to me than Milton Yale. We'll create a new organization, separate from HANA, and we won't make Milton a part of it."

I went to Milton and told him exactly what had happened. I explained that I needed to create another agency and he couldn't be a part of it. The man cried. I told him I could resign in protest, but that that wouldn't really help, and that it would be better for me to be there and guide the thing, even though he couldn't be part of it. I told him I'd stay in touch with him and get guidance from him. He stayed on as executive director of HANA and we created HARYOU (Harlem Youth).

Kenneth Clark of Northside Center became the executive director of the newly formed HARYOU and I was chairman of the board. HARYOU was a great idea. It was well conceived and well put together. It had an educational component, it had a jobs component, and it had a cultural component.

Ken hired two men from Columbia and City College, Kenneth Marshal as project director and James Jones as research director. I wasn't keen about these choices because I feared that their approach would be laden with academic studies that would drain the funds and not accomplish what we wanted and needed to do. I was a student of Saul Alinsky, the sociology professor at the University of Chicago, whose basic concept of community organization was that the participation of the people who were suffering from the existing system and who fought for change also needed to be part of the solution.

One of the most profound documents ever written at that time on the topic of social reform to improve lives of impoverished youth of the inner city, *Youth in the Ghetto,* was created by HARYOU. The primary focus of this document was to provide a roadmap and execution plan to enable opportunities for young people in the ghetto to get better jobs. The demographics are dated now, but the ideas and some of the programs were fantastic and are relevant today. The group that Kenneth Clark put together produced this document, so while my fears were steeped in reality, Ken and his team really understood our mission.

One of the consistent problems that affected youth in the large ghetto communities was declining progress in education. More and more kids were dropping out of school, especially in Harlem. That was one of the reasons we developed HARYOU, a program sponsored by the federal government to improve the opportunities for black youth in education, art, and employment.

The kids hated the word "school," so we called our program the "Academies of Transition." Its purpose was to get kids from the streets back into the schools. We focused on instilling basic personal responsibilities, tutoring, and believing and hoping in something greater than themselves. We also taught them about the consequences associated with breaking the law and the valuable opportunities that could be available with hard work and an education.

While I was developing the plan for the Academy of Transition, the associate pastor at Church of the Master was a young Caucasian fellow named Ed Fiske. Ed Fiske met Harv Oostdyk, also white, who was working with the Young Life Program down on the Lower East Side. But Harv always wanted to work in Harlem. He had gone through Young Life training, established as a Christian youth ministry in Texas in 1938. Harv was deeply interested in working in an urban area. He knew that Young Life worked well in suburban areas, but he wanted to try it out in urban areas. So he moved to Harlem and brought a team of young dedicated men and women from Young Life to Church of the Master.

In addition to the volunteers from Young Life, we were able to get corporate foundation grants for people who would work as tutors, mentors, counselors, and advisors in the program. They were all white, but that did not matter to me. It was my desire that these young men and women would hang out around the playgrounds where the young teenagers of Harlem gathered to play. At first the neighborhood youngsters of Harlem were reluctant to become too close and familiar with the Young Life team because they thought they were cops in disguise. We identified and picked neighborhood kids who were leaders. We selected sixteen of the top basketball players in Harlem to join this Academy of Transition in the church. The Young Life kids became the street kids' motivators. They were what we called "street workers." We opened two apartments on Manhattan Avenue, because most of these kids had no place to live, since their parents had kicked them out when they started using drugs.

When I was searching for teachers to help us with the tutoring in the Academy of Transition, I looked for retired teachers through a teaching sorority in New York City, giving the pitch that we were seeking special teachers who were not looking for a lot of money, but who loved kids and who were patient. I explained that the kids couldn't read well, if at all, and didn't have any discipline. I said we'd get street workers to handle the discipline, but we needed creative and patient educators to help these kids rise out of their life on the streets of New York. I made it clear that teaching at the school would not be a traditional nine-to-five job. Dr. Susie Bryant was the first lady to raise her hand.

She was our first teacher, with sixteen boys. They loved her. She was like a mother to them. She took a real interest in them and spent time with them. Susie taught reading and English, while another teacher, Mr. Griffith, taught math and science.

This program flourished until politics got in the way. While we were doing great things in Harlem with HARYOU and the Academies of Transition, Adam Clayton Powell went to Bobby Kennedy and told him, "You gave those guys $250,000! I want $250,000 for my own program in Harlem. He got the money. He created an agency called Associated Community Teams (ACT). So now we had two programs in Harlem, totaling $500,000 in grants. We had HARYOU and Powell had ACT. There was nothing I could do about it.

There was a lot of tension between HARYOU and ACT. We felt that we were a legitimate organization committed to making changes in Harlem. We followed policies and procedures. We suspected that ACT was a figurehead organization, formed by politicians who we thought were lining their pockets with money intended for the community.

At one point someone came to me and said, "Gene, you've got a snake in the grass."

Someone had been meeting with ACT and telling its leaders everything we were doing. I couldn't believe it. Who on our staff would do that? It felt like such a betrayal that we were doing all of this hard work at HARYOU and that anyone would give our ideas away to ACT. I told Ken Clark about it. He couldn't believe it either. We were extremely upset.

We went back to Henry Cohen, who was still serving as deputy mayor, and told him about the situation. Henry got in touch with David Hackett, and David Hackett got in touch with Bobby Kennedy. Hackett came back to us and said he didn't want us to jeopardize our work with Harlem with a scandal about bad politics; we had to find a way to move on.

Meanwhile, HARYOU presented our *Youth in the Ghetto* report and findings to Sargent Shriver of the Office of Economic Opportunity. Adam Powell came back and said he didn't want two programs in Harlem. He only wanted one program and he wanted it to be his. He said his committee would block any money coming to us if he didn't get his way.

To overcome the political stalemate, we agreed to merge the two organizations, the two boards, and the two grants to create HARYOU-ACT. Somehow, we managed to maintain two separate organizations under one new umbrella. I was the chairman of HARYOU and Ken Clark was the executive director. Livingston Wingate remained the executive director of ACT.

HARYOU-ACT had some successes in Harlem, including the creation of an arts-and-culture program headed by Art Taylor and Julian Yule. They worked with youngsters between the ages of twelve and fourteen. They taught them music and acting. Some of these young people became professional musicians and actors. Others went on to dance for Alvin Ailey and work on Broadway. One success story of the program was saxophonist Rene McLean, whose father was Jackie McLean, who augmented his studies of music and education, which supported his strong foundation to reach the world with music to transcend boundaries.

Another program implemented by HARYOU-ACT was a jobs-and-opportunity program to provide kids economic training. We found work for them at gas stations, butcher stores, and furniture manufacturing factories. We trained a lot of kids under this program.

We tried implementing an education program, but with little success.

Everything seemed to be working OK until it was decided that we should indeed merge both boards (HARYOU and ACT) and elect one executive director.

Ken Clark was so upset by this turn of events that he resigned as executive director of HARYOU. Several other professionals left with him.

I became chairman of the newly merged board, but unfortunately I had no say in day-to-day operations. After the organizations merged, the new board voted to elect Livingston Wingate executive director of HARYOU-ACT. Wingate won the election by one vote.

In my opinion, that was the beginning of the end of HARYOU-ACT as an effective agency. I stayed on as chairman because I had a personal interest in the success of the community programs that I helped spearhead. HARYOU-ACT had a lot of hope, but unfortunately, petty politics got in the way of servicing the needs of others.

The tragic part of it was that in a period of five years, over $55 million dollars came into the central Harlem community through HARYOU-ACT—and the community was in worse shape than ever. What happened to that money? We institutionalized the hustle, led by selfish career politicians. There were many people on the HARYOU-ACT payroll who worked hard, and there were others who never did a day's work.

On a positive note, we did raise the salaries of social workers in Harlem. When HARYOU-ACT hired Wingate as the director in 1964, we paid him $25,000 per year. At that time, the highest salary for a social director was about $15,000 dollars. At first, all the social work agencies jumped on us, saying, "What are you doing?" But later, other agencies had to raise their salaries for social workers in Harlem to meet the salaries that we were paying. This meant that Harlem could attract better quality social workers.

Apart from this, sadly, nothing substantial really happened, from the point of view of social change in Harlem, with the merging of HARYOU and ACT. In my opinion, as a social experiment it didn't work, or rather, it stopped working because there were more people lining their pockets instead of really making a difference to the public by whom they were elected and swore to serve.

Bumpy Johnson

During my time as chairman of the board at HARYOU-ACT, I was having some difficulty with some of the young hustlers in Harlem who wanted our organization to give them large sums of money without making legitimate requests through written proposals. I had given explicit instructions to Livingston Wingate, the HARYOU-ACT executive director, "Don't you ever give those guys any money!"

The most serious of these groups was led by a local writer who lived in the Village. They came to Wingate and insisted that he give their organization $150,000. Wingate told him that he'd been given instructions by me that they were not to get any money at all. The writer from the Village and a friend of his paid me a visit at Church of the Master and threatened me at gunpoint, saying that if I did not give them the $150,000, they would kill me.

I told them, "You can shoot me all that you want. But that's not going to get you the money. If you shoot me, everyone in this building would know it was you because I'd alerted the staff of the church that you were coming, and I had mentioned your names."

They left in anger, and with a parting threat. "We'll get to you."

Indeed, it was frightening, and I had no confidence that the police could handle the situation. I went to dinner at my favorite restaurant at the time, *Obie's*, run by Mr. Obadiah Green. Obie told me, "Doc, don't worry about it. I'll see to it that you get the best guardian in the community."

"How will you do that?"

"Let me handle it."

Two days later, I got a call from a man who identified himself as Bumpy Johnson.

I had heard the name; I'd heard of his notorious reputation. Bumpy has been called "The Harlem Godfather." He had a big reputation of being the only black gangster in Harlem who was recognized by and frightened the Italian mafia that dominated the criminal element of New York City. He had a number of legitimate businesses. When the 1968 riots broke out after Dr. Martin Luther King was assassinated, Bumpy came to Harlem to try to calm the rioters down. His favorite restaurant was Obie's. Obie had known Bumpy since the late 1930s.

Later that week, Ellsworth "Bumpy" Johnson came over to my apartment in Lenox Terrace. Lemoine and I had moved there with her two kids. I took two apartments: one was five-and-a-half rooms, and the other three-and-a-half rooms. I took down the wall between them, which gave us eight rooms, two terraces, twelve closets, three bathrooms, and three bedrooms.

It turns out Bumpy and I were neighbors. He lived in the building next to ours. He came over to meet my family and me. He was a sharp dresser. He told me a lot about his involvement in criminal activity. He told me about the time he had spent in jail and how he was walking around with eighteen bullets in his body.

He said to me, "Obie wants me to be your bodyguard and be with you wherever you go to speak. That will keep those thieves away from you!" That's how our friendship began. It lasted the entire time I was at HARYOU-ACT and included one summer's vacation in Saratoga, New York. After that, everywhere I walked in Harlem, Bumpy or some of his fellows watched over me. I felt perfectly secure.

During the 1960s, I used to play golf every Tuesday and Sunday morning. On one Sunday morning, my golfing group met at Marshalls Café on Seventh Avenue at six thirty for our pregolf breakfast. As we were eating, a gentleman named Patty came in and said, "Fellas, guess what just happened?"

"What?"

"Bumpy Johnson just died."

Our automatic response was, "Who killed him?"

"Nobody killed him. He died of a heart attack."

We all ran to Harlem Hospital, which was across the street from Lenox Terrace, where I lived. One of Bumpy's friends, Junie Byrd, was outside and he was crying. I looked at him and said, "Junie, he's gone, isn't he?" And Junie said, "Yeah, Rev, he's gone."

Years later, there was a movie starring Denzel Washington that changed the ending of Bumpy's life. The picture was based on the life of Frank Lucas, one of Bumpy's biggest competitors in the gangster world, who, in the movie, told people that Bumpy died in his arms. That was not true.

Articles were written about Bumpy's death and funeral in *The New York Times*. Some people found it hard to believe that he was gone, knowing how he had narrowly avoided death so many times in the past. Some of them kind of hoped Bumpy was going to get up from the casket and start raising hell. Sugar Ray Robinson came to the funeral. So did Joe Lewis and Count Basie and Eddie Small and Juanita Poitier, Sidney Poitier's first wife. Georgie Rose, one of my golf companions, was there, as was Spanish godfather Raymond Marquez. They were among the pallbearers, along with Hoss Steel and Pop Gates. One celebrity who attended was the jazz great Billy Daniels, who was also a good friend of Bumpy's. He sang a stirring rendition of "My Buddy." That brought even the hard-nosed street players to tears. Bumpy was buried in an opulent mahogany coffin and was driven slowly all the way to Woodlawn Cemetery in the Bronx. Bumpy had left Harlem forever.

Chapter 18:
Campaigning for Bobby Kennedy

Bobby Kennedy was a champion for equality. He demonstrated this early in his career when, in the fall of 1962, Kennedy ordered U.S. Marshalls to go to Oxford, Mississippi, to enforce a federal court order that allowed James Meredith to attend the University of Mississippi. James was going to be the first African American student admitted to "Ole' Miss," and because of this there was a dangerous amount of tension between the black and white citizens of Oxford.

This tension manifested in the form of riots, and a couple of people were killed during the violence. Bobby Kennedy believed that all citizens should have access to education. He also was an outspoken advocate of workplace equality, and he knew that insuring black citizens could vote without harassment or other barriers was essential to racial justice. Bobby was actively involved with President Kennedy and then President Johnson in creating the Civil Rights Act of 1964, which effectively began to eliminate Jim Crow laws.

One area that did trouble him was the growing tensions due to racism. Often, riots broke out, especially if a remarkable incident such as an unjust death occurred. The police certainly never intervened on the behalf of black citizens; instead, they compounded the problem—and sometimes they *were* the problem.

It was this recurring pattern of civil unrest that spurred the JFK National Reelection Committee to give our campaign committee in New York $2.5 million to pour into the communities that had a high concentration of colored people, to meet some short-term social, economic, and basic needs, and thus to release some of the mounting tension. Bobby was really worried that riots would erupt in many urban areas, especially in communities like Harlem, because of racism and social injustice. He wanted to use the money to reduce the likelihood of riots during the election year.

On November 22, 1963, President Kennedy was assassinated. Somehow, Bobby found a way to press on. He remained U.S. Attorney General for nine more months to assist in the transition for President Johnson, and then resigned so that he could run for U.S. Senate in New York.

I worked on Bobby's senatorial campaign and President Johnson's reelection campaign. President Johnson and Bobby Kennedy were often at great odds with each other, both politically and personally, yet Johnson gave considerable support to Bobby's senatorial campaign. Bobby's opponent in the 1964 race was Republican incumbent Kenneth Keating, who attempted to portray Bobby Kennedy as an arrogant carpetbagger from Massachusetts. Bobby emerged victorious in the November election, helped in part by Johnson's huge victory margin in New York.

In June 1966, Kennedy visited apartheid-ruled South Africa. At the University of Cape Town, he delivered the Annual Day of Affirmation speech. A quote from this address appears on his memorial at Arlington National Cemetery: "Each time a man stands up for an ideal, or acts to improve the lot of others, or strikes out against injustice, he sends forth a tiny ripple of hope."

Senator Kennedy sent more than just ripples of hope through Brooklyn's poverty-stricken Bedford-Stuyvesant area, where he helped begin a successful redevelopment project. Kennedy did not limit his compassion to just one region, but instead cared about the entire nation, both North and South; he visited the Mississippi Delta to check the effectiveness of War on Poverty programs. Nor did he limit his compassion to one racial group, but instead worked for equality for all Americans, including immigrants and Native Americans as well as African Americans.

Senator Kennedy was able to help bring about social changes that reflected his values. Among these were The Voting Act of 1965, busing desegregation, health care, and the integration of public buildings.

In the race for president in 1968, Bobby was one of the leading Democratic candidates. I served as a consultant on his National Campaign Committee. I did everything I could to help him meet as many black people as possible. Bobby accepted my invitation to speak at the Church of the Master and asked me if I could also invite James Baldwin, author of *The Fire Next Time*, a terrific essay about the role of race and religion in America.

I spoke with James and he said he'd come under one condition. "I can't speak without having something to drink."

"I'll get you some water."

"I don't want any water. I want scotch. I'm not speaking without it."

So I made sure he had his scotch before he started speaking.

This was right after *The Fire Next Time* came out, and James made a fantastic speech. It was James who introduced Bobby Kennedy.

Bobby Kennedy got up and said, "Who else but Gene Callender would bring together in Harlem a radical writer, like James Baldwin, and a New England aristocrat?"

After the program was over, we went downstairs for a small reception and several people immediately volunteered to work on Bobby Kennedy's campaign for president.

I fully expected Bobby to win and I believed that he was going to be one of the greatest president's that our country would ever have. But he was to die on June 6, 1968, like his brother, the victim of an assassin's bullet, while campaigning in Los Angeles.

Chapter 19:
Leaving Church of the Master

Meanwhile, work continued at Church of the Master. We had a membership of eleven hundred people. We had two camps in New Hampshire, a farm in Chatham, New York, a co-op store, credit union, social group work, and the Academy of Transition. We had sixty-two people working full time and we were popping.

While working at Church of the Master, I moderated the New York City Presbytery. At that time there were 150 Presbyterian churches in New York City, spread throughout the five boroughs. Those churches made up the members of the New York Presbytery. The Presbytery managed the reports, growth, and special programs carried out in these churches. I was twice elected moderator, and twice sent as a delegate to the National General Assembly. Years later, the National General Assembly elected me the first black Presbyterian Minister of the Year, and I delivered a sermon in the National Presbyterian Church in Washington DC.

Sadly, our congregation did not reach out to the community, to "ruffians," as they were called. Church members would say things like, "They are not our kind." The church membership consisted primarily of middle class blacks with a few whites. The church leadership offices were integrated between blacks and whites. When I first arrived, I wanted to continue the work I had been doing before with the addicts, alcoholics, and troubled youth. This brought a different crowd into the church. Many of the church members were not pleased. They didn't like the way these folks dressed and they thought they were a bunch of crooks and thieves. I didn't care. I wanted to help change lives. At every session meeting, the elders of the church would ask me, "When are you going to get rid of those kids?" I told them I was not going to get rid of them, that this was the whole purpose of the church. Jesus said that we should minister to the least of the community.

The five hundred teenagers who came to the Young Life program every Wednesday night were street kids, and they were not like the congregation. Truth be told, the church members feared them. Most of the congregation had left Harlem and moved to Queens because they wanted to escape the violence and the drugs and the despair these youngsters could bring into *their* church.

One time we arranged for three hundred youngsters between fourteen and nineteen years old to attend two Young Life camps for three weeks. We asked the children to come to the church on Saturday morning and be prepared to leave by ten. The youngsters showed up as typical young street kids from Harlem. They did not remove their hats. Two of the elders of the church arrived and, feeling the disrespect of the youngsters for the traditions of the church, chased all of the young people out of the building and told them never to come back again.

Our church was indicative of the declining reach and power of the church in America because it had become insular, each congregation becoming its own private club. For me, it felt as if Sunday morning at eleven was still the most segregated hour in America. I thought our congregation was hypocritical, and they weren't really serious about being the church, being like Christ. I felt as if I had not made a bit of progress on influencing the congregation to get involved in the community, let alone the critical needs of the youth in Harlem.

So in April 1966, I left the Church of the Master and accepted the invitation to become the new executive director of the New York City Urban League. I wasn't even sure I wanted to stay in the ministry because the Presbyterian churches I had dealt with up to this point did not tend to reach out to the poor people in the community. I was invited to speak at Columbia University, at Princeton University Chapel, and Yale University, and during those sermons I talked about how the church had turned its back on the poor and the hungry in New York City.

Chapter 20:
The New York Urban League

The New York Urban League supported a professional social work staff that tried to find jobs for talented blacks in the telephone company, banking industry, or with major corporations. Its main purpose was to help black people find white-collar employment.

I was still the chairman of the board of HARYOU-ACT, and when I became the executive director of the New York Urban League, I had to resign from the board. Since HARYOU-ACT gave grants to the Urban League, it was seen as a conflict of interest.

This was the first time the board of the directors of the New York Urban League had gone outside the Urban League family to hire an executive director. Prior to my hiring, most people worked their way up the Urban League ladder. The board selected me because of my reputation for community service, including my work with rent strikes, detox programs for addicts, working for different presidential candidates, and the Academies of Transition.

Because I hadn't "come up the ranks," the staff was initially hostile to this newcomer in their midst. I had a tough time winning their confidence.

I observed and assessed the mission, structure, and accountability of the organization and I didn't like what I saw. Many staff members were not doing the job for which they were getting paid. The League was staffed by some professionals who were comfortable in their positions and weren't worried about being fired. I soon began to realize that a man who had applied for my job was undermining me with the staff. I made a point of giving him a lot of attention. I met with him and the rest of the management team and delegated a lot of assignments to him. At the same time I was planning my own agenda for necessary change.

After six or seven months had passed, I started to clean house. We would still meet the mission of helping talented blacks find corporate jobs. We would also raise the importance of the mission by developing programs for the youth so that we could cultivate an even greater population of talented blacks worthy of competing for future corporate positions. This idea had the full support of the board. Once we streamlined the team, I started raising money on my own to fully establish new community goals, such as employment training and engaging the Street Academies in a public service partnership with the private sector. All of my past experience with my missionary ministry, with HANA, HARYOU, and HARYOU-ACT proved valuable and led to quick results.

When I arrived at the Urban League in 1966, it had a budget of $200,000. My first year there I increased it to two million dollars. We completely redesigned the initiative of the New York Urban League. Instead of maintaining little offices in five boroughs, we ran everything from a main office in Manhattan, and we brought corporate people onto the board. We started the annual Frederick Douglass Awards Dinner in 1966. This fundraiser was Ann Kheel's idea, and we named it after that dynamic former slave, Frederick Douglass, who ran away at the age of nine, taught himself how to read, and wound up in Rochester, New York. We raised a lot of money at that dinner, with most of the funds coming from corporations and foundations. This annual dinner continues today.

Street Academies of Transition

When I left Church of the Master and came to the Urban League, I brought the Street Academy program and its staff with me. In addition to Susie Bryant, our faculty consisted of Sister Ruth Dowd, a PhD and professor of philosophy at Manhattanville College, which at the time was a very well-known Jesuit school for women. Her assistant also came and joined our faculty. Another nun, Mother O'Brien, brought three of her nuns from the Sacred Heart Order, and they became the faculty of the Academy. They were an outstanding team of educators. They loved those kids, and the kids truly loved them.

We saw tremendous progress and true transformation happening in the lives of those youngsters. We knew we could and had to do more. But to do so would require financial resources. So I approached a couple of foundations and several major corporations and each corporation put up $50,000 to start a street academy, a storefront school for high school dropouts. As a result, we had several corporate branded academies: Union Carbide Street Academy, Pfizer Street Academy, First National City Bank Street Academy, Chase Manhattan Bank Street Academy, Time Inc. Street Academy. They not only had to provide the money to fix up the storefront, but also to provide equipment, and enough funds to supply all of the needs of the schools and students.

We provided the teaching staff. We also provided support services, which were the responsibility of the Young Life street workers. The Young Life workers would see to it that the kids got out of bed in the morning, went to school, and would help them meet their needs outside of the classroom, like making sure they were well nourished.

When we began the street academies, those kids could barely read or write. They knew no math at all. We began with *The Autobiography of Malcolm X*. Sometimes it took them eighteen months to read the book. But that's how we taught them English. They liked the book because it was about blacks and Malcolm. They could connect to it, so they were interested in it. Their interest in Malcolm and the social challenge he posed, with which they could identify, inspired a desire for learning.

They were then given *Manchild in the Promised Land* by Claude Brown. Every word they didn't know, they had to look up and use in a sentence. Their vocabulary rapidly grew, and with their improved command of reading, writing, and speaking, their confidence began to soar. It was amazing to experience. Before the academies, their lives were spiraling into hopelessness. Now they had gained and could apply the knowledge they received at the academies. For many, it was a long journey, but they flourished.

I cannot overstate the tremendous contribution of the Young Life street workers. The majority of them were students of Union Theological Seminary, and others were from Princeton Theological Seminary. A few came from schools in the Midwest and the South. They were really big brothers and big sisters to the disoriented and disinherited youth of Harlem. They began a program of transformation for the students' lives through religious programs, as well as taking students to camps in Minnesota and Colorado and retreats in New Jersey and the New York area. From time to time, they would tell me how much they were learning from this experience. They were not only helping the kids improve their situations, but the youngsters gave them insight into their own lives in ways they had never known before.

Harlem Prep

Our mission to get kids off the streets and back to learning was a success, but we hit a wall once they were ready for higher learning. A few returned to the public schools to finish their high school education. Many of our children did not have a home to go back to, so we sent these kids to Newark Prep, in Newark, New Jersey. It was very expensive to send these kids to Newark Prep. We had to provide transportation to and from New Jersey, buy them books, and pay tuition. When we looked at those expenses, we felt it would be better for us to develop our own high school in Harlem, Harlem Prep. Only students who completed work at the street academies would be admitted.

It was going to take a major commitment and financial backing to bring Harlem Prep and our concept to fruition. What made our approach different from public schools is that we would allow each student to stay in the Harlem Prep program until that youngster was admitted to a college, regardless of how long it took. For the kids' parts, they had to commit to stay clear from substance abuse, be responsible and law-abiding citizens, good neighbors in the housing we provided, and good stewards of all that we provided to them.

I invited McGeorge Bundy to come visit us and see what we were up to. I had met Mr. Bundy when I was at HAR-YOU and he was an advisor in the Kennedy administration. He later became president of the Ford Foundation. It was from his position at the Ford Foundation that I introduced him to the concept of Harlem Prep as the next step beyond the street academies.

Mr. Bundy came to Harlem and took a tour of our street academies. As he walked the streets of Harlem with me, he met and talked with the kids. He was very impressed with what we were doing. He took me to lunch afterward and asked how he could help. I gave him more details about the unique nature of our proposed alternative high school in Harlem and its importance as the next step that would bring the kids from the academies to a special high school. He asked how much money I would need. I told him it would take at least a half million dollars.

In two weeks' time we got a big check from the Ford Foundation for $535,500, along with a letter from McGeorge Bundy telling me to go get my high school. We started Harlem Prep with that money. Two thousand former high school dropouts went from the streets of Harlem through the street academies to Harlem Prep. And every one of them went to college. Every one!

Our first graduation consisted of two students. We had the graduation in the boardroom of the Ford Foundation, and McGeorge Bundy was the speaker. I remember him saying to the kids, "Maybe one day you guys will be sitting in these chairs"—these chairs, where Robert McNamara and Henry Ford III once sat.

After five years, the foundations and corporations that contributed to Harlem Prep decided to end their financial support. Not because they were displeased with the results or lost interest in the cause. Quite the contrary, they believed we proved a successful approach to education and had reached the point that the Board of Education should be able to use our blueprint and execution plan to assume responsibility of our program through the better allocation of public funds. The foundations asserted that they already paid taxes and that public funding should pave the way for the next generation of Harlem Prep graduations. Their decisions made logical sense. But I told tell them that if we turned Harlem Prep over to the public sector, I feared that the program would be mismanaged, funds would be wasted, and petty politics would eat away at the fabric of what had been achieved. I was concerned that if we were no longer in charge, the school would go back to being a traditional public high school—and we knew that this kind of school just did not work for many of these kids.

We established a transition period from year five to year six and turned Harlem Prep over to the city when our funding dried up. It died a quick and extremely painful death. Just like that, Harlem Prep was gone.

I believe that the street academies and Harlem Prep are forerunners of the charter school movement in New York City. Charter schools are independent schools that can hire their own staff. Their teachers do not have to be approved by the Board of Regents, but salaries are paid by the city Board of Education, which gives them consistent support to continue year after year. I'm a strong advocate for charter schools for a couple reasons: They tend to attract better teachers and management, and they have less crowded conditions and good learning atmospheres in their classrooms.

I believe this approach to education deserves a growing consideration in our country's imperative to improve, innovate, and lead across all sectors and stations of life.

Operation Open City

One of the other exciting programs I was able to develop at the New York Urban League was called Operation Open City. I selected a young lady from the community, Betty Hoeber, to be the executive director because of her knowledge of the real estate community in New York City.

The goal and purpose of Operation Open City was to create opportunities for nonwhites to live in areas such as Park Avenue, Madison Avenue, the East Side, and the West Side. We'd take the *New York Times* and see which apartments were vacant in those areas. We'd send a black couple to those apartments. Sometimes we sent two or three black couples. Every time, they were each told by the real estate agent or the broker that that the apartment had already been rented. Then we'd send interracial couples to the same three apartments. They were also told that the apartments had been already rented. Then we'd send a white couple. They were allowed to fill out paperwork; they could have left their check, but we had them tell the landlord they needed a day or two to think about it. This always happened on the same day the other couples were turned down.

This all transpired after the City Council had passed the Sharkey Brown Isaacs Bill, which was sponsored by the only Jewish man on the council, Mr. Isaacs, the only black man, Mr. Brown, and Mr. Sharkey, an Irishman. This bill was supposed to eliminate housing discrimination in New York City.

Even though this bill was on the books, none of those apartments were rented to minorities. Many experiments proved that these expensive and luxurious apartments would not take people of color (and few Jews were ever accepted).

The result of our work was that thousands of minorities were able to move into homes throughout the five boroughs and suburbs. We were so successful that the New York City Council Against Poverty provided over $200,000 in grant money that enabled our agency to continue another year.

Chapter 21:
Mayor John Lindsay

Shortly after my work with Operation Open City, I received a call from John Lindsay, the mayor of New York City. He asked me to leave the Urban League and become the deputy commissioner of housing for the City of New York. I was conflicted. So I called my friend Ann Kheel and met with her and her husband Ted, a prominent lawyer in New York City and chairman of the Republic National Bank.

Ann said, "I don't think you should take the job. I think you should stay at the Urban League and continue your work here."

Her husband, Ted, said, "Go!" And then he asked Ann, "How can you ask this young man to turn down a request from the mayor of New York?"

Then Lindsay's people leaked to the press that this offer was made to me. I didn't want word to get out yet because I was still busy working on some important projects for the Urban League. I was in Cleveland, Ohio, when I saw a copy of the *New York Times* claiming that I had already accepted the position. I guess this is how people try to get you to do what they want you to do.

I decided to leave the New York Urban League. I thought I could do more for the Urban League and other organizations as a member of Lindsay's staff. I had arrived at the Urban League in June 1966 and I left eighteen months later in December 1967. My departure would change the whole course of my life.

John Lindsay was a courageous, young successful Republican congressman in a Democratic city. He was the first Republican mayor in New York City since 1945. I've only voted for a Republican three times in my life: John Lindsay, Stanley Isaacs, and Louis J. Lefkowitz, who was the New York Attorney General for 22 years.

Occasionally Mayor Lindsay invited my wife, Lemoine, and me to visit him and his wife, Mary, at Gracie Mansion. On these occasions, he asked me about my vision for Harlem. He was impressed with the success of the street academies and Harlem Prep.

My work with Mayor Lindsay was mostly managerial. The commissioner of housing was the public person who made the speeches, while the deputy commissioner ran the office. I had seventy-five employees to manage. I had become the city's landlord. Nobody could build anything without my signature.

I worked with all the developers for anything that we needed built in the city. I found it so interesting that on every contract, there was a line item that said, "Miscellaneous," with maybe a half million dollars on it. I would ask, "What's that for?"

"Well, in case we have some unforeseen expenses."

"A half a million dollars' worth? Don't you guys plan well?" And I would scratch it out.

One day the union rep in my agency asked me to have a meeting with union leaders. They took me to lunch at a fabulous restaurant and we were just chitchatting for a while. Then they said, "Deputy Commissioner Callender, you keep turning down our proposals because we won't spell out to you what's in the 'Miscellaneous' line."

"That's right. I'm not going to spend the city's money foolishly like that."

"But that's how we've always done it. It's always been acceptable."

"Well, it's not going to be if I'm the one making the decision."

They said, "Well, don't you like money?"

"Yes, I like money."

"Well, a portion of that is for you." They were honest about it—that was the payoff for getting the contract.

"I'm sorry," I replied. "I like money but I don't like jail."

After that lunch, instead of coming to me they started going to the budget director. They went over my head and got their contracts approved.

I wanted to demonstrate to the people in the budget office why I would not approve these contracts. By this time I had gone to MIT and Columbia Business School, where I learned something about management. I did an internal study of the agency and found we could do the same amount of work and be as productive, if not more so, if we fired fifteen hundred staffers. So I drew up a proposal. I had a budget whiz kid from Harvard Business School with me. Together, we did a very thorough productivity study. I took it to the Bureau of the Budget, because it had to approve everything on budget and personnel. I said I had found a way to save the city a lot of money.

I started by telling the budget managers what happened on a daily basis. First of all, several people came to work late. They brought their coffee and rolls to work and the first thing most folks did at their desk was eat. They spent the first half hour eating breakfast. They would not eat breakfast at home. They then took their breaks at ten thirty; they were supposed to get twenty minutes but many took forty-five. Several got ready for lunch a half hour before it was time to go, and they came back half an hour late. Others took their afternoon break and, a half hour leaving at five o'clock they would stop work and get ready to leave.

I detailed all of it.

I presented my conclusions to the Bureau of the Budget and thought surely that the managers would be pleased and want to take immediate action. To my shock they said, "Leave it alone." The reason: Those workers were unionized and the city didn't want any trouble from the unions. The budget director didn't want to take responsibility for people losing their jobs. I said, "If you're not going to approve it, I'm going to the mayor."

"The mayor?" the budget director asked. "The Mayor? Let's see? LaGuardia, O'Dwyer, Impellitieri, Wagner. I've seen them all come and go. I've been here thirty-seven years. Go ahead and go to the mayor. It's not going to get you anywhere."

I went to John Lindsey, the mayor, and he asked, "Did you go to Budget?"

"Yes."

"What did they say?"

"They said they don't want to do it."

"Then it's not going to happen," the mayor said.

I liked working in the community and with the community groups, but it was a very frustrating job. I became very disillusioned with the lack of progress we were making through the entrenched bureaucracy.

Chapter 22:
The Emergence of Black Power

Meanwhile, progress was being made on national civil rights front. In 1967, Dr. Martin Luther King's message suddenly shifted beyond civil rights when he started speaking out against the Vietnam War. In a sermon in Riverside Church in New York City, Dr. King pointed out that America was the first country in the world to use the atomic bomb, which claimed hundreds of thousands of casualties. And now in Vietnam, without any express purpose for freedom or democracy, thousands of American young men and women were being killed on a regular basis because of what he called "this unnecessary war." In his speech, he declared that America was a vicious nation.

On March 4, 1968, Dr. Martin Luther King Jr. and I received awards and lifetime membership in the NAACP. We shared many things together, but a moment I will never forget is the joy on my stepson Billy's face when I introduced him to Martin Luther King. He was so proud to meet him and get his autograph.

The last words Martin said to me were, "See you in Memphis." I never got to see him again because he was killed before I got there. He was assassinated exactly one month later, on April 4, 1968, at the Lorraine Motel in Memphis, Tennessee.

When Martin Luther King was shot in 1968, Deputy Mayor Barry Gottehrer called me up and said, "Mayor Lindsay is coming to Harlem tonight to walk the streets with the community and he wants you to walk with him."

"I'm not going," I said.

"Why not?"

"Barry, if I go to those streets tonight I'm going to do the same thing those people are going to do because I share their rage. If I go out to the streets, I will be right alongside them throwing bricks at windows and who knows what else. That is how angry and lost I feel right now."

He said, "I understand."

Mayor Lindsay came and he walked the streets that night and kept riots from taking place in Harlem.

The following day, he came back to Harlem to thank people for not rioting. My wife, Lemoine, took his arm as he marched through Harlem and together, we honored the life of Dr. King.

From a theological point of view, I wondered why God had let King's murder happen. It happened right at a critical point in the civil rights movement. I listened to all the speeches, marched in the funeral marches, and instead of flying to Memphis to help Martin fight for the rights of sanitation workers, I used my ticket to fly to Atlanta and march in his funeral. I came back to New York, empty and broken.

I guess like most black people, I wondered what was going to happen now with our leader gone. Our worst fears had come to fruition. The civil rights movement, its campaign of nonviolence, and its call for equality and justice, ground to a halt. There were no more peaceful marches and demonstrations.

This was at a very dynamic and volatile time in our nation's history, both domestically and globally. From the mid-1960s through early 1972, America experienced the assassinations of key political and social leaders, the ravages of the Vietnam War, and the emergence of the Black Power movement.

Two organizers for the Student Nonviolent Coordinating Committee (SNCC), Stokely Carmichael and Willie Ricks, were the first to use the term "Black Power" as a sociopolitical slogan. Stokely was my mentor when I participated in peace marches with Martin Luther King. But he had finally reached his breaking point.

Stokely was participating in The March Against Fear, which was a protest march between Memphis, Tennessee, and Jackson, Mississippi, held to renounce the shooting of the first black student at the University of Mississippi, James Meredith. When the marchers began to be harassed, Stokely said, "This is the twenty-seventh time I have been arrested and I ain't going to jail no more! The only way we gonna stop them white men from whuppin' us is to take over. What we gonna start sayin' now is Black Power!"

For Stokely, the term "Black Power" articulated the desire for solidarity among oppressed African Americans. He later said, "For the last time, 'Black Power' means black people coming together to form a political force and either electing representatives or forcing their representatives to speak their needs."

The emergence of Black Power brought along with it retaliatory violence. With the emergence of retaliatory violence came increasing incidents of planned aggression to make a statement. A campaign of riots sent several inner cities into chaos and flames.

That is when the Urban Coalition was created. The corporate community finally said, "We have got to do something about this, we can't have people burning up our factories!" So the private sector took the lead to create the framework for the start of the National Urban Coalition, and John Lindsay started the New York Urban Coalition. Saul Wallen was selected to be the first president of the New York Urban Coalition.

One day Mayor John Lindsay called me into his office and said, "Saul Wallen has died. Gene, can you keep the coalition functioning smoothly?"

"Yes."

Chapter 23:
New York Urban Coalition

When I got to the New York Urban Coalition, I ran into a hornet's nest. One of the vice presidents, Linc, was black,
and another, Frank, was Hispanic. They were given these positions by Saul Wallen, a very bright, competent Jewish labor ne-
gotiator, in order to pacify the blacks and Hispanics. Lincoln
and Frank had never finished high school. They were, however,
wise and connected with life in the cultural streets of New York
City.

Andrew Heiskell, who was chairman of Time Inc., was
chairman of the board of the Urban Coalition as well. He called
me and told me that my first assignment as president was to fire
Linc and Frank.

"Are you kidding?!"

"No."

I warned him that that could cause problems. He said,
"Let's see how you do."

I brought my friend Luther Gatling in with me as my
assistant, and met with him to brainstorm a plan for the task I
was given. I invited all the black members on the board out to
dinner. I said to them, "I'm a black man, and I'm a black man

265

who wants to get things done. I have had enough of the jiving and shucking in other organizations I've worked in. We have an opportunity here. The corporate community of New York City has said they are willing to put the money up if we are willing to come up with some significant plans and programs, not just a hustle doling out money just for the sake of some community group that says they've got some little program going. We want to make constructive, significant changes."

They said they agreed.

I told them, "The first thing we need to do is let go of Linc and Fran." They were shocked. I went on, "You guys know as well as I that Linc cannot do the job. He is not competent for the job. If he was competent I'd fight for him. But I cannot have a vice president behind me that cannot fill my job if I were to leave it. I can fire him without you, but I'd rather do it with you."

Finally, they agreed. So we all went to see Linc to ask him to resign. He said he wouldn't step down, and that the community would back him, that I should go ahead and fire him. I fired him and nobody raised a voice.

Next I had to fire Fran. I called on Johnny Olivera and Manny Diaz. Johnny and Manny were from the Bronx, and were leaders in the Hispanic community. I told them and a few others, "Look. I'm black; you guys are Hispanic. They picked me to be the president, and you guys should have representation here. I would like to have a Hispanic vice president, but I want a competent one. I don't think Fran can do the job. You guys know that. I'll take any one of you instead. You need to get rid of Fran, and then give me the names of some Hispanic candidates for vice president." They did. Manny Diaz picked himself to be the vice president. He did a good job.

It is not unusual for a new leader to make changes in the management structure. But the political and cultural considerations had to be managed very carefully. I was now in a position to start building a productive organization. Once in place, the team and I would be able to start making a real difference. Through the Urban Coalition, we built brand new housing in Red Hook, a community in Brooklyn. We started several types of drug rehabilitation centers in Brooklyn to meet the swelling needs of a population that had been ignored for so long. We grew Harlem Prep significantly through corporate and foundation funding, and we opened new channels of opportunity for black professionals in the media.

We partnered with large companies so we could develop a strategy and business plan, replete with a detailed and compelling cost-benefit analysis, to become the first prefab company in New York. We even obtained letters from the building trade union saying it would support us, which was unprecedented. We spent a lot of money to develop a workable plan. We had really done our homework.

When I brought the idea to the members of the Urban Coalition Board, which I thought would be a pleasant formality, I was met with resistance. Mr. Wilcox, the vice president of the NYC Urban Coalition Board said, "This will never happen." He went on to make a speech that began, "Gene Callender, we didn't bring you here to be an entrepreneur. We brought you here to solve social problems."

Mr. Wilcox was also an executive with Citibank. It was not the project that he was opposed to. He objected, I later realized, because we got Chase Bank committed as a partner. He did not want to let Chase become associated with anything that he and Citibank were a part of. Citibank was providing us with several hundred thousand dollars a year and was the Urban Coalition's biggest contributor. By contributing in this way, Citibank was gaining good will, and clearly they would not want to share this with a competitor.

Once again I learned a lot from this process. We still were able to do a lot of good during the time while I was at the Urban Coalition, and as time went on, I became pretty adept at understanding the corporate and market landscape to not only manage surprises, but also to open doors for new opportunities.

Essence Magazine

In the late 1960s, during my presidency of the Urban Coalition, four young men, all college graduates—Edward Lewis, Clarence Smith, Cecil Hollingsworth, and Jonathan Blount—came to see me with the idea of publishing a fashion magazine for black ladies. The first name they had picked was "Sapphire." That made me think of the comic strip *Amos & Andy*, so I recommended that they consider changing the name. They chose *Essence.*

They had exhausted their options for publishers to give their plan serious consideration. They presented their idea and business plan to me and I liked it, so I sponsored them through the Coalition, allowing them to create a more professional layout and advance their business plan. I brought the proposal to the Urban Coalition board, whose chairman was Andrew Heiskell, also the chairman of Time Inc. Coincidentally, Gardiner Cowles, who had been the publisher of *Look* and *Saturday Evening Post,* was also on the board. It was a bad time in the magazine publishing business. Subscriptions were way down, and *Life, Saturday Evening Post,* and *Look* had recently folded. It was probably the worst of times to present a new magazine proposal, but I believed in this idea. I presented the proposal with the principal creators of the concept and requested $150,000 to help these guys create a new magazine for black women.

The board members each took turns expressing the same theme: "This is not a good time for magazines to get started." We sat quietly and listened. I thought the cause was lost and I felt truly discouraged.

I stood up and said, "Gentlemen, you created this organization, this Urban Coalition. You created it because you felt that the business community had not played a significant enough role in dealing with the social issues that have kept blacks out of the mainstream of America. You created this coalition because you were committed to giving blacks equality of opportunity. Sure those magazines have all failed, but blacks have a right to fail just as much as you have! If you think it's going to fail, give them the opportunity. I don't think it will. But if we're going to have equality of opportunity, let's have it on both sides of the fence."

The board was stunned. They didn't know what to say, so they called for an immediate vote. They voted unanimously for the proposal, and contributed to help start *Essence*.

We gave them the $150,000. *Playboy* gave them $250,000 and promised them editorial help. *Essence* magazine not only was launched, but it thrived. I attended the twenty-fifth anniversary celebration of the magazine in the mid-1990s, and it is still going strong today. *Essence* is now owned by Time Warner Communications. And to think that it almost never saw the light because the creators could not get access to the right people at a time that defied logical business sense. At that time, conventional business, market, and corporate wisdom did not even consider the black female population as a viable market.

Positively Black

With the successful launch of *Essence*, the next media barrier that we addressed through the Urban

Coalition was television. I went to the New York City NBC affiliate and said, "You need a local black television show to inspire young black people to get into the television industry."

So I went back to the Urban Coalition and we decided on a format that addressed cultural, arts, corporate, political, and social interests of the black community. From there we laid out a business plan, programming concepts, and management structure. One day I was driving, when the name *Positively Black* came to me. We submitted our proposal to NBC, which loved the idea and in June 1970, we began an initial thirteen-week run. I cohosted the early shows. My first interview was with Alex Haley.

Positively Black was well received. We had a black management team and production staff, including our director, Henry McNeil, from Baltimore. Tom Johnson, who was a writer for the *New York Times*, became a cowriter for the show. Shortly after our show aired, another channel started a new show titled *Like It Is*, hosted by Gil Noble, with a similar focus on issues concerning African Americans and those within the African diaspora.

Our main purpose was to chronicle and point out to the viewing population black influences in the arts, literature, American and African cultures, the rise in corporate leadership, the rise and militancy of the Black Power movement, and the devastating impact of heroin addiction on the black community, especially in Harlem. These two shows were important pioneering efforts not only for blacks, but also for all of New York.

While I was working for the New York Urban Coalition, the U.S. Chamber of Commerce hired me to go around the country to give lectures to corporations about the value of equal opportunity and community stewardship. I was invited to lecture at Columbia Graduate School of Business on social justice and corporations, and I was appointed by President Johnson to a commission to study urban employment policy. That was how I met George Shultz, a native son of New York City, who later became the secretary of labor, the first director of the Office of Management and Budget (OMB), U.S. secretary of the treasury, and the U.S. secretary of state in the Nixon and Reagan administrations. He and I became good friends. He was chairman of the President's Committee on Urban Unemployment. I was the only black on the committee. I was an influential member of that committee because I could bring them into the black communities. We visited twenty-five cities in the United States on a campaign for education and change in our cities. George Shultz was my roommate. We were partners in every activity, in every city we visited.

It was on one of these trips, on June 6, 1968, that I got the news that Bobby Kennedy had been assassinated. I was in Arizona at the time, and heard the news at two in the morning. I was supposed to get up and give a speech the next morning on economics and unemployment. My first thought was, "Oh God, not again." Within months we'd lost Martin Luther King Jr. and Bobby Kennedy. I was heartbroken.

I did not give the speech I'd planned to give. Instead I talked about how brutal a nation we had become. America is a violent nation, I said; it has a history of being violent. It was violent when it took over the land from the Indians. It was violent during the riots. It killed Abraham Lincoln, John F. Kennedy, Martin Luther King Jr., and now Bobby Kennedy. We should ask God for mercy.

I asked if I could leave early to return to New York. Bobby Kennedy was a dear friend of mine and I wanted to be in New York to be part of any memorial service. I had believed in my heart that Bobby Kennedy would have become the best American president. He really cared about America. He cared about civil rights. And he cared about people.

President Johnson was considered by many to be a civil rights hero. So much legislation that started under President John F. Kennedy was enacted under President Johnson's administration, including the Civil Rights Act of 1964, the Voting Rights Act of 1965, the Immigration and National Services Act of 1965, and the Civil Rights Act of 1968. This led people like Adam Clayton Powell to call him "our first black president." Many positive acts linked to civil rights and social reform that came to fruition during Johnson's administration, but almost all of them had Bobby Kennedy's fingerprints on them.

In 1968 Nelson Rockefeller Jr. challenged Richard Nixon for the Republican nomination for president. John Lindsay had just been elected mayor of New York City. Members of John Lindsay's staff were assigned to different states to canvass the delegates at the National Republican Convention. Our message was that if neither Rockefeller nor Nixon got enough votes to be nominated, the delegates should consider casting their ballot for John Lindsay on the second ballot. In the end, Nixon trounced Rockefeller, and Lindsay continued his first mayoral term in New York City.

National Appointment

When Richard Nixon was elected president of the United States in 1968, he appointed my friend George Shultz secretary of labor. This was quite a surprise to me because I always thought George was a Democrat. We had served together on a committee under President Johnson's administration and traveled across the country talking about unemployment in the ghetto. It never occurred to me he could be a Republican.

When George was appointed by President Nixon, he asked me to become his deputy. This was my chance to serve my country at the national level, but I had to say no because I still had so much to do with the Urban Coalition.

In 1969, Mayor Lindsay ran for reelection as mayor of New York City. This time he ran and won as an Independent. Shortly after he won, John Lindsay invited Lemoine and me to dinner with his wife, Mary, at Gracie Mansion. He shared with us a secret that he made us promise not to tell until it became public. He was making plans to run for president in the 1972 election. More shocking, he said he would not be running as an Independent, but as a Democrat. He asked me to be part of his team because he knew I was such a confirmed Democrat.

I told him that he'd spent his whole life campaigning against Democrats and that he would never win. Still, he tried. In 1972, Hubert Humphrey won the Democratic nomination for president, but lost the election to Richard Nixon.

Chapter 24:
Transition

God placed a desire in me to be educated, to enable others the opportunity to get a good education, and to provide educators with the opportunity to make a difference. One of the people I enjoyed working at this time was Mrs. Havermayer, president of the board of trustees at Barnard College.

During one of our meetings at the Urban Coalition, the conversation turned to equal opportunity and possible needs she had for faculty and staff. I asked her if she had any black faculty and she said no. I said, "How can you exist in the world today without having a black faculty member?"

She said, "I know, but we just can't find anybody that's qualified right now. In fact, I think we ought to have a black dean of students and dean of faculty as well."

"I think so, too," I said. "I have just the person for you, my wife. Do you want to talk to her?"

She agreed to interview Lemoine, and she and the staff loved her. She had many of the key qualifications that they had been looking for, such as multiple roles as an educator, communication, and leadership skills, so they hired her as assistant dean of faculty at Barnard College.

This was early 1970. Lemoine's father worked for the post office, which was a top job for blacks in those days. She had been brought up in a housing project. Her father saved his money and bought a house in Rahway, New Jersey, and she and her sister were brought up in a very middle class black community. She knew nothing about the struggle for civil rights.

I advised her that if she was going to take that job, she ought to get familiar with the inner workings of the black mentality and black psyche. I suggested she spend the summer at the Institute of the Black World, with which I was associated. Vincent Harding, a native son of Harlem, a renowned historian, civil rights activist and author of acclaimed works chronicling Dr. King's life, was head of the Institute and I really thought it would be a great experience for Lemoine.

She spent six weeks there. When she returned, she had cut off all her hair and wore only African clothes. She insisted that I give up my job at the Urban Coalition because I was nothing but an "Oreo" (white on the inside, black on the outside) doing a white man's work. Furthermore, she wanted me to give up *Positively Black* because she felt I was selling out to the white monopoly.

I was not willing to give up the work that I believed in and strived so hard to do. "This is my life," I said. A huge chasm formed in our marriage and it continued to unravel.

One day I returned from a business trip for the U.S. Chamber of Commerce. I employed a driver to get me to and from the airport. He was talkative and engaging, and I enjoyed his company on the drives home after a long trip. He was unusually silent on this particular drive home from my trip. I asked, "Ted, why are you so quiet?"

When we got to my house, he said, "Doc, I got something to tell you. Your wife is gone."

"What do you mean she's gone?" I inquired frantically.

"She called me yesterday and wanted to use the car to move stuff out of the house, and I said I wouldn't do it."

I could not comprehend what he was saying. When I got home I saw she had taken almost everything. I was crushed. She left her two children, Billy and Leslie, whom I loved dearly and had tried to adopt when I first married Lemoine. They waited for her to return. The haunting feelings of abandonment enveloped me again.

I called her father who told me she was with him. I asked if I could speak to her and she refused. Three weeks went by. I came home one day and the doorman handed me a note from Lemoine. She wanted to get the children.

So I cooked dinner for the kids. Afterward, I told them that they needed to go back to their mom. They asked if they could come back and see me and I told them they could come any time. They asked if they'd still have their room and I said, "That's your room whether you sleep in it or not."

Single Again

When my first wife, Gladys, and I separated, our daughter, Renee, was eight years old. During that time I'd see Renee on weekends and during school vacations. I'd take her to the circus and all that stuff I thought a daddy was supposed to do with a daughter. When Renee was twelve, Gladys became the secretary to African missionaries and took her to Kenya. I didn't see Renee again for seven years.

On December 19, 1970 Renee gave birth to Roshon— my grandson. As the door to my life with Lemoine closed, God reopened the door to my life with Renee. We became best friends.

Chapter 25:
Return to Church of the Master

In 1971 Ulyssis Taylor, an officer from the Church of the Master, came to my office at the New York Urban Coalition and asked me, "Doc, would you consider coming back to the church?"

I said, "No, Mr. Taylor."

Taylor had brought me into the Masons Lodge, and I often used to see him at meetings. Afterward we would have a drink together. I knew him quite well and could be frank with him. I said, "I can't go back to the church. It's just not in me. I don't want to be fighting with people."

"We need you," he said. "We're having problems."

"I'm sorry, Mr. Taylor, I just can't do it. I've found my niche. I like what I'm doing at the Urban Coalition because it gives me the opportunity and the means to do what I was trying to do at the Church of the Master. I appreciate that you are asking me to come back, but I just don't want to do it."

"Well," he said, "will you come and preach for us? We don't have a preacher for the first Sunday in November."

I said I would.

Just before I left the church in 1966, I planned to build a school as well as an apartment house next to the church. But my successor decided to build a new church and sold the camps and farm we had in New Hampshire to do so. The new church was built but the congregation never worshipped in it. The junkies came in and stole all the plumbing, and as a result the church was awash in water. I was devastated when I saw the disarray and the destruction. The church was dying. I could not believe what had transpired in five short years.

So we went back to the old church. When the church service started, no one was available to play the organ. Including several of the Urban Coalition staff members I invited, a total of twenty-five people were in that church. I could not believe it. I was so disheartened, I tried to compose myself and find comfort in God. I told Pru Pemberton, a member my staff with the Urban Coalition, "You play the piano. Will you play this morning?" And that's how our church service got underway.

After the service I said to Mr. Taylor, "Why didn't you tell me?"

"Doc, I tried to tell you but you wouldn't let me."

"You said you were doing bad, but I had no idea it was like this. Where are all the people who once belonged to this church?"

"They're gone," he said. "That's why I'm begging you to come back."

I said, "I am not coming back as your pastor. But I tell you what I will do. I will preach for you every Sunday until we build this congregation back up again. I don't want money. I'll be your preaching minister. I make a good salary. You won't have to pay me."

Starting in the spring of 1971, I preached every Sunday, and people started to attend. As president of the New York Urban Coalition, I had the authority to write thousand-dollar emergency grant checks to any community organization I chose, and my board of directors gave that right to me. So I used grant checks to pay some overdue bills and to hire some necessary staff. My first hire was Waldo Parish. He ran church operations. We printed a monthly newsletter at the Coalition as well as the Sunday bulletin. It got to the point that people would say, "What is this, the downtown office of Church of the Master?"

I'd reply, "Yes, it is. Got any problems?"

Then I went back to the Presbytery and raised hell. That's when I really became a Mau Mau. I told them, "If this church had been on Fifth Avenue at Fiftieth Street you wouldn't have let this happen. But because it's in Harlem, you ignored it; you put up a brand new building that you haven't even used in three years." I threatened to publicly expose how the director had allowed their church in Harlem to die.

They voted and approved $60,000 to finish the building. They had loaned the church $300,000 out of their mission fund to rebuild it. I told them we weren't going to pay the money back.

They said, "What do you mean?"

"We're not paying it back because you owe this to us. You're responsible for allowing the church to die."

Cities in Schools

The church regrew to about eight hundred members over a couple of years. We started community services again, and this time the congregation became fully engaged. We brought back Young Life and created Cities in Schools (CIS).

Essentially we took the street academies without the storefronts and got permission to have the programs implemented in some of the borough schools. CIS became a national program that President Carter adopted and Rosalyn Carter instituted, and eventually, the nation's largest nonprofit dropout-prevention organization. A national leader, Cities in Schools promoted and facilitated the coordinated delivery of existing health, social, education, and other support services at educational sites for the benefit of youth and their families. It is needed as much today as it was when it started.

I was the preaching minister, not the pastor. A pastor needs to be at a church full time. I told the deacons and elders they should go visit the sick, I wasn't going to do it. I had a full-time job, and I had a television program to produce every week. I showed up on Sunday mornings and stayed there most of the day. The church grew again and we had a grand reopening with Patti LaBelle singing worship, and lots of other stars came because I knew them all through my television program. It was a divine transformation for the church, the congregation, the community, and for me.

Given my full-time job at the Urban Coalition and the time I spent at Church of the Master, I was reaching a point where I had to choose. I was not able to honestly and credibly commit and serve both responsibilities. I had to make a decision. In 1975 I left the Urban Coalition after serving eight years to once again become the pastor at the Church of the Master full time. This meant I traded in my $50,000-a-year job to take a $15,000 pastor position. Everybody said I was a fool. My friends said, "What are you going to do that for?"

"Because I know that is where I'm supposed to be."

"How are you going to live?"

"I'll make it," I said.

Another step in my journey of understanding was one of my more humbling experiences. I became the first black to be named Presbyterian Minister of the Year in 1978. While it was an honor, what made this humbling was the fact that the Presbytery showed me unconditional love and forgiveness in spite of my departure from my pastor position in the mid-1960s.

Office of Aging

I had toyed with the idea of getting a law degree. In the beginning, it was out of pure interest and fascination. In the end, interest still intact, it was also driven by the fact that I was dealing with lawyers most of my career, especially in my public service roles at HARYOU-ACT, the Urban League, and the Urban Coalition. I was busy with contracts, zoning, buyer-seller agreements, and human resources. I was always giving lawyers my money. I used to say to them half-jokingly as the ink was drying, "One of these days I'm going to be on that side of the table and you're going to be handing me checks." I decided to give my half-joke a basis of reality by going to law school. I worked by day and went to law school in the evenings. I really enjoyed it.

I graduated in 1982. Around this time there was a hotly contested race for governor of New York between Mario Cuomo and Ed Koch. Most experts expected Koch to win, just as he did when he defeated Cuomo for mayor in 1977. It was during that mayoral race that I got to know Mario Cuomo, and I liked him a lot. The race for governor had a different result. Mario Cuomo defeated Ed Koch.

At the end of 1982, Mario Cuomo was setting up his administration and asked me to work for him. I thought about it for what seemed like minutes but was probably more like nanoseconds and accepted the job. Governor Cuomo told me I could have my pick of any position not yet filled in his cabinet. I chose the Office of Aging.

I liked the opportunity to be creative, I liked older people, and I liked the opportunity to be the spokesperson for the elderly community. It gave me a chance to travel all over New York State. I didn't work too closely with Cuomo in this role, but I had access to him. We enjoyed a good relationship personally and professionally. He came to my church a couple of times and it made a difference to our congregation and it meant a lot to me that he supported me and what we were doing in Harlem. I felt he really cared.

As commissioner of the Office of Aging, I was responsible for managing a bureaucracy that covered all the sixty-two counties in the state of New York. My task was to make sure that the local and city councils were effectively and efficiently managed and received sufficient financial support from the federal and state governments to carry out meaningful programs for the elderly. Governor Cuomo and the state budget office increased the Office of Aging's budget by over $7 million, and we were able to do significant things pragmatically in the senior citizen centers throughout the state.

Some of the unique initiatives I was able to implement were rent reduction programs for senior citizens and a drug prescription program to help seniors purchase their drugs at discount prices throughout the state. In addition, we ran senior citizen programs at state fairs, including golf matches, marathon races, and cooking competitions. I was very much interested in the elderly people who were sick and fought hard for them to receive a significant increase in their Medicaid supplemental checks. My responsibilities included speaking throughout the state, and I created an interracial advisory council that dealt with issues that affected minorities, particularly immigrant seniors, seniors of color, and seniors from broken homes.

Board of Parole

Three years later, Governor Cuomo appointed me as a commissioner of the New York State Board of Parole. Governor Cuomo attended my eightieth birthday celebration at City College of New York, where I was then serving as the first Life Leader in Residence for the Colin Powell Center for Policy Studies. He generously said, "One of the most superb decisions I ever made as governor was asking Dr. Callender to join me in government." I served as the head of the Office of Aging and the commissioner of parole in Governor Cuomo's administration.

Chapter 26:
How Baba Transformed My Life

In 1974, I happened to be in a meeting with an old friend, Barbara Ann Teer. When I saw her, I could not believe how much she had changed. "Barbara," I said, "you look radiant. Something must have happened to you. Whatever you did, I want that, too!"

"Yes, I feel very different," Barbara replied. "I have just been introduced to the most masterful person I've ever met in my life. His name is Swami Muktananda…"

When I heard the word "swami," that did it for me. I couldn't hear anything else she said. I certainly wasn't going to go and see some swami, and that was the end of that. And I forgot all about Swami Muktananda until five years later.

In 1979, I got a call from Janet League. At this time, I was chairman of the Negro Ensemble Company, a black repertory theater, and Janet starred in *First Breeze of Summer*, one of our productions on Broadway. Janet said, "I need your help, Eugene. I would like for you to come to my house for brunch on the seventeenth of June and bring some of your friends."

I said, "Oh, yeah? What's the occasion?"

"Well, my spiritual teacher from India is coming to New York and he's going to be speaking at Carnegie Hall that day and I'd like you all to meet him. I think he could help you in the work you are doing."

"OK. What's his name?"

"Swami Muktananda."

I turned livid. I accused her of insulting my intelligence. How dare she waste my time calling me about "some old swami"? I went on for about twenty minutes in the most vitriolic fashion. "You want to see swamis, Janet? Come on, I'll take you up to 125th Street and Lenox Avenue. They're a dime a dozen up there."

I was struck by her silence. Finally I said, "Janet, you're not talking. Say something."

"All I can say is you're not being fair. You never met this man, you've never seen him, you've never heard him, and you're making all these negative comments about him. That's not fair."

She had a point. I asked her what she wanted me to do. She said to forget the brunch, and that I should just come and hear him speak and make up my mind. I promised to come.

The seventeenth of June showed up and it was Father's Day. We had a great service in the church and I had completely forgotten about Janet's event at Carnegie Hall. The phone rang in my office in the church. It was Janet. "Don't forget you promised you were going to be at Carnegie Hall this afternoon!" I had forgotten about it, but I had given my word. So I called up Bunnie Clarke, a good friend of Janet's and mine, and told her I had been invited to a program at Carnegie Hall, and asked if she wanted to go with me. I didn't give her any details.

When we got there we saw hundreds of people outside. I figured we must be early and that the hall wasn't open yet. Bunnie said, "Maybe the hall is full."

I laughed and said, "You're out of your cotton-pickin' mind. That many people to see some swami?" When we walked into the hall, I saw three thousand people. The event had been sold out. It was standing room only. Bunnie and I met up with Janet and she brought us to a guest section, where we sat behind some bald-headed men dressed in orange and women with buns on the backs of their heads.

I said to myself, "Oh my God, crazy swamis!" because they were the only people I saw dressed like that on the streets of New York. "What am I doing here?" But there I was, so I sat down.

The first person that came onto the stage was Marsha Mason, the movie actress. She talked about how she had met Baba Muktananda and how he'd transformed her life. Then she introduced somebody else I knew, Paul Zweig, chairman of the English Department of Queens College. He spoke about how he met Baba and how Baba had transformed *his* life. Despite my negative preconceptions, I had to admit that I was impressed. Then he introduced Baba.

Baba stood behind the curtain and when he came out, he was wearing a red ski cap. It was a hot June day, so I thought that was kind of strange, although I later learned that Baba often wore knitted caps. Then he came to the end of the stage and waved his hands. When he moved his hands, I said to Bunnie, "Do you feel that?"

"Feel what?"

"Well, when he waves his hands my nerves begin to tingle."

Baba walked to the center of the stage, to a chair waiting for him. Gurumayi, Baba's assistant, was standing next to him so she could serve as his translator. Baba jumped into that chair and assumed a full lotus position.

You know how when you're on a plane sometimes how your stomach drops? That's exactly what happened to me. I said, "Bunnie, did you feel that?"

"Feel what?"

"There is something about that man that affects me with his movements."

Bunnie asked me if I was feeling OK.

Baba spoke for an hour and forty minutes on love. It seemed as if the whole hall emptied out and he was just talking to me. I was captivated, not only by his words but also by his whole being. This seemed to affect me totally. And he said something that I had never heard in all my years in church, all my years in Sunday school, in seminary, in ministry—nobody ever said this before: "God dwells within you as you."

I sat there dumbfounded. Those words were very powerful. Before this, I had only heard that God was somewhere up in heaven. God was up there, out there, somewhere, but not in here, not in my own heart. And now, here I was being told that God was in me, too. I was astonished. At the same time, I could feel the awesome truth of this teaching. Despite all my previous doubts, I knew that Baba was onto something huge. I was drawn to his message and wanted to dive deeper. For the first time in my life, I began to feel the presence and the meaning of being created in the image of God and God's Holy Spirit dwelling in me. The walls that I had built around my compartmentalized spiritual life were beginning to melt away, and I was filled with hope.

After he spoke, Janet asked me if I would like to meet Baba. I said, "I'm not getting near that guy. If he can do this to me from that far away, I'm not going to go near him." But after a few moments' thought, I changed my mind and Janet took me downstairs to introduce me to Baba. I saw people were taking off their shoes, and I didn't mind doing that. But I noticed they were bowing down. It is Indian custom to bow down, *pranam*, to someone out of respect. I said, "Janet, I don't mind taking my shoes off, but I'm not bowing down before him." She said I didn't have to.

When we got up there, Baba stuck out his hand. I thought, "Oh, he must want to shake my hand." I shook his hand. He said something in Hindi and Gurumayi translated to Janet. "Baba says to bring him to the ashram." I never saw Baba look at me—though later I realized he had seen me very well. He just kept talking.

Janet was so happy that she got this little mission to take me to the Siddha Yoga ashram in upstate New York. I had never heard of this ashram. I was outraged because I thought the man was rude.

I said, "Janet, I wouldn't go around the corner to hear him again. The man doesn't have any manners! He never really looked at me, or said hello, or thanked me for coming. I've been in the White House with King Hussein and with Tito from Yugoslavia for state dinners. I met Haile Selassie when he was in New York meeting with Lindsay, and in the reception line *they* greeted *me* and said, 'Hello, nice to meet you, thank you for coming.' Your spiritual leader never looked at me. I wasted my whole afternoon coming down here to listen to be treated badly by this old swami. I told you that swamis were a bunch of hustlers."

Before I left, Janet handed me a little magazine called *Meditate* that was put out those days by the SYDA Foundation,

Baba's organization. I took it and went home, made myself a cup of tea, and started to read.

As I began to read the magazine, all the powerful, wonderful feelings I had in the hall came back. As I read about other people's experiences with Baba, I remembered the profound revelation that I'd received from him: "God dwells within you as you." I read that magazine four times that night; I almost memorized it. At midnight that Sunday I called Janet at home, apologized for being such an arrogant ass, and said, "I want to thank you for the nicest Father's Day I've ever spent in my life. Please take me to this ashram place, since it is obviously something I am supposed to do."

So the following Saturday she took me to the ashram. I remember sitting outside of a room called the Namaste Room, where Baba met with people. I met a lot of people I knew from Harlem and New York City. I said, "What are you guys doing up here?" They told me they were meditating and chanting. I told them they should go back to Harlem. If they had all this love in their hearts they should go teach in the public schools in Harlem and bring all the love and understanding to the schools. They said to me, "You'll see."

At nine thirty that Saturday morning, the door opened to the Namaste Room and someone told me to come in. Something struck me. I had the same feeling when the Holy Spirit washed over me in the Pentecostal church so many years ago. My first conscious thought was, "I'm going to have another one of those experiences!" I was not afraid, but I was filled with wonder and anticipation. With all the stirring going on inside of me I could do nothing but be still.

Baba was sitting down in front and he was waving his arms, indicating that he wanted me to come forward. But I couldn't move. There were about fifteen other people who were there who had also been invited to meet with Baba. I tried to walk to where Baba was and I couldn't walk. All I could feel was a fantastic, warm electricity moving through me. I could hardly lift one foot in front of the other. All I could think of was, this must be the way Moses felt when he saw the bush on fire, but not consumed by the fire, and he heard the voice of God say, "Take off your sandals, for the place in which you stand is holy ground." I knew I was in the presence of a very, very special person. I didn't need any theology or philosophy to tell me that.

Who was this special person? I had been told he was a guru—a spiritual master who has attained oneness with God and who is able to initiate seekers and to guide them on the spiritual path to liberation. This, though I didn't know it at the time, was the beginning of my initiation.

So here I was, with the energy of delight coursing through my body, and hardly able to move. Finally, others in the room saw my predicament. They helped me up. I fell on my knees in front of Baba. My head was down. All I can remember is this beautiful white pillow that my head was resting on. I lifted my head and Baba's eyes and my eyes met, and when he looked at me it was as if fire was coming out of his eyes to my eyes.

The thought went through my head, "Gene, this man knows everything there is to know about you. There's no time for shuckin' and jivin' now. This is *it*!" He started stroking my head. When he touched me, it was like bolts of lightning, powerful shocks, but no shocks of pain—just a raw energy that I had barely experienced consciously in the Pentecostal church. This time I was aware of what was going on, or better said, I was connected to what was going on.

Then he said, "You are so full of love." He said it three times. Then he told me just to give him two days, and he'd really have me doing the Lord's work. When he said that, he was touching the top of my head and I was feeling all this beautiful energy pouring through me and I broke out in tears. I started to cry.

With those words—"You are so full of love"—he broke through fifty-three years of negative feelings toward myself, fifty-three years of lack of self-esteem. He went right through it, *bam!* The walls around the compartments of my personal and spiritual life crumbled. I had never thought I was truly lovable. I had always thought that if people really knew me, they wouldn't like me. I never realized that I did not really love myself, which was the root of why I did not feel lovable. My emotions swelled and I sobbed.

Later, I found out that what had happened to me was known as *shaktipat*, which is Sanskrit for "the descent of grace." Shaktipat, which is bestowed by a guru, gives the seeker the direct experience of knowing God. During the process of shaktipat, I learned, old patterns and habits may get dislodged. I'm talking about major habits here—and one of mine had been my inability to love myself.

When Baba had said, "Give Baba two days," I really had no idea what he was talking about. I thought, "Really do the Lord's work? What am I doing now?" Then I went upstairs and thought about it: "He knows." Every Sunday morning when I got up in the pulpit of the Church of the Master, I felt like a hypocrite. I rarely read the Bible. I rarely prayed during the week. I prayed on Sunday morning in church and I could preach lovely sermons, but I had little devotional life. I was a guy about town. I felt that Baba was helping me change my life so that I could legitimately serve God.

I was emotionally and physically exhausted after my encounter with Baba. Two people kindly helped me go upstairs to my room. I fell to the floor and stayed there for five hours, crying and crying. Not sad tears—just a lot of pent-up stuff that had been in me for a long time that just had to get out—a sort of "detoxifying" shedding of tears for things that I had tried to suppress or control either by trying to forget or by avoiding the reality of the painful events of my life, self-inflicted or otherwise.

As I said, I learned later that this detox was a natural part of shaktipat—part of a spiritual purification that occurs after the direct experience of God's grace. At the time I didn't know this, but I knew that what was happening to me was good. I felt a sense of relief and opening.

Later in the day, a young black man, Lester Strong, came in and said, "Mr. Callender, Baba wants you to sit up front tonight."

I was scared, because in the Pentecostal church, where I grew up, you sat up front where everybody could see you when you were bad. I thought, "Oh, my God. I must have done something wrong."

Then a young man named Robert Jacobs came into the room and asked how I was doing. I asked him what I had done wrong because I was told to sit up front that night. He said that I was very fortunate. He asked, "Do you know how many people would love to be in that position?"

I replied, "I know nothing about any of this. This is my first time here."

Lester came and took me into the meditation hall at five o'clock. He introduced me to a young man in a business suit who said, "Oh, you're the minister from New York City." He escorted me down the center aisle. He sat me right next to Baba's chair, on the floor. I closed my eyes and had no idea what to expect. The lights were muted and it was silent.

Then the lights went out altogether and they started slowly chanting a Sanskrit mantra. At first it seemed eerie. I feared I was the sacrificial lamb getting ready for the sacrifice, I really did. In spite of my fears, my trust in my previous experiences with Baba kept me there.

Then Baba came into the hall, walked down the center aisle, sat in his chair at the front of the hall facing all of us, and waved at me. When he did that I knew everything was OK. We continued to chant the mantra, which turned out to be a beautiful experience. I could feel great joy and love. The whole room seemed to be filled with God's grace, though I could not explain it.

When Baba got ready to leave the hall, he started to get out of his chair and then he reached back for something. It looked like a blanket, but it was a prayer shawl. He walked right past me, took the shawl, and wrapped it around me. He was honoring me and I could not understand why. It was very humbling. That was my first trip to the Siddha Yoga ashram. Later, I understood that Baba was loving God by serving and honoring, and he was serving as God's hands and voice so that he could help me fulfill God's destiny for me. He was inspiring me to do the Lord's work as a pastor to the people to whom I was ministering.

When I went back to church the next day, I scrapped the sermon and told them everything about my experience at the ashram. My congregation found me a different human being. I finally had a sense of humor. My relationship with my officers changed. I had always found them slow and I would get impatient. Instead, I remained calm, knowing that things would work out for the best. I became more patient, more loving, more human, and more present. Everyone wanted to know, "What happened to *him*?"

What happened was a transformation from having had some knowledge about God to experiencing a full, loving relationship with God. The meditation that I learned from Baba gave me the fullness of a relationship with God because it helped me to be still and listen to the voice of God within. This was a big step to removing the walls of my compartmentalized and "me-controlled" life. The transformation of learning to love who is in me, God, led me to love myself, which led me to see myself as lovable. This was so important for me because for the first time in my life, I was open to receive love and be in love with all that God had created. This radical change was noticeable to those around me, especially my congregation.

One Sunday morning, before the sermon, I addressed the congregation because I indirectly heard and sensed that there were a lot of questions that had been going around about "What's up with Rev?" I told them that I had added prayer and meditation into my spiritual walk and if anyone really wanted to find out about meditation, they should come to my house that afternoon.

I thought maybe five or six people would show up. Thirty people came. I talked to them about meditating. After this, many people started meditating and it made a difference to their lives. The spiritual life of our church really changed because people had more *experiences* of God, in addition to knowing about God. Before I met Baba, the Sunday morning prayers I offered in church were something I was supposed to do. God may have worked through me anyway, but I felt no inner connection. After meeting Baba, my prayers became inspired. I would meditate before each service. And then, from a state of stillness and tranquility, the prayer would come forth from within me.

In my sermons, I would let people know that God dwelled within them. "You do not have to accept the definition

297

that society has placed on you," I'd say. "Each of you is a divine being. You are a portion of the divine." For many Harlem people who did not necessarily think of themselves very highly, this was an inspiring and hopeful statement. In these ways, Baba helped me become a better pastor.

I felt very close to Baba. I'd go up to the ashram every weekend. Baba gave me new understanding about life, and above all, he gave me an inner relationship with God. Having the experience of God dwelling within me, I treated myself with greater respect and I could drop the unnecessary mental burdens that chipped my shoulders. And recognizing that the same was true for all human beings—that God dwelt within them, too—enabled me to treat others with more respect and compassion.

On September 30, 1979, Baba went back to Carnegie Hall. Raul Julia, the actor, and I introduced him. Raul gave a ten-minute talk on his relationship with Baba, and then he introduced me. I gave a ten-minute talk and then I introduced Baba. We had been instructed that when Baba appeared we were to go take our seats. I started to do so when Baba came over to me and put out his hand. I thought he wanted to shake my hand. When he got my hand he pulled me to him and grabbed me and hugged me and patted me on the back in front of thirty-five hundred people, as if to say, "So you don't think you're lovable, huh? I'll show you!" I lit up like a light. Baba was like a spark plug to shock me into consciousness of the Holy Spirit.

I had invited my friends from all walks of life to Carnegie Hall to share this experience with them. Nearly all my relationships with my friends changed for the better. My closest friends didn't think what I was doing was so strange. I guess that's because I was always a little "different" to most of them, which is what many of them liked about me in the first place. I was always there for them. I was also there for the church members. I remained involved. So they had no reason to worry.

In the winter of 1980, I was invited to be on the Board of Trustees of the SYDA Foundation, the organization that protects, preserves, and disseminates the Siddha Yoga teachings. One of the businessmen on the board found a place in Santa Monica, California, with grounds where we could put up a magnificent tent where Baba could hold programs on meditation for hundreds of people. I was able to use some contacts I'd made in California to help them make the arrangements. After all I had received, it was satisfying to be able to make a contribution.

The Santa Monica facility was a great facility. It was peaceful and inviting. It was a perfect setting for prayer and meditation. Being removed from the normal daily routine, the toils of maintaining a home, an office, and a job, was the best way for me to remove the distractions that normally appear when I sweat out the small and large details of everyday life. Santa Monica was a place for me to focus on God and me. Being there with Baba helped me intensify my prayers and meditation.

I spent seventeen days with Baba in Santa Monica. I was convinced that that was where I was supposed to be for the rest of my life. I resorted to my past experience and to the religion I knew. I got down on my knees every night and every day and prayed and said, "Lord, if you want me to stay with Baba, give me two signs." That thought came from a Bible story of Gideon, what he did when God told him to fight the hundred-thousand-person army of the Midianites and Amalekites with three hundred men. Gideon said, "Oh no, I can't do that. We can't fight those people." And God said, "Yes, you can with me, I have chosen you." And Gideon said, "Well Lord, if you really want me to do it, give me two signs," and God gave him two signs and the three hundred people destroyed their enemy.

So I asked for two signs to show me if I was supposed to be with Baba full time. I was ready to give up Church of the Master and law school. I had never felt so much peace and contentment. I didn't want the big apartment I had at home; I didn't want the fast life in New York that I had enjoyed. I just wanted that peace and contentment.

I meditated every morning, went to the chant every morning, chanted every afternoon, went to programs every night, and read nothing but spiritual literature all day long. I gobbled it up from the day I met Baba. I read the Bible again. I got a whole new insight on Biblical understanding and interpretation.

So I prayed. The next morning after I started my prayer mission with the Lord asking for direction and two signs, this young man came to me at the breakfast table and told me that he was a former Lutheran minister who met Baba in 1974. He had such a powerful awakening with Baba that he went back to his congregation and tried to get his whole congregation involved in Siddha Yoga. They kicked him out of the church.

My congregation's response, open-mindedness, was completely different. This may have been partly because I was able to accept Baba's teachings as an aid to help me go deeper in my own Christian understanding. But still, I so wanted to be with Baba full time that I convinced myself that I had to leave the church. I used the Lutheran minister's experience with his church instead of my own to be my sign, and I said to myself, "Sign one."

That evening I got a call from George Shultz. Ronald Reagan had been elected president in November 1980, but he had not yet been inaugurated. The inauguration was to take place in January and this was December. There was a lot of talk of who was going to be in Reagan's cabinet, and one of the prominent names was George Shultz. So George called me in Santa Monica and said, "Gene, I had a tough time tracking you down." He said, "I guess you've been reading the newspapers. I might be going to Washington. It depends on what the President offers me. But I've been thinking, if I go, who do I want to go with me, and your name is at the top of the list. I just want to let you know that if it comes up, I hope you will join me."

I said to myself, "Sign Two," indicating that I didn't have to go back to the church because there was other work I could do. God had answered my prayers; my destiny was to leave the church and eventually I could stay with Baba. I had made up my mind.

The next morning, I got a call at eight thirty that Baba wanted to see me right away. So I went to meet him. He was sitting at his desk, writing, and when I came in, he kept on writing; he didn't pay any attention to me for several minutes. I didn't mind at all because I just liked being there with him. In his presence, I could feel love in my soul.

After many minutes, he turned around to me and pointed his finger at me and said, "You're a good priest. Go back to your church." That was God at work.

I asked myself, "How did he know?" I hadn't told anybody. Then he said, "You needn't worry. We will always be together. We were together before, we're together now, we will always be together." He pointed to a picture of Bhagawan Nityananda, his guru, and said, "You dream about him a lot, don't you?" I asked how he knew that.

He said, "He's going to take care of both of us. Don't you worry." I haven't worried since.

.

Chapter 27:
My Guru Comes to Harlem

I felt so buoyant and happy in my spiritual rekindling that I asked Baba to come to Harlem. I said, "I love your teachings and know what they've done for me, and if you would just come and give your shaktipat to people in Harlem, their lives would be transformed. They'd take more responsibility for their lives and change would happen."

I was kneeling in front of him. He was sitting in his chair. He had his little nightcap on. He stood up and lifted me up and grabbed me and hugged me and he said, "You are my child. I'll do what you've asked."

I was buzzing. I came back and gathered all the black people I knew in Siddha Yoga together and told them the Guru would be coming to Harlem. We had introductory programs at The Tree of Life, at the National Black Theater, at my church—any place that we could find in Harlem. In these programs we taught people chanting, the words of the mantra, and how to meditate.

I had a big Sunday service at the church with a swami speaking. "Swami" is a term of respect for a monk. Baba was called Swami Muktananda because he was a monk as well as a guru. There were many other Siddha Yoga swamis who were not gurus, but who had taken the vows of monkhood—dedicating their lives to God. If you had asked me before I met Baba if I was ever going to have a swami speaking in my church, I would have thought you were speaking blasphemy. But Baba taught me that you don't have to give up your religion to practice Siddha Yoga. Meditation brings you closer to God, whatever your spiritual path.

It was a great service. Powerful! The church was jam-packed with six hundred people. Some days later, I invited people from the Harlem community to come to the Siddha Yoga ashram in upstate New York. Sixty people came. Baba met them all and talked to them of universal brotherhood. He said that God did not see racial differences. When I watched my guests meet Baba, my mind went back to the sixties freedom rides—sitting in Birmingham, Alabama, being washed down by Bull O'Connor's hoses and pricked by his cattle prodders.

When I saw these Harlem people experience Baba's enormous respect and love for them, I wept. I thought, "This is what it is all about. Universal brotherhood will only come when every one of us looks within and discovers the divinity within. Universal brotherhood will come when we recognize that every race, every sect, belongs to God—when we can respect each other as Baba respects us."

In these ways, we were preparing for the Guru to come to Harlem. I did not know when this would be. When I heard that Baba would be going back to India soon, I assumed the Guru's visit to Harlem would be sometime after his visit to India.

In 1981 Baba left the ashram in upstate New York and returned to his home ashram in India. I went to Baba's ashram in India in order to see Baba again and also to update him on our progress. I arrived in India at five thirty in the morning. I remember walking into the courtyard and people were arriving for the morning chant that everyone in the ashram is expected to attend.

I was wearing a cap. I took it off and sat down at the base of a tree, The Bhagawan Nityananda statue was facing me. This statue honored Baba's Guru, Nityananda. I sat there and said, "This is my family. I've come home." I really felt that.

Every day after that, Baba would sit in the courtyard in the morning and every day I would go up to him and he'd say, "What are you doing today?" I'd say, "I'm going to be with you, Baba." Then I would sit close by him, along with many others. In his presence, I felt like I was connected to God's love. It was an indescribably beautiful feeling. Over time, I learned that this feeling, which so palpably emanated from Baba, was something that I needed to develop from within myself. Baba taught us that we all could know God from within, as we learned to listen to the God that dwells in our hearts.

A few times Baba took me to the outskirts of Ganeshpuri where he had built homes for the poor. One time we went into the home of a very old couple. I've been in slums in Harlem, but this was much more basic than any slum there. Baba sat down on the bed. The old woman came to him and started speaking in their language. He just smiled. Gurumayi translated. She told me that the couple used to cook for Bhagawan Nityananda and Baba. The old lady asked if Baba would like to have tea and he agreed. When she brought the tea, I looked at that little tin teacup. I knew that Baba had high standards of cleanliness. I was thinking, "Oh please, Baba, don't drink from that cup." It looked so dirty.

Baba drank the tea in one swallow then handed back the cup, saying *"Bahut'acha"* ("Very good"). He began to tell me something. Gurumayi translated that he wanted me to know that he would always be a child in the presence of those two people.

Just before I left the ashram to go back to America, I was standing in the courtyard. Gurumayi and two or three others were there. I was supposed to leave at nine thirty that night. At nine fifteen, the door to Baba's house opened and Baba came out in his nightgown and knit cap. Baba used to get up before three every morning, and he went to bed pretty early. Baba beckoned us to him. When I approached, he wrapped his arms around me and squeezed me tight. "I was asleep," he said, "but I knew you were leaving, so I woke up because I wanted to say good-bye to you personally."

Those were the last words I ever heard Baba say. I was touched that he got up to say good-bye to me. Soon after I had left India, I received a letter from Baba in which he wrote: "Don't worry about anything. You will be with me in October." I did not know what he meant by this, until October came.

I was in New York in October 1982 when I got a call from Joan Friedlander, the wife of one of the SYDA trustees. She let me know that Baba had died. I immediately knew why Baba had wanted to say good-bye to me in India; he knew I'd never see him again. I was touched by this memory, and I felt pain in my heart at losing Baba. I opened the Bible and felt guided to Psalm 139. Then I went into meditation and felt Baba's presence in an astoundingly vivid way. The Psalmist had written, "This is too glorious, too wonderful to believe. I can never be lost to your spirit." This is what I experienced. I knew that Baba's gift to me would never die. I would never lose that belief, that certainty that God dwells within me as me.

Before his death, Baba had named Gurumayi as his successor, and I was to learn later that Gurumayi was able to transmit the same divine love as her guru, Baba. Joan told me that Gurumayi had asked if I would like to come to India for the burial ceremony. It was the first Sunday in October; worldwide Communion Sunday. I told my congregation that I was leaving and that I didn't know when I'd be back. I told them where I was going; they knew I was involved with Baba. I left that night.

Once I arrived in India, I was taken to Baba's house where they were preparing for the ceremony. While Gurumayi and others were going through the Hindu rituals for burying the dead, I thought to myself, "Baba, you promised me you were going to come to Harlem. I've done all the preparation; the people are practicing, and were so looking forward to seeing you come. What am I going to do?"

In August 1984, Gurumayi came to the United States from India and one of her stops was Washington DC. I was then president of the SYDA Foundation, and I met Gurumayi in Washington. It was during this stay in Washington that she told me that Baba had told her that he had promised me that the Guru would come to Harlem. She said, "I'll be coming to your church next week."

I was deeply touched that Baba had remembered me before his death and that Gurumayi was carrying out his promise. When I came back to New York, I began the preparations immediately and made all of the arrangements for her arrival the following Sunday.

That following Sunday, there was a huge crowd. All of the local Siddha Yoga devotees came to Harlem to see the Guru, but we'd reserved the space for church members and people from the community. The others had to wait outside or else go to the overflow space in the basement. We put up sound systems in both these areas so people who couldn't get into the church could hear Gurumayi speaking.

We had a regular worship service where we sang Presbyterian hymns, and gave readings from the Bible. When it came time for the morning prayer, I asked Gurumayi, "Would you like to do the morning prayer?"

She politely declined.

So I gave the morning prayer. After that, one of the church members sang "Amazing Grace." Then I introduced Gurumayi as the morning's speaker. When I returned to my seat she told me that she was not going to speak.

"What? You are not going speak?" I said, taken aback.

Gurumayi told me that it would be better for us to chant, and she explained why to the congregation. She said to everyone that she had looked down at Eugene's notes and all she had seen was, "In the beginning…" With a hint of a smile, she asked what the "dot dot dot" meant.

I got up and said, "That's where I was supposed to ad lib and speak my prayer without reading my notes."

Everyone laughed.

Gurumayi said: "The presence of God is so powerful in this church, there is no need for speaking. We'll chant."

The harmonium player began playing the same tune to the Sanskrit mantra that I had sung in the ashram in upstate New York. Then my organist picked it up. I'm willing to bet this was the first time this chant was played by a pipe organ in any church. That whole congregation, plus the people outside and the overflow of people downstairs, chanted the mantra for thirty minutes.

It was a moving experience. Everyone felt very together and there were tears of joy all over the place. For me, the chant was a beautiful prayer. I had never thought of chanting or meditation as prayer before; the awareness just unfolded in that very moment. I thought, "This is communication with God; this is what I have been reaching for in my prayers." We closed the service with the benediction.

I was told that Gurumayi had to leave right away to go back to the ashram in upstate New York for an evening program. I led her out of the church to go outside and get in her car. When we got to the church lobby, she saw the stairway downstairs and said she had to go there to see the people. She went down the stairs. I remembered that I had asked the custodian to remove all the chairs to handle the overflow. People downstairs had stood through the whole service. When Gurumayi got down there, I realized there was no place for her to sit. She found one broken chair, which leaned a bit. She sat in that broken chair for nearly two hours, individually meeting every single person who wished to meet her, the people from downstairs, the people from the church upstairs, and the people who had been outside.

Gurumayi then answered questions from the audience. After nearly three hours, she turned to me and said that she would like to see the Siddha Yoga meditation center near the church. It was obvious that she was not leaving to get to the ashram in time for the evening program, and I felt honored by the love and respect she was giving to all the people of the parish. I also observed how she was able to change her schedule in the moment, in response to the hearts of the people. By now it was three o'clock. We walked to the center, and there she met everyone and answered questions until five, when she finally left.

Chapter 28:
The Chance to Say I Love You

I spent that summer at the ashram in upstate New York. One day, Gurumayi called me to meet her and the conversation that I remember went something like this, "Eugene, I don't know anything about your family. Do you have a mother?"

"Gurumayi, you know everything there is to know about me."

"No. Do you have a mother?"

I told her my mother had died in 1958.

"Do you have a father?"

I looked at her and said, "Gurumayi, I don't talk to my father. I don't talk about my father. I've hardly spoken to him in forty-seven years. When he came to my college graduation at Boston University, I walked off the stage. I do not talk about my father."

She pointed her finger at me and said, "Tell me about him."

"I do not talk about my father!"

This time she shook her finger at me and said, "Tell me about him."

I unraveled the litany of his brutality; I told her the story about my baseball team, Patsy's Midgets, and the missed piano lesson. I told her about the time I tried to protect my sister from his brutality. I told her that when I was in therapy, I flat out and with conviction told the therapist, "I will never speak to him again; as far as I'm concerned, my father does not exist."

"You're never going to get well," the therapist had replied. "You can't live with all that anger and hatred."

"Eugene, why are you blaming him?" Gurumayi asked. "Don't you know that you chose him before you came into this world? All of these experiences were a part of the journey to get you to where you are right now."

I sat there, completely shocked—you talk about blowing your mind; that blew my mind. One of the things we always talked about in psychology class is how the behavior of parents impact upon the lives of children, consciously and unconsciously.

She continued, "Look at where you are now. Look at your relationship with Baba. You had to go through all that, Eugene. That was all part of the process of making you who you are today."

Then she got up, went to her drawer, pulled out this gorgeous purple shawl—my favorite color—trimmed with gold. She folded it, handed it to me, and she said, "Here, I want you to give this to your father from me."

I thought, "She wants me to reward that bastard for beating the shit out of me?" But I didn't say that. Instead I said, "Gurumayi, my father will be ninety years old in November. He doesn't go anywhere. He just sits in my sister's house, I am told. He doesn't need it. Can I have it?"

"No," she said. "It's for your father."

So I went to Boston on Labor Day. I said to my sister, "I've got something for Daddy."

"You've got something for Daddy?"

She knew I did not speak to him and I never even asked about him when I visited her. In fact, I would avoid visiting my sister if I knew he was there.

I explained, "It's not really from me. Gurumayi sent this for Daddy. Will you take it and give it to him for me?"

My sister had wisdom enough to say, "If Gurumayi gave you that to give to him, you have got to give it to him."

So I walked in the room. My father looked wrinkled, old, and frail. He was watching the television screen. I said, "I've got something for you." I handed him Gurumayi's package. I didn't ask him how he was. I didn't care. I turned around and walked out of the room.

That November, Gurumayi asked me what I was doing for Thanksgiving.

"I hope to be with you, Gurumayi, in the ashram. My sister in Boston called and asked me to have Thanksgiving dinner with her and the family, but I want to stay in the ashram and be with you."

Her reply changed my life. She told me I should go to Boston for Thanksgiving, and that when I saw my father this time, all of that bad karma would be gone, all the hostility would be over. She also said I'd have a good time.

So I went to Boston, because she wanted me to go. When I got off the plane, my brother, Leland, came to meet me at Logan Airport, and suddenly all those old songs we used to sing in the gospel chorus started coming back. I hadn't thought of those songs for years. I started singing them when we got into the car, and we were singing them together. I felt so happy and light all of a sudden. When I was on the plane I kept thinking, "My father is going to be there, and I'm dreading the time with him." But I got off the plane and these songs started coming back to me.

I was in a very lighthearted, joyful mood when I arrived. My sister said, "What's wrong with you two?"

Leland said, "Gene started singing these songs."

All of a sudden it just came out of my mouth, "Where's Daddy?"

My sister looked at me blankly. I thought she was going to faint.

"Where's Daddy?" I repeated.

She finally said, "He's in his room."

I walked into his room. Thanksgiving came on November 25 that year. It was his birthday. I looked at him and said, "Do you know why God allowed you to live to be ninety years old today?"

"Why?"

"Just so I could have the opportunity to tell you I love you."

We embraced for the first time in our lives. I felt lighter than air, I felt safety, I felt joy, I felt peace, and I felt love in the arms of my father for the first time. He started to cry. I started to cry. My brother started to cry. I did not realize how paralyzed and suspended the life of our family was until the moment we were liberated through forgiveness.

My sister said, "I've got to meet this Gurumayi. If she can do this, I've got to meet her."

That was the beginning of a more humane and kinder relationship between my father and me. It all happened so easily, so spontaneously. I knew that this had happened through Gurumayi's grace. I had eight good years of his life. It was during this time that I learned most of the stories about him, his childhood, and his experiences in Barbados. Every year after this, Gurumayi sent my father a present on Father's Day.

As I've told this story over the years, many people have been moved to tears, and have been inspired to perform their own acts of forgiveness. They have been touched by Gurumayi's act of compassion that reconnected me to my father, and also by my willingness to follow her suggestion, and to forgive.

I believe that the *you* Gurumayi referred to when she said, "Don't you know that you chose him to be your father..." is my own higher wisdom, the God that dwells within me. In this sense, I chose my father so that I could become the man that I am. What my father did was not right. But I was given a choice—the choice to forgive. And by taking that path, I was led to love. I found and experienced love and God through those who were His hands, His feet, and His voice, so that I can share and serve the same for others. That is why, I believe, we were all created.

I was at the ashram in Oakland in 1993 when my father died. When Gurumayi was informed, she asked Janet League, who had originally invited me to meet Baba at Carnegie Hall, to tell me. I was in the chanting hall and Janet asked me to come out. I told her I wanted to stay and chant. She said she needed to talk to me about something very important.

I came out and she and her husband told me what had happened. I really felt a sense of loss. She left me alone for a while. Then I went back into the program and joined the chanting and listened to Gurumayi's talk.

Afterward, there was a time when everyone could meet the Guru. I went up to see Gurumayi and I remember her saying: "Ah, Eugene! Our father died today. He was ninety, wasn't he?"

I said, "He was ninety-eight."

She said, "Oh, that's good. Just think of the thousands of souls that have been inspired to compassion through your father's story. He did his work well."

That weekend I was to give a talk at the Siddha Yoga program on Easter Sunday. I was rehearsing my talk when I just broke down. Gurumayi walked into the room. She asked me if I was OK and patted me on the back.

I was able to finish rehearsing and then share my story with everyone at that weekend's program. After the talk Gurumayi sent for me. I was just about to leave and take the plane to Boston. She looked at me seriously. Then she broke into a big smile and said that I was "fantastic"! She hugged me. Then she handed me a big, soft, stuffed bunny.

I thought back to the shawl she first sent my father and then the presents that she had sent him every Father's Day. All these gifts were filled with love. They had helped open my heart and my father's heart. That bunny was buried with my father.

My life had come full circle. I was at peace.

EPILOGUE
"Nobody Is a Nobody"

A sermon originally delivered in 1966
at Cathedral Church of Saint John the Divine
New York, New York

by

the Reverend Dr. Eugene S. Callender

Biblical References:

OLD TESTAMENT LESSON:
Psalm 42:1-11

NEW TESTAMENT LESSON:
Luke 19:1-10

Nobody Is a Nobody:
A sermon.

In the Middle Ages, there was a type of intellectual sickness known as acedia, which seems to have afflicted students, monks, and others committed to scholarship and contemplation. Its symptoms, we are told, were loss of faith, undue retreat into one's self, a sense of futility, and a paralyzing estrangement from the source and man. The prescribed cure for acedia was hard and unremitting prayer.

For almost 250 years now, there has been a similar malaise we call alienation. Originally, the church spoke about man being alienated from God. Rousseau felt men were alienated from nature. Karl Marx said the worker was alienated from society because he did not share in the profits of his work. Kierkegaard believed man was alienated from himself. In any case, hard and unremitting prayer is definitely not prescribed because prayer and the religious life belong among those things persons feel most alienated from. Today, countless men feel alienated from God, from nature, from society, from themselves. Not just intellectuals and artists and sensitive people, but millions of ordinary people feel cut off from one another and cut off from themselves. They feel pushed around. Nothing seems more ridiculous than those lines we used to quote so bravely from Henley:

> I am the master of my fate,
> I am the captain of my soul.

That is precisely what I do not feel, because technology made it impossible for me to master the conditions of my life and very difficult even to reflect seriously on who I am, what I believe, and what I want to do.

The Nothing Life

This sense of alienation is aggravated everywhere you go. One specific place is on the campus. Some fifteen hundred students commit suicide each year, it is said, and another ten thousand attempt it. The causes of this distressing figure include the "pressure cooker," emotional stress about exams, grades, and admission to grad school; absentee ownership of the classroom by the moonlighting faculty; and the "professionalism" that values the student's expertness higher than the student himself. The size of the campus adds geometrically to the problem. The student finds that the university may spend larger sums to recruit him, register him, finance, feed, house, entertain, equip, employ, counsel and cure him of his diseases than it does to teach him. Nor can he see how the university cares about him as a person behind his ID card. Memorizing a mass of material makes him feel meaningless and wears him down to resentment. He is forever being tested and evaluated, studied and talked about. Rarely does a faculty person relate to him as a person. As a consequence, he feels, "hung up." "I don't belong here." "Nobody cares."

To elaborate this sense of what we all feel, Philip Wylie wrote about the "Generation of Zeros." His theme is that everything seems to add up to nothing. In our homes, there is no privacy, hence no living. The new morality really means no morality, which engenders an alarming trend in our society to purge ourselves of our humanity.

This nothing life includes noninvolvement, with the notorious instance when a woman was attacked on the street and spent a full hour screaming and dying; thirty-eight people heard her cry and turned back to their televisions and did not even report it, much less go to help her. They didn't want to get involved. She was nobody to be bothered about.

The nothing life has gone so far that responsible men say God has died, causing one to quip, "God is not dead, He simply doesn't want to get involved." Thus, from the trivial to the profound, we humans seem to be cutting ourselves off from other humans, human experiences, and spiritual experience. We are oriented toward nothing. In short, with no intense expectations, no values, no moral compass, and no faith in something greater than ourselves, each person feels like nobody. I spent nearly fifty years of my life hiding from the fact that I feared, and at times believed, that I was nobody.

Escapes From Nothing

Alarming escapes from the emptiness of feeling like a nobody drive some people to drink, and others take drugs, to experiment with exhilaration and dreams. These "disaffiliates" withdraw from encounters that are not encounters. They try to intensify their inner experiences because they have no valid outer experience with people. Others escape into sex, to find a moment of solace and a sense of mattering to someone. Still others turn to public action to escape from private emptiness. They demonstrate and shout, often against the establishment.

Other people protest against their nothingness through study and the effort to excel as a student, thus to prove their existence by standards that society erects. I remember, as a high school student, saying aloud to myself, "If I can only make that debate team, then I'll amount to something and really count. Then, I'll be somebody, no longer a nobody." Thus do various people try to escape from the emptiness of modern life?

Staking Out the Inner-Space

Ah, woe is me, I am undone; I have an unclean soul, and I live among other people of unclean souls. What am I worth? I am a nobody, living in a world of nobodies. And nobody cares. In the face of all this alienation, how is a person to protect the sanctity of our created life? To quote from W. H. Auden:

> The inner-space of private ownership,
> The place that each of us is forced to own,
> The landscape of his will and need,
> Where he is sovereign indeed,
> And even if he findeth hell,
> May neither leave it or rebel."

How indeed is a person to admit his alienation, yet not accept it as incurable? How is he to be alert and humanized enough to live with his alienation? As e. e. cummings says:

> To be nobody-but-yourself
> in a world which is doing its best,
> night and day to make you everybody else,
> means to fight the hardest battle
> which any human being can fight;
> and never stop fighting.

Some people try to confront it head-on. They say, "I want to know my friends as persons…I want a few close friends…Society must recover its humaneness…We need to make human life human. What we are talking about is love." This is exactly right.

How to Go About It?

First of all, you must believe in yourself. Accept your own distinction; be the person you are. Stop trying to be some-body else. Stop fretting about how people don't like and don't appreciate you. Stop complaining that the world will not devote itself to making you happy. Realize your own distinctive charac-ter and know it is good. You are what you are, and that's that. And that's good. Rejoice for it.

Then, stand up for something. I learned from Dean Howard Thurman's sermon about a professor who found himself in a faculty split over a hard issue involving a colleague. Eventually, the trustees became involved. At last, the faculty had to take positions, pro and con. This professor took a positive stand that made him become unpopular with his colleagues, and next fall he taught elsewhere. Then, he commented, "For the first time in my life, I felt I was a man. I could not hedge. I took sides according to my convictions—I became a new person, way down deep."

When the French artist Henri Matisse was a young man, he went through a period in which he painted still lifes in an uninspired and academic style. He found a dealer who would buy those paintings for four hundred francs a piece. Matisse was married and had three children, and this kind of work provided a livelihood. One day came a moment of decision. Matisse says, "I had just finished one of these pictures. I knew that on delivery, I would get the money I really needed. There was a temptation to deliver it, but I knew that if I yielded, it would be my artistic death. Looking back, I realize that it required courage to destroy that picture, particularly since the hands of the butcher and baker were outstretched for the money. But I did destroy it. I count my emancipation from that day." When a person decides he will not subvert his talents for any foundation grant, or compromise his integrity to keep a job, or play safe just to stay in the game, there comes a wonderful sense that he is somebody, not a nobody. Things are different because of him. He stands for something. He counts.

Third, recognize the sacred. More and more is desacralized these days, until almost nothing feels sacred. Yet, you cannot deny the sacred. If you saw a madman shoot up children at play, you would scream. You would be horrified if young toughs beat up an old woman. Not only was what happened illegal, but something sacred, a taboo, had been violated. Every person is valuable, supremely valuable, and not because he is right or virtuous but because he is a person, a child of God, a being made in God's image, a being who must never be violated for any reason. A child must be fed, however imbecilic he is. A prisoner is not to be tortured, however guilty. Every person is a somebody and not a nobody. And if he is, so are you. You are somebody because:

(1) You believe in yourself, because...

(2) You stand for something, and because...

(3) God made you; as Christians know and believe, "Christ died for you."

Three People Whom Jesus Respected, Plus You

This Jesus, who is called Christ, this Christ who was once embodied in a man named Jesus, had indeed a profound, uncalculating respect for people. Look at three of them.

Peter, to begin with. Peter was a vacillating fellow. After professing commitment and friendship to God through God's own son, Jesus, he hid behind trees as soldiers brutally tormented an innocent Jesus; and when a soldier recognized the cowering Peter as one of Jesus's followers, Peter denied that he even knew the man. Yet, Jesus said to him, "Peter, you are a rock. I will build my church on you." You are solid ground, you are dependable, and I can count on you.

Goethe warned that if we take a man as he is, we make him worse; if we take him for what he might be, we help him to become that. Had Jesus said to Peter, "You are a vacillating character, you blow hot and cold, you'll never amount to much," that would have been the end of Peter. Instead, Jesus spoke vision into the life of Peter, "You are the rock, the solid man I need and count on." So He speaks also to you. We all need to be listening for His call of destiny for our lives.

Fortunate is any man who has a friend who knows his potential. Luckily, I have such a friend, a man who believes in me. He mentors and shares with me the power and intent of Christ's words to Peter, and makes it personal for me: "You are a man worth betting on, I believe in you, you are solid stuff." And that is precisely what God and Christ says to you.

Now let's consider the woman taken in adultery. Jesus spoke destiny to her when he said, "I do not judge you. Go and sin no more." That is exactly what she needed to hear. She knew she had sinned. She didn't need to be told that. She needed only understanding, love, and forgiveness—that was the only thing that could make her whole again, a new person. The love of Jesus and His sacrifice for our sins is the ultimate forgiveness that completes each one of us; once and for all. It is a gift that we only need to acknowledge and receive to be permanently whole.

Finally, Zacchaeus, the little man whose small stature matches our emotional feeling. We feel too small to see, too little to count, and we cannot get near the excitement of life because we are blocked out by the shadows of society striving to forever dim the light within each of us.

I often share Zacchaeus's disappointment with life, for when I am judged, by my job performance, I don't amount to much, and were I to drop out, the world would go on gaily without me. But Jesus said to Zacchaeus, "Come down out of that tree. I don't care if you are a failure. I will dine with you today." Jesus saw him as a person. He was somebody, not nobody.

Never Without God

There is a parchment fragment, dated about AD 200, which says, "Wheresoever they may be, they are not without God; and where there is one alone, ever thus, I am with him. Raise the stone, and there thou shalt find me; cleave the wood and I am there." This fragment is reported to consist of lost sayings of Jesus. They may belong to the document, now lost, that Paul quoted at a certain time. In any case, it points up to the great fact that wherever you may be, you cannot possibly be without God. "Raise the stone, there you find me; cleave the wood, there I am."

Our fear of isolation seems to be a penetrating fear. It eats away at our sense of worth, because God and God alone is the final ground of our worth. Therefore, all the aloneness that we feel, all the distress of spirit that results from being cut off, all doubts about our own worth, all the panic that churns up when the props are knocked out—all this is God's way of reminding us that wherever we are, whatever our condition, God is present and ultimately in control. Our panic and fear are really our cry of recognition. Raise the stone, wherever you are, whatever you are, God knows and hears. To God, you are never a nobody.

Eugene O'Neill once said, "This is the secret for today: man is born broken. He lives by mending. The grace of God is glue."

I believe this to be true. Life is broken and makes sense only when we can mend it. The grace of God is glue. It is by the grace of God that my life has been daily mending, molding, shaping to the somebody he created me to be. I, like you, am a testimony that *nobody is a nobody.*

Praise be to God!

ABOUT THE AUTHORS

Eugene S. Callender

Dr. Eugene Callender's career covers a broad span of social, political, and devotional activism for over seventy years, from serving as a long-time civil rights and community leader in Harlem to serving our nation on five presidential commissions under five separate presidents. His tireless work for his ministry is rooted in his deep conviction that the dignity of human beings is sacred, and that people should not be judged by external conditions that are arbitrarily assigned in life, but rather by the possibilities inherent in being a child of God.

As head of his ministry, he has been described by the *New York Daily News* as one of our "contemporary superstars," and by the *New York Times* as one of the twenty-six most outstanding clergy members in New York City. His focus and concerns have been the "disinherited," the voiceless who have needed a voice, the oppressed who have needed a liberator.

Motivated by his passion for social justice, Dr. Callender began his work in Harlem in 1950. With an understanding of the most critical problems in Harlem at the time, he created a ministry for addicts, alcoholics, welfare recipients, ex-convicts, battered women, and brutalized children. On the fifth floor of the church building, he began the first community-based clinic to detoxify heroin addicts with the help of doctors, nurses, psychologists, and social workers that he himself recruited.

Because he was a minister to people who were not church-oriented, he took his worship services out onto the asphalt of 121st and 122nd Streets.

Subsequently, Dr. Callender has served on presidential commissions under Presidents Johnson, Nixon, Carter, Bush Sr., and Clinton. From 1983 to 1989, he served as commissioner for the New York State Office for the Aging under Governor Mario Cuomo, and from 1989 to 1991, he served as a member of the Parole Board for the State of New York, also under Cuomo.

From 1982 to 1993 he served as president of the board of directors of the SYDA Foundation, an international organization that teaches people to live from their inner strength and love so that they can transform their everyday world.

Dr. Callender served as pastor at the Christian Parish for Spiritual Renewal from 1991 to 2000. In 1996, he was national chairperson of the Senior Citizen Council for the Clinton-Gore presidential campaign. For many years, Dr. Callender was an active participant in The Hunger Project and served as a senior advisor to its global board of directors.

From 2001 to 2006, Dr. Callender was the pastor at Saint James Presbyterian Church, which was founded in 1895 and is the oldest African American Presbyterian Church in Manhattan. While at Saint James, Dr. Callender was instrumental in creating the Harlem 40 and the Harlem 50.

The Harlem 40 are forty students "adopted" each year from the sixth grade at PS 123 who are nurtured, tutored, and coached to reach for goals and become mentors for others. From the beginning, they are told they can go to college and are surrounded with support and direction while they are at school, in their neighborhood, and with their families. Committed participants develop into a vital peer group in their community.

The Harlem 50 are young men from the community who had dropped out of school, who could be identified as "street-addicted" but also as street leaders. They are brought together into a GED. College Prep program at Saint James. They men are given support and direction and commit to going to college and to help other young people follow their example.

In August 2007, Dr. Callender was appointed Leader in Residence at the Colin Powell Center at The City College of New York (CCNY). Dr. Callender gave seminars and colloquiums to graduate students on emerging issues involving race in the United States. Since 1976 he has been the chairman of the board of the National Black Theater of Harlem, and in 1992 he served as the chairman of the Senior Coordinating Committee of the Democratic National Committee.

He served as pulpit guest minister at Church of the Master, the church he began serving in 1959. He formally retired from preaching in October 2010.

A native of Cambridge, Massachusetts, Dr. Callender holds a BA from Boston University; a master of divinity degree from Westminster Theological Seminary, cum laude; a master's degree in theology from Union Seminary; a doctor of divinity from Knoxville College; and a Juris Doctor from New York Law School. He has taught at Columbia School of Business, New York University, The New School for Social Research, City College of New York, and CUNY York College in Queens.

He currently lives in Manhattan near his daughter Renee, grandson Roshon, and great-granddaughter, Shanice. He continues to perform weddings and funerals and to touch lives around the world.

Lorena K. Rostig

Lorena met Reverend Callender at a book-signing event for *Eat, Pray, Love,* by Elizabeth Gilbert. While having lunch, she asked, "Sir, why haven't you written a book?" His answer, "I've been too busy preaching and teaching." Lorena offered to collect the stories, and they found George Zdravecky to help write the story.

Lorena lives in Germantown, Tennessee, with her husband of twenty-six years, Markus. Together they have two grown children, Annelise & Sebastian, and one grandson, Jude.

She dedicates this book to Alan Gompers, the author of *Maximum Security: The True Meaning of Freedom,* who introduced her to Reverend Callender and to the power of meditation. She credits him with changing her life profoundly.

Lorena would like to thank the following people for their support throughout this journey (in alphabetical order): Hillel Black; Patty Black; Lori Bishop; Debbie and Mike Brennan; Baxter Buck; Carolyn Clements; Lynn Franklin; Good Enough to Eat Restaurant (and staff); Jacques Granger; Karim Adeen-Hasan; Annik LeDouaron; La Mirabelle Restaurant (and staff); Debbie Mahoney; José Mestre; Jeanine Nitzel; Carrie Levin-Perly; Kimberly and Steven Rockefeller; Miska Shaw; Cyndy and David Tucker; John and Elizabeth van Merkensteijn; Kathleen "Shivani" Walker; Willa and Saul Waring; Renee Callender-Williams; and Gil Winter.

And she extends special acknowledgments to Janeen Koconis for holding Eugene's vision and making it real and to Phyllis Dubrow for her partnership in the final dotting of i's and crossing of t's.

George A. Zdravecky

George is humbled and blessed by collaborating with Dr. Eugene Callender and Lorena Rostig in capturing the journey of Eugene's life experiences in some of the most socially compelling times of recent American history and his continued path of spiritual reconciliation. It is a great honor to present *Nobody Is a Nobody* as a team. Eugene's story is our story when we are willing to see and live beyond our circumstances in a fellowship of love, a fellowship of forgiveness, and a fellowship of serving for changed lives.

George has been married to Rebecca since March 2, 1991 (oh happy day!), and they enjoy their three children, Liam, Xander, and Elizabeth. The Zdravecky family enjoys fellowship and worship at The Life Church of Memphis.

INDEX

Made in the USA
Charleston, SC
30 August 2012